Opinion Writing and Drafting in Tort

Cavendish
Publishing
Limited

Opinion Writing and Drafting in Tort

Valerie Beardsmore
and
Adele Cox

Cavendish
Publishing
Limited

Published in Great Britain 1996 by Cavendish Publishing Limited, The Glass House, Wharton Street, London WC1X 9PX.

Telephone: 0171-278 8000 Facsimile: 0171-278 8080

British Library Cataloguing in Publication Data. A catalogue record for this book is available from the British Library.

Beardsmore, Valerie
Opinion Writing and Drafting in Tort
I. Title II. Cox, Adele
808.0663441063

ISBN 1-85941-032-4

Printed and bound in Great Britain

Preface

For a number of years we have taught students taking the Bar Vocational Course how to write opinions and to draft pleadings, injunctions and affidavits. In doing so we have often felt the need for a book which would enable students to learn step by step how to construct those documents and would give them an opportunity to practise their skills in self-testing exercises.

Opinion Writing and Drafting in Tort is our attempt to produce such a work. In it basic practice in writing opinions and the rules and practice relating to drafting pleadings, injunctions, affidavits and other court documents are discussed in relation to tort generally and to a number of specific torts. While the book is not intended to serve as a book of precedents, annotated sample documents are given to help students to understand the application of the principles discussed in the text.

Although basic principles are explained and illustrated in the context of tort actions, they are largely applicable to opinion writing and drafting in other types of civil action. We hope, therefore, that the book will prove generally useful to those seeking to acquire the opinion writing and drafting skills.

The approach to opinion writing and drafting presented here is in large measure derived from our experience as teachers. We wish, therefore, to record our debt to our former students, whose difficulties and successes have helped to shape our ideas on the skills involved in these tasks and on the process of learning such skills. Valerie Beardsmore also wishes to thank her former pupil master, Stephen Boyd of 29 Bedford Row Chambers, and all those members of Desmond De Silva's Chambers at 2 Paper Buildings, Temple, who gave invaluable guidance and encouragement during her early efforts at drafting and opinion writing. A further debt is owed to the colleagues at the Inns of Court School of Law with whom we have discussed these skills and, in particular, to George Cumming, for both ideas and encouragement, and to Alexander Hewitt, whose views on the importance of the logical development of a pleading find expression in Chapter 3. Special thanks are due to Joanna Toch of Warwick Chambers for the advice which she gave us on the pleadings in this book, to Edna Beardsmore and Ralph Ruby who painstakingly read our proofs and to our editor Jo Reddy who originally conceived the project. Finally, our thanks to John Cox, without whose help our work would not have made it onto the computer. We need only add that the blame for any errors lies, of course, with us.

March 1996

Contents

Table of Cases

Table of Statutes

Table of Statutory Instruments

Chapter 1

Writing as a Lawyer

In daily life few of us, perhaps, give any great thought to the way in which we use words. The rapidity with which we formulate and communicate ideas through speech precludes any careful weighing of words in most situations. Even when writing, the extent to which we consider our choice of words is likely to be limited.

Within our society there are, however, many for whom the process of communication through words does require careful consideration. Those for whom words are, pre-eminently, the tools of their trade must of necessity choose their words with care. Journalists, advertising copywriters, authors and poets, for example, must all be skilled in the use of words and, more particularly, must be skilled writers.

Both speaking and writing are also central to a lawyer's work. Oral skills are crucial not only in the courtroom but also in conferring with clients and negotiating with opponents. However, part of the work of a lawyer, and for many it is the major part, is concerned with writing.

It is therefore vital that the would-be lawyer develops relevant writing skills. The word relevant is significant here. Since in Britain a university degree is nearly always a prerequisite for training as a solicitor or barrister, those entering professional legal training ought by definition to be capable of writing effectively. However, it is not merely the ability to write, or write well, that is required. What must be learned is to use words in the ways that skilled lawyers do. It is therefore necessary to grasp the essential characteristics of legal writing.

The primary purpose of all writing is, of course, communication. Yet though, for example, both the poet and the lawyer communicate through writing, and both may demonstrate skill in the use of language, the effect will be very different.

Consider for a moment a few lines far removed both in content and in style from legal writing:

When will you ever, Peace, wild wooddove, shy wings shut,
Your round me roaming end, and under be my boughs?
When, when, Peace, will you Peace?

In the poem 'Peace', Gerard Manley Hopkins communicates by using words to seduce both the ear and the mind of his reader. In this, as in his other poems, Hopkins shows how, in the hands of an artist, words can stimulate the senses, evoke memories and stretch the imagination of a reader.

To achieve such an effect, Hopkins selected words and structured sentences with precision. Exactly the same approach characterises the work of a writer engaged in drafting a statute. The effect, however, is very different, as the following extract from s 19 Landlord and Tenant Act 1954 shows:

> (1) Where on the coming to an end of a tenancy at a low rent the person who was tenant thereunder immediately before the coming to an end thereof becomes (whether by grant or by implication of law) tenant of the whole or any part of the property comprised therein under another tenancy at a low rent, then if the first tenancy was a long tenancy or is deemed by virtue of this subsection to have been a long tenancy the second tenancy shall be deemed for the purposes of this Part of this Act to be a long tenancy irrespective of its terms.

Here, while the primary purpose remains to communicate, words are selected for their power not to stimulate but to confine the imagination, not to play upon but to exclude shades of meaning. It is the draftsman's task to use words not to convey to or create for the reader an emotional experience but to inform him or her clearly, accurately and concisely of the legal consequences which follow from specified circumstances or events.

This comparison has highlighted qualities which ought to be apparent in any piece of legal writing: clarity, accuracy and conciseness of expression. In addition it suggests that a further distinctive quality of such writing is the neutral presentation of facts and ideas, that is, the elimination of emotive words and phrases.

This is crucial. A lawyer must be capable of thinking objectively. He or she must understand that the task of analysis requires an awareness of the way in which preconceptions and emotions influence not only the perception of events by those who take part in or witness them, but also the interpretation of those events and the assessment of the accounts of them by both participants and observers which is undertaken by lawyers.

Perfect objectivity may be unattainable and preconceptions and emotional responses doubtless give valuable insights into given situations, but a lawyer, at least, must recognise them for what they are. This knowledge is a precondition for the proper utilisation of such preconceptions and emotions in, and where appropriate their exclusion from, the process of legal analysis.

This ability of the lawyer to think objectively must be reflected in what he or she writes. It is this characteristic which, perhaps above all others, gives legal thought and writing its force. Even in drafting an affidavit, which puts a witness's evidence before the court in written form and may properly express that witness's views quite strongly, the lawyer should avoid unnecessarily emotive language.

Chapter 2

Preparing a Writ or County Court Summons

Scope of chapter

When an action is to be commenced, the plaintiff's solicitor, or the plaintiff if he or she is not legally represented (ie a litigant in person), must undertake the task of completing any forms and/or preparing any other documents required by the Rules of Court.

In the High Court actions in tort are usually heard in the Queen's Bench Division and must, with the exception of actions for trespass to the land, be commenced by writ. In the county court tort actions are commenced by default or fixed date summons depending on the relief sought. The summons must be accompanied by particulars of claim.

The present chapter will examine how to prepare a writ and an originating summons in a High Court tort action and both default and fixed date summonses in a county court tort action. Drafting particulars of claim is dealt with in Chapter 3 below.

Preparing the writ

A writ must be in the form prescribed by the Rules of the Supreme Court (RSC Ord 6 r1 and Prescribed Form 1 in SCP Appendix A). This means that while the lay-out of the writ may be varied to suit the circumstances of a particular case, the operative words of Form 1 must be retained (SCP 6/1/1). The appropriate form may be obtained from a law stationers or produced on a word processor by the plaintiff's solicitor.

Set out on pp 6-7 is a completed writ; notes explaining what must be inserted by the solicitor follow.

Writ of
Summons
[Unliquidated
Demand]
(O6 r1)

IN THE HIGH COURT OF JUSTICE   1995.–M.–No.¹

Queen's Bench Division

[*Brighton*   **District Registry]** ²

Between

ELAINE ALICE MACDONALD ³   Plaintiff

AND

ALISON RUTH JONES ⁴   Defendant

(1) Insert name **To the Defendant** (1)   *ALISON RUTH JONES* ⁵

(2) Insert
address
of (2) *25 Fowley Street, Lewes, Sussex* ⁶

This Writ of Summons has been issued against you by the above-named Plaintiff in respect of the claim set out on the back.

Within 14 days after the service of this Writ on you, counting the day of service, you must either satisfy the claim or return to the Court Office mentioned below the accompanying **Acknowledgment of Service** stating therein whether you intend to contest these proceedings.

If you fail to satisfy the claim or to return the Acknowledgment within the time stated, or if you return the Acknowledgment without stating therein an intention to contest the proceedings, the Plaintiff may proceed with the action and judgment may be entered against you forthwith without further notice.

(3) Complete
and delete as
necessary
Issued from the (3) [~~Central Office~~] [~~Admiralty and Commercial Registry~~] ⁷
(*Brighton*   District Registry] of the High Court
this   day of   19

NOTE:– This Writ may not be served later than 4 calendar months (*or, if leave is required to effect service out of the jurisdiction, 6 months*) beginning with that date unless renewed by order of the court.

IMPORTANT

Directions for Acknowledgment of Service are given with the accompanying form.

The Plaintiff's claim is for *8*

1. *An injunction to restrain the Defendant whether by himself, his servants or agents or otherwise howsoever, from obstructing the entrance to the Plaintiff's land at number 26 Fowley Street, Lewes, Sussex.*

2. *Damages for nuisance.*

3. *Interest on the said damages pursuant to section 35A of the Supreme Court Act 1981 at such rate and for such period as the Court thinks fit.*

---

(1) If this Writ was issued out of a District Registry, this indorsement as to place where the action arose should be completed.

(2) Delete as necessary.

(3) Insert name of place.

(4) For phraseology of this indorsement where the Plaintiff sues in person, see *Supreme Court Practice,* vol 2, para 1.

(1) (2) [The cause] [~~One of the causes~~] of action in respect of which the Plaintiff claims *9* relief in this action arose wholly or in part at (3) *Lewes 10* in the district of the District Registry named overleaf.]

(4) **This Writ** was issued by *Walters and Roberts* of *35 Poole Street, Lewes, Sussex 11*

[Agent   for

of

Solicitor   for the said Plaintiff   whose address (2) [is]~~[are]~~ *12*

35 Poole Street, Lewes, Sussex

Solicitor's Reference   Tel. No:

7

OYEZ The Solicitor's Law Stationery Society Ltd., Oyez House, 7 Spa Road, London SE 17 3QQ.   11.92 F23559

High Court A1   5044019

Notes

1   Insert the year of issue and the first letter of the plaintiff's surname. If the plaintiff is a company, insert the first letter of the company's name omitting 'the'. The case number should be left blank as this will be allocated and entered on the writ by the court.

2   Either insert the name of the appropriate District Registry (see the list in the Supreme Court Practice (SCP) at 4008) or, if proceedings are to be commenced in the Central Office in London, delete the reference to the District Registry.

3   Insert the plaintiff's name, giving the surname and first names (SCP 6/1/2). For the practice with regard to particular types of plaintiff, see below at p 17.

4   Insert the defendant's name, giving the surname and first names if known. If only the surname is known, the sex should be added if known. Initials may be used if known, as in the example below.

	J L PETERS (Male)	<u>Defendant</u>
or		
	Mr J L PETERS	<u>Defendant</u>

For the practice as to particular types of defendant, see below at pp 17-20.

5   Insert the defendant's name, in capitals for clarity.

6   Insert the defendant's usual or last known residential or business address, as appropriate.

7   Insert the name of the District Registry. The court office inserts day and date of issue.

8   The writ must be indorsed with a statement of claim or with a concise statement of the nature of the claim made or the relief or remedy required in the action: RSC Ord 6 r2. The example on this writ is a concise statement of the plaintiff's claim for damages for, and an injunction to restrain the defendant from committing, nuisance. Where the plaintiff issues a generally indorsed writ, a claim for interest may be indorsed on the writ, but this is not essential as interest may be awarded even if the claim for interest is not indorsed on the writ. Indorsement of the writ is discussed more fully at pp 11-13 below.

9 Remember to add 's' to the word plaintiff if there is more than one plaintiff, and 's' to the word claim if there is only one plaintiff.

10 Where a writ is to be issued out of a District Registry it should be indorsed to show the place in which the cause of action arose.

11 Insert the name and address of the plaintiff's solicitor. Where the plaintiff sues in person, the indorsement should state that the writ was issued by the plaintiff in person and should give his or her place of residence (SCP 6/5/2) as in the example below.

This Writ was issued by the said Plaintiff who resides at [address].

12 Insert an address for service on the plaintiff. Where a plaintiff sues in person this must be his or her place of residence, but where, as is usually the case, the plaintiff acts through a solicitor, the address will be that of his or her solicitor's office.

Indorsing the writ with the plaintiff's claim

As noted above, the writ must be indorsed with a statement of the plaintiff's claim: RSC Ord 6 r2. This indorsement may be in one of two forms:

- a full statement of claim; or

- a concise statement of the nature of the claim or the relief or remedy sought.

Indorsement with a full statement of claim

When the indorsement takes the form of a full statement of claim, the writ is sometimes described as 'a specially indorsed writ'. Although a writ is not a pleading, a statement of claim indorsed on the writ, rather than produced as a separate document, is a pleading: SCP 6/2/3. When drafting such an indorsement of claim you should therefore consult Chapter 3. However, it will usually be appropriate to indorse the writ with a full statement of claim in a straightforward case.

Indorsement with a concise statement of the plaintiff's claim

When the indorsement takes the form of a concise statement of the plaintiff's claim it is described as 'a general indorsement' and the writ is sometimes referred to as 'a generally indorsed writ'.

The general indorsement relating to an action in tort should include the following information:

- the relief or remedy (or remedies) sought: eg damages, an injunction, interest;
- in relation to a claim for damages:

    (1) the nature of the cause of action: eg negligence

    (2) concise details of the alleged wrongdoing sufficient to enable the defendant to identify the occasion of the wrongful conduct: eg date, time, place and nature of a road traffic accident allegedly caused by the defendant's negligence

    (3) concise statement of harm suffered by plaintiff as a result of the defendant's wrongful conduct: eg personal injuries, damage to goods

    (4) in a fatal accident claim, in addition, the capacity in which the plaintiff sues, the names and dates of birth of any dependants on whose behalf a claim is brought and the Acts under which the action is brought;

- in relation to a claim for an injunction:

    (1) the nature of the order:

        (i) *if prohibitory*: an order restraining the defendant from some specified conduct

        (ii) *if mandatory*: an order that the defendant do some specified act or acts

    (2) concise details of:

        (i) *if prohibitory*: the wrongful conduct to be restrained

        (ii) *if mandatory*: the act or acts to be undertaken.

The example below shows the general indorsement in relation to a claim for damages for personal injuries and loss and damage suffered by the plaintiff in a road traffic accident caused by the defendant:

> The Plaintiff's claim is for damages for personal injuries and loss and damage suffered as a result of a road traffic accident on 28 November 1995 in High Street, Boddington, Oxfordshire caused by the negligent driving of the Defendant.

Further examples of indorsements relating to the types of tort action covered in this book are set out below, and may be used as self-testing exercises. You should note, however, that if an action is brought in the High Court, interest is claimed under s 35A of the Supreme Court Act 1981.

Types of general indorsement

Claim in negligence for property damage

(a) Damage to motorcycle [see county court claim at pp 154–55]

The Plaintiff's claim is for damages for damage to his motorcycle suffered as a result of an accident on the 1st May 1995 at the junction of Bristol Road and Albert Road near Wilsdown, Somerset caused by the negligent driving of the Defendant and interest pursuant to section 35A of the Supreme Court Act 1981 at such rate and for such period as the Court thinks fit.

(b) Damage to greenhouse and contents [see claim at pp 176-77]

The Plaintiff's claim is for damages for damage to his goods and premises suffered on 10 October 1995 which was the result of the negligence of the Defendant in the felling of a tree on his premises at 6 Wingate Lane, Old Fordham, Shropshire and interest pursuant to section 35A of the Supreme Court Act 1981 at such rate and for such period as the Court thinks fit.

Claim in negligence for personal injuries, loss and damage [see claim on pp 207-8]

The Plaintiff's claim is for damages for personal injuries and loss and damage suffered as a result of the negligent driving of the First Defendant as servant or agent of the Second Defendant on 26 May 1995 at High Street, Westchester and interest thereon pursuant to section 35A of the Supreme Court Act 1981 at such rate and for such period as the Court thinks fit.

Claim in negligence for damages in a fatal accident case [see claim on pp 220-22]

The Plaintiff is the widower and administrator of the estate of the late Rebecca Jane Ramsey who died in an accident on 1st September 1994 in Lime Road, Northam caused by the negligent driving of the Defendant and the Plaintiff claims on behalf of himself and the Plaintiff's estate and on behalf of her children, Richard Alfred Ramsey, date of birth 11 August 1982, and Sarah Rebecca Ramsey, date of birth 1 March 1986, under the provisions of: (a) The Fatal Accidents Act 1976 and (b) The Law Reform (Miscellaneous Provisions) Act 1934.

Claim under the Occupiers' Liability Act 1957 [see claim at pp 252-54]

The Plaintiff's claim is for damages for personal injuries sustained and loss and damage suffered when she was, on 21 April 1995, a visitor at the First Defendant's premises, the Wisteria House Nursing Home, Saleworth, caused by the negligence and breach of duty under the Occupiers' Liability Act 1957 of the Second Defendant as servant and agent of the First Defendant and/or the negligence of the Third Defendant in the carrying out of his duties as maintenance manager and/or the negligence of the Fourth Defendant in the carrying out of plumbing work at the premises.

Claim in nuisance for an injunction and damages [see claim at pp 287-88]

The Plaintiff's claim is for:

(1) An injunction forbidding the Defendant whether by himself or by instructing or encouraging any other person from playing or permitting to be played a record player on the Defendant's premises at Flat 3, Rose Court, Park View, Parksea, so as to cause a nuisance by noise to the Plaintiff or other occupiers of the Plaintiff's premises.

(2) Damages for nuisance and interest pursuant to section 35A of the Supreme Court Act 1981 at such rate and for such period as the Court thinks fit.

Claim for damages for trespass to the land [see claim at pp 310-11]

The Plaintiff's claim is for:

(1) A declaration that the Defendant is not allowed to occupy the Plaintiff's land at Lime Cottage, Green Lanes, Oldbury.

(2) An injunction forbidding the Defendant whether by himself or by instructing or encouraging any other person from occupying the said land.

(3) An order that the Defendant do forthwith pull down and remove the greenhouse erected by the Defendant on the Plaintiff's said land.

(4) Damages for trespass to land and interest pursuant to section 35A of the Supreme Court Act 1981 at such rate and for such period as the Court thinks fit.

Claim for an injunction and damages in respect of trespass to the person [see claim at pp 333-34]

The Plaintiff's claim is for an injunction forbidding the Defendant whether by himself or by instructing or encouraging any other person

(a) to assault, molest or otherwise interfere with the Plaintiff,

(b) to enter or attempt to enter the Plaintiff's property known as Flat 2 Frimley Buildings, Hodge Street, Halifax.

Indorsement with a statement of value

It should be noted that where a claim is brought for damages for personal injuries, and this includes a claim for damages resulting from the death of any person, the action may only be commenced in the High Court if the value of the claim exceeds £50,000. See below at p 146. The writ must therefore also be indorsed with the following statement:

This writ includes a claim for personal injury but may be commenced in the High Court because the value of the action for the purposes of Article 5 of the High Court and County Court Jurisdiction Order 1991 exceeds £50,000.

This indorsement certifying the value of the claim must be signed by the plaintiff's solicitor, or the plaintiff if he acts in person, and follows immediately after the indorsement of the claim.

Preparing the county court summons

In the county court an action for damages in tort will normally be commenced by issuing a default summons. This is the type of summons which the plaintiff must issue when his or her claim is for money: CCR Ord 3 r2(2). In an action in tort the plaintiff is often seeking damages which will be assessed by the court. Consequently no fixed sum is claimed and the default summons is in Form N2 for an amount which is not fixed. The annotated sample summons at p 14 shows how to complete a default summons on Form N2.

Where the plaintiff's claim consists of or includes a claim for a non-money remedy, such as an injunction, the plaintiff must issue a fixed date summons: CCR Ord 3 r2(1). The sample summons at p 16 shows how to complete a fixed date summons.

These forms may be obtained from a law stationers or a county court, or generated on the solicitor's computer. Alternatively a form of request for summons may be obtained from a county court or a law stationers and the summons will be prepared by the court on receipt of a completed form of request together with the particulars of claim: CCR Ord 3 r3(1).

County Court Summons	Case Number	*Always quote this*	1

Plaintiff's full name address	JAMES KIERAN O'DOWD 4 1 FIELD ROAD LEETON MANCHESTER M50 4RT

In the   2

MANCHESTER

County Court

The court office is open from 10am to 4pm
Monday to Friday

Plaintiff's Solicitor's address Ref/Tel No	FORSTERS 5 24 MANCHESTER ROAD LEETON MANCHESTER M50 3DR

THE COURTS OF JUSTICE   3
CROWN SQUARE
MANCHESTER
M60 9OJ

Telephone *0161 954 1900*

Defendant's full name (including title eg Mr Mrs or Miss) and address	FASHIONS LIMITED 6 UNIT 1 THE INDUSTRIAL CENTRE ILVERLEY M30 2NP

seal

This summons is only valid if sealed by the court.
If it is not sealed it should be sent to the court.

Keep this summons, you may need to refer to it.

What the plaintiff claims from you

Give brief description of type of claim	DAMAGES FOR 7 NEGLIGENCE

Amount claimed   see particulars

Court fee	*80*	*00*	10
Solicitor's costs	*TO BE TAXED*		
Total Amount			

Particulars of the plaintiff's claim against you

SEE ATTACHED PARTICULARS   8 OF CLAIM

Summons issued on   *4 NOVEMBER 1995*

What you should do

You have 21 days (16 days if you are a limited company served at your registered office) from the date of the postmark to either
- **defend the claim** by filling in the back of the enclosed form and **sending it to the court;**
  OR
- **admit the claim** and make an offer of payment, by filling in the front of the enclosed reply form and **sending it to the court.**

If you do nothing judgment may be entered against you

My claim is worth	£5000 or less ☐	over £5000 ☑

All cases over £3000

I would like my case decided by	trial ☑	arbitration ☐

Signed

Plaintiff or plaintiff's solicitor   9
(or see enclosed "Particulars of claim")

Please read the information on the back of the form. It will tell you more about what to do

N2 Default summons (amount not fixed) (Order 3, rule 3(2)(b))

Notes

1 The case number is inserted by the court office and should be left blank.

2 Insert the name of the county court in which the proceedings are to be brought.

3 Insert the address of the court. This can be found in the county court directory at the back of the *County Court Practice* (the *Green Book*), or in the telephone directory.

4 Insert the plaintiff's full name and address.

5 Insert the plaintiff's solicitor's name and address.

6 Insert the defendant's full name and address.

7 The type of claim must be concisely described.

8 Concise particulars of the plaintiff's claim may be indorsed on the summons. In many cases, especially where the facts need to be set out in detail, it will be more convenient to attach particulars of claim. Drafting particulars of claim is discussed in Chapter 3.

9 The appropriate box must be ticked to indicate whether or not the value of the plaintiff's claim exceeds £5,000. This is because the court officer needs to decide whether the claim should be heard by a district judge or a circuit judge. If the claim exceeds £5,000 it is outside the district judge's jurisdiction and should be heard by a circuit judge. If the value exceeds £3,000 the plaintiff must also indicate whether he or she wishes the case to be decided by trial or arbitration by ticking the appropriate box. A claim that is for £3,000 or less will automatically be allocated for arbitration if the defendant files a defence, and so will be dealt with by the arbitration 'small claims' procedure governed by CCR Ord 19. Personal injury claims exceeding £1,000 are an exception to this rule.

10 The court fee is determined by the amount of money claimed by the plaintiff. Where the amount claimed exceeds £5,000, or where, as here, there is no fixed amount claimed (ie the claim is an unliquidated claim) the prescribed fee is £75 if the summons is issued at the Summons Production Centre and £80 otherwise. See CCR Ord Part II; Sch 1 County Court Fee Order 1982, set out in the *Green Book* at p 1698 as updated 30 October 1995. The initial solicitor's costs also depend on the amount of the claim, but where the amount is not fixed (an unliquidated sum) the words 'to be taxed' should be inserted. CCR Ord 38 r18(2).

N. 4
Fixed Date Summons
[*As substituted* 1991]
Order 3, Rule 3(2)(b)
[Royal Arms]
[*General Title – Form N. 1*]

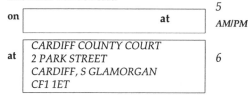

seal

To the defendant *MEGAN WILLIAMS   1*

- The plaintiff claims *an injunction   2*   (see particulars enclosed)

Court fee	80	00
Solicitor's costs		
Total amount		
Summons issued on		

3

4

- **The claim will be heard**

on | | at

5

AM/PM

at | CARDIFF COUNTY COURT
2 PARK STREET
CARDIFF, S GLAMORGAN
CF1 1ET |

6

when you are summoned to attend. Failure to attend may result in judgment being entered against you

Important—for instructions turn over

Please read this page: it will help you deal with the summons

Instructions

Within 14 days after the date of service (which is explained under the heading **General Information** below) **you must complete the enclosed form of reply and send it to the court. Delay in returning the reply form may add to the costs.**

General Information

- If you received this summons through the post the date of service will be 7 days (for a limited company at its registered office, the second working day) after the date of posting as shown by the postmark.

- You can get help to complete the enclosed form and information about court procedure at any county court office or citizens' advice bureau. The address and telephone number of your local court is listed under 'Courts' in the phone book.

- If you dispute the claim, you may be entitled to help with your legal costs. Ask about the legal aid scheme at any county court office, citizens' advice bureau,

legal advice centre or firm of solicitors displaying the legal aid sign.

- When corresponding with the court, please address forms or letters to the Chief Clerk and quote the case number.

Registration of Judgments

If the summons results in a judgment against you, your name and address may be entered in the Register of County Court Judgments. **This may make it difficult for you to get credit.** A leaflet giving further information can be obtained from the court.

Interest on Judgments

If judgment is entered against you and is for more than £5000, the plaintiff may be entitled to interest on the total amount.

[*How to Pay*—N. 1]
[*Certificate of Service*—N. 12]

Notes

1   Insert defendant's full name.

2   If particulars of claim are enclosed only a concise description of the nature of the claim need be given here. If the claim is a very straightforward one, the particulars may be indorsed on the summons in the space provided.

3   Insert the information required as shown. The court fee and the solicitor's fixed costs depend on the value of the claim. Where proceedings are commenced for a remedy or relief other than a claim for money or a claim under the Companies Act 1985 and Insolvency Act 1986, the prescribed fee is £65, *Green Book,* p 1699 as updated 30 October 1995.

4   The court will insert the date on which the summons is issued so this box should be left blank.

5   The court will fix the date and time of the hearing, so this box should also be left blank.

6   Insert the name and address of the county court in which the summons is to be issued.

Particular types of plaintiff and defendant

In each of the sample documents set out above the action is brought by an individual plaintiff. However, various types of defendants are sued. As this indicates, it is important to know how to describe commonly encountered types of plaintiff and defendant, and examples illustrating this are set out below.

Co-plaintiffs and co-defendants

Where there are a number of plaintiffs or defendants these may be clearly and concisely set out as follows:

In the case of plaintiffs:

(1) Pauline Rose Marcey

(2) Elizabeth Firth

(3) Henry Willis   Plaintiffs

In the case of defendants:

(1) Justin Peterson

(2) William Thomas Peek   Defendants

Partnerships

Two or more partners can sue or be sued in the name of their firm, avoiding the need to set out the names of all the partners, as in the example below:

HUTCHINS AND POOLE (a firm)   <u>Plaintiffs</u>

GEORGE McWILLIAMS AND SONS (a firm) <u>Defendants</u>

The address given in the writ or summons may be the partnership's place of business.

Sole trader

A person who carries on business in a name other than his or her own may be sued in that name: RSC Ord 81 r9. The corresponding County Court Rule sets out explicitly the practice with regard to suing such a person. By CCR Ord 5 r10 he or she may be sued:

• in his own name, followed by the words (trading as AB); or
• in his business name, followed by the words (a trading name).

These two forms are illustrated below:

ROBERT JENKINS (trading as Bobs Snacks)   <u>Defendant</u>

BOBS SNACKS (a trading name)   <u>Defendant</u>

However, a sole trader cannot sue in a trading name, but only in his or her own name, and consequently only the first of these two forms may be used, as in the following example:

ANNA BURTON (trading as Anna's)   <u>Plaintiff</u>

Service on a body corporate

A corporate body should sue and should be sued in its full corporate name, for example:

• The Post Office
• London Regional Transport

Companies

A company registered under the Companies Act 1985 must, whether a plaintiff or a defendant, be described by its full name. A company search may be carried out by the plaintiff's solicitor to establish the correct name of a defendant company.

If the company is a public company, it should be described as in the example below:

JONES PARRY PHARMACEUTICALS PLC   <u>Plaintiff</u>

A private company should be described as in the following example:

ALISON YARROW INVESTMENTS LIMITED <u>Defendant</u>

Note that while in practice 'Public Liability Company' is abbreviated to 'plc' the word 'Limited' is generally written out in full, although there is no rule on these matters.[1]

Building societies

An incorporated building society sues and is sued in its corporate name, for example:

• The Cumbershire Building Society

If unincorporated a building society should sue or be sued through its trustees or officers as the representatives of the society's members.

Trade unions

A trade union may sue or be sued in its own name.

Persons under a disability

An 'infant' or a 'minor', that is a person who has not yet reached the age of 18 years, or a 'patient', that is a person who by reason of a mental disorder within the meaning of the Mental Health Act 1985 is incapable of managing and administering his or her property and affairs, is defined in RSC Ord 80 r1 as 'a person under a disability'.

A plaintiff who is a person under a disability must sue by a next friend, and this information must be inserted on the writ or summons as follows:

<u>Minor:</u>   PHILIPPA SUSAN REYNOLDS
            (an infant, suing by Rosemary Reynolds
               her mother and next friend)   <u>Plaintiff</u>

---

1   Most books on drafting appear to support the view expressed by Anthony Radevsky in *Drafting Pleadings* (2nd edn, 1955) 134 that 'Limited' should not be abbreviated. For a contrary view see Jacob & Goldrein, *Pleadings: Principles and Practice* (1990) 30. The SCP uses 'Ltd' at para 6/1/7.

Patient: WILLIAM JOHN LAWLEY
(by Anne Roberts his next friend)   Plaintiff

- No reference is made to the fact that the plaintiff is a patient.

A person under a disability can only defend proceedings, or bring a counterclaim, by acting through a guardian ad litem. The infant defendant must be described as follows:

PHILIPPA SUSAN REYNOLDS (an infant,
by Rosemary Reynolds her mother
and guardian ad litem)   Defendant

A defendant who is a patient should be described as in the example below:

WILLIAM JOHN LAWLEY
(by Anne Roberts his guardian
ad litem)   Defendant

Personal representatives

In fatal accident cases, an action is often brought by a spouse who sues not only in a personal capacity as a dependant of the deceased, but also as the executor or executrix or administrator or administratrix of the deceased person's estate. In the example given below, Mrs Halden sues on her own behalf as the widow of the deceased and also as the executrix of her late husband's estate.

ELLEN HALDEN
(Widow and executrix of
the estate of Peter Halden,
deceased)   Plaintiff

Chapter 3

Drafting Pleadings: Basic Rules and Practice

Part 1: Introduction

Scope of chapter

In writing this chapter we have assumed that there will be at least some readers who have little idea of what a pleading is and no idea at all of how to go about drafting one. The chapter is therefore intended to be a basic introduction to drafting pleadings in tort cases. It will explain what pleadings are and the rules and conventions which must be understood if pleadings are to be effectively drafted. At the same time the chapter provides a basic framework within which the skill of drafting in relation to particular areas of tort can be examined in later chapters. Finally, the chapter has been organised so as to facilitate reference to it for guidance on particular points of pleading that may arise.

Pleadings generally

Purpose of pleadings

Neither the Rules of the Supreme Court nor the County Court Rules specifically and fully define pleadings. However, the notes to RSC Ord 18, which governs the practice with regard to pleadings, defines them as:[1]

> The written statements of the parties of all the material facts on which each party relies for his claim or defence as the case may be.

The purpose of such written statements is twofold. Firstly, a pleading is intended to make clear to every other party in the case the facts which the party pleading intends to and must prove at trial in order to establish a claim or defence. Secondly, by setting out the facts on which each party relies, pleadings should clarify, both for the parties themselves and for the court which hears the case, the facts on which they disagree, that is, the facts in issue between them.

---

[1]   RSC Ord 18 at 18A.

Types of pleading

STATEMENT OF CLAIM/PARTICULARS OF CLAIM

The first pleading in an action sets out the claim or claims made by one or more plaintiffs against one or more defendants. In the High Court this pleading is called a statement of claim and in the county courts it is known as the particulars of claim.[2] As the rules which govern drafting a statement of claim and the particulars of claim are often identical, the term 'statement/particulars of claim' is used throughout where reference is made to both pleadings. It should be noted that a statement of claim indorsed on a writ is a pleading.[3]

DEFENCE

In both the High Court and the county courts a defendant who wishes to contest any claim or claims made by the plaintiff must do so in a written defence.[4]

REPLY AND SUBSEQUENT PLEADINGS

In the High Court the rules also provide for further pleadings, but except for a reply, these are rarely drafted.[5] Even a reply is unnecessary if the plaintiff merely takes issue with the defence. It is only where the plaintiff wishes to rely on some affirmative case of his own in answer to the defence that a reply must be drafted and served on the defendant.[6]

The County Court Rules do not expressly provide for a reply, but presumably this is a lacuna in the rules which could be remedied by invoking s 76 County Courts Act 1984. This section provides that, in a case not expressly provided for under the Act, the general principles of practice in the High Court may be adopted and applied to the

---

2   RSC Ord 18 r1; CCR Ord 6 r1(1).

3   See RSC Ord 18 at 18/A. A statement of claim may be indorsed on the writ by virtue of RSC Ord 6 r2(1)(a).

4   RSC Ord 18 r2; CCR Ord 9 r6.

5   Pleadings subsequent to the reply are as follows: rejoinder (by the defendant), surrejoinder (by the plaintiff), rebutter (by the defendant), and surrebutter (by the plaintiff). You should also be aware of a further document which, though not a pleading in its own right, is nevertheless part of the pleadings in an action. This is the document which sets out replies to a request for further and better particulars of a pleading. Sometimes a party who has been served with a pleading asks the party whose pleading it is to clarify his or her case by supplying further particulars of one or more matters pleaded. The party from whom particulars are sought replies by producing a single document containing both the questions and his or her responses. The particulars given, whether provided in response to a letter or a court order, become part of the pleadings to which the request relates. See further, RSC Ord 18 r12.

6   RSC Ord 18 r3.

proceedings.[7] Pleadings subsequent to a reply are unlikely to be required in a county court case, but s 76 would seem to apply again if necessary.

COUNTERCLAIM

A defence may be accompanied by a counterclaim. As its name suggests, this pleads a claim made by a defendant against a plaintiff. Such a claim may arise out of, or independently of, the facts on which the plaintiff's claim is based. In either situation, however, the defendant's claim is a separate and distinct action which could be brought and heard as a separate action in its own right.

Such an independent cross-action is brought as a counterclaim in the plaintiff's action for convenience and to save costs, as this procedure enables the court to deal with all the claims between the parties at the same time. In the county courts a counterclaim must be made in the defence and in the High Court must be contained in a pleading and is normally contained in a single document with the defence.[8] In both courts the composite pleading is described as a defence and counterclaim.

DEFENCE TO COUNTERCLAIM

In High Court proceedings, a plaintiff who wishes to contest a counterclaim must do so in a defence to counterclaim.[9] When, as is often the case, the plaintiff also wishes to serve on the defendant a reply, taking issue with the defendant's defence, both of the plaintiff's pleadings must be contained in a single document.[10] This composite pleading is described as a reply and defence to counterclaim.

Pleadings in tort cases

Pleadings are only required in actions begun by writ in the High Court or by summons in the county court. This, however, covers all actions in tort. Consequently, when a lawyer's analysis of the facts of a client's case results in the advice that an action in tort should be brought, or resisted, it becomes necessary to draft the appropriate pleading. If the case is not settled at an early stage, it may be necessary to consider drafting further pleadings.

---

[7] See s 76 and the notes thereto in the *Green Book* at pp 70–71.
[8] CCR Ord 9 r6; SCP at 15/2/3 citing *Impex Transport Aktieselskabet v AG Thomas Holdings Ltd* [1981] 1 WLR 1547.
[9] RSC Ord 18 r3(2).
[10] *Ibid* r3(3).

A lawyer handling tort cases must, therefore, be capable of drafting effective pleadings. To do so he or she must have a knowledge and understanding of the rules, conventions and tactical considerations which shape the way in which pleadings are drafted. Consequently it is to a consideration of these matters that the remainder of this chapter is devoted.

Part 2: Formalities

The Rules of the Supreme Court lay down a number of formal requirements which relate to every High Court pleading.[11] These have helped to shape the conventional lay-out of a pleading into a heading, which includes the title of the action, a description of the pleading, the body of the pleading and its closing sections. The example below illustrates and explains the operation of the relevant rules.

---

[11] *Ibid* r6.

Sample pleading
(1) High Court: statement of claim

IN THE HIGH COURT OF JUSTICE a   1995 F No b
QUEEN'S BENCH DIVISION c
[DISTRICT REGISTRY] d
[Writ issued the   day of   1995] e

BETWEEN f

JAMES ROBERT FOSTER   <u>Plaintiff</u>
and
ALICE ROSE CARTWRIGHT   <u>Defendant</u>

1

STATEMENT OF CLAIM 2

1.
2.
3.   3
4.

AND the Plaintiff claims:
(1)
(2)   4

                             (signed)_____ 5

Served the   day of   199   by
Messrs _____ & Co of _____
solicitors for the Plaintiff 6

Notes

1   Heading.
  (a) The court in which the action is brought is stated in capitals in the top left-hand corner of the pleading.
  (b) The pleading must show the year in which the writ was issued, the letter and the number of the action: RSC Ord 18 r6(1)(a). The letter used is the first letter of the surname of the plaintiff (or first plaintiff if there are several) or, if the plaintiff is a company, the first letter of the plaintiff's name omitting 'The'. The number of the action is given by the court when the writ is issued and should be left blank when drafting before the issue of the writ. The required information appears in the top right-hand corner of the pleading.

(c) RSC Ord 18 r6(1)(c) requires that the pleading shows the division of the High Court to which the action is assigned and the name of the judge (if any) to whom it is assigned.

(d) If the writ is issued out of a district registry, the name of the district registry must be inserted here.

(e) A statement of claim must be indorsed with the date on which the writ was issued. This line should be omitted if the statement of claim is indorsed on the writ pursuant to RSC Ord 6 r2(1)(a) and does not appear on pleadings subsequent to the statement of claim.

(f) The pleading must state the title of the action: RSC Ord 18 r6(1)(b). The conventional way to set out the parties is shown here although the word 'Between' sometimes appears in lower case. The parties' first names and surname should be stated in full: SCP 6/1/2, 6/1/5. If the defendant's first names are not known, the surname alone may be used, indicating the defendant's sex if known: SCP 6/1/5.

2   RSC Ord 18 r6(1)(d) requires that a description of the pleading appears on its face, namely, statement of claim, defence, reply etc as appropriate.

3   A pleading must, if necessary, be divided into paragraphs which are numbered consecutively: RSC Ord 18 r6(2). Since r6(2) also requires that each allegation is, so far as is convenient, contained in a separate paragraph, it will invariably be necessary to number paragraphs.

4   A statement of claim must plead specifically the relief or remedy sought by the plaintiff: RSC Ord 18 r15(1). The practice is to end the pleading with the prayer setting out each head of relief or remedy claimed in separate numbered paragraphs: SCP 18/15/1. Note that the numbering of the paragraphs in the body of the statement of claim and the prayer is not continuous. Costs need not be specifically claimed and the practice is to omit costs from the prayer in the Queen's Bench Division. Both costs and 'further or other relief' are claimed in the prayer in action in the Chancery Division.

5   A pleading must be signed by the barrister or solicitor who drafts it, or by the party if he or she is suing in person (ie conducting his or her own case): RSC Ord 18 r6(5). The signature is conventionally located at the bottom right-hand corner of the pleading.

6   A pleading must be indorsed with the name and address of the party if he or she is acting in person, or with the name or firm, and business address, of the solicitor who serves it: RSC Ord 18 r6(4)(a) and (b). The indorsement conventionally appears on the bottom left-hand corner of the pleading, together with the date of service which is required by RSC Ord 18 r6(1)(e) to be stated on the pleading.

Sample pleading
(2) County court: particulars of claim

IN THE COUNTY COURT [1]   Case No [2]

BETWEEN [3]

(1) BARBARA HARRIS

(2) JOHN WILLIAM LEWIS   Plaintiffs

and

PETER FRENCH & SONS LTD   Defendants

PARTICULARS OF CLAIM [4]

1.

2. } [5]

3.

AND the Plaintiff claims:

(1)   } [6]

(2)

(Signed)_____ [7]

Dated this   day of   199 [8]

Messrs Wall, Tobin & Roberts,
Solicitors for the Plaintiff, of
2 Bridge Street, Norwich, N15 2PZ
where they will accept proceedings
on behalf of the Plaintiff. [9]

To the District Judge of
            County Court [10]
and to the Defendant.

Notes

1 The name of the county court in which the action is brought is
   stated, in capital letters, in the top left-hand corner of the pleading.
2 Every pleading must bear the number allocated to the action by the
   court, CCR Ord 3 r7(1). When drafting particulars of claim the case
   number should be left blank so that it can be inserted by the court
   office. The number allocated should be reproduced exactly in
   subsequent pleadings.
3 Every pleading must bear the title of the action: CCR Ord 3 r7(1).
   The title identifies the parties, and the practice with regard to
   setting out the title is as in the High Court.
4 Following High Court practice, a description of the pleading
   appears on its face, namely particulars of claim, defence or defence
   and counterclaim etc as appropriate. This may be referred to as the
   title of the pleading.
5 and 6 The basic lay-out of the body of the particulars of claim
   follows High Court practice. Costs are omitted from the prayer in
   the county court.
7 A pleading must be signed by the party whose pleading it is if he
   or she is acting in person or by the party's solicitor if he or she is
   acting through a solicitor: CCR Ord 6 r8, Ord 9 r19. The signature is
   conventionally located at the bottom right-hand corner of the
   pleading. When counsel settles a pleading, the draft must be signed
   by counsel and his or her name must appear on every copy of the
   pleading used in the proceedings: CCR Ord 50 r6.
8 The date of the pleading is stated at the bottom left-hand corner of
   the pleading, preceded by the word 'Dated'. Note that in the High
   Court, the date given is that of service, and is preceded by the word
   'Served'.
9 The pleading must state the address for service of the party whose
   pleading it is: CCR Ord 6 r8, Ord 9 r19.
10 This indorsement indicates to whom the pleading is addressed.

Sample pleading
(3) County court: defence

IN THE   **COUNTY COURT**   **Case No**

BETWEEN   (1)   BARBARA HARRIS
               (2)   JOHN WILLIAM LEWIS   Plaintiffs   1
                            and
                  PETER FRENCH & SONS LTD   Defendants

DEFENCE   2

1.
2.
3.   } 3
4.
5.

                                    (Signed)_____   4

Dated the   day of   199 5

                        Michael Walsh, solicitor for
                        the Defendants, of 14 Bridge Street,
                        Norwich, N15 2PZ
                        where he will accept proceedings
                        on behalf of the Defendants. 6

To the District Judge of the
             County Court 7
and to the Plaintiff

Notes

1 Heading as in the particulars of claim. The case number allocated
   by the court office is taken from the particulars of claim.
2 The description of the pleading, following High Court practice.
3 As in the High Court, the body of the pleading must be divided
   into consecutively numbered paragraphs, each containing, so far as
   is convenient, a single allegation.

4   Signature of barrister, solicitor or defendant acting in person who drafted the pleading: CCR Ord 9 r19.

5, 6, 7 Indorsements as in the sample pleading (2) above.

Note: If the action was brought in the High Court, the lay-out of the heading and the indorsement following the signature would be as in sample pleading (1) above with the case number allocated by Central Office being taken from the statement of claim. The description and the lay-out of the pleading would be as in sample pleading (3).

Sample pleading
(4) High Court: defence and counterclaim

IN THE HIGH COURT OF JUSTICE   1995 F No 56678
QUEEN'S BENCH DIVISION
[DISTRICT REGISTRY]
BETWEEN

JAMES ROBERT FOSTER   Plaintiff

and

ALICE ROSE CARTWRIGHT   Defendant

3

DEFENCE AND COUNTERCLAIM 2

DEFENCE

1.
2.
3.   4
4.
5.

COUNTERCLAIM 5

6.
7.   6
8.

AND the Defendant counterclaims:

(1) 7
(2)

(signed)_____ 8

Served the   day of   199
by Messrs _____ & Co of _____
Solicitors for the Defendant.9

Notes

1 Heading as in the statement of claim. The case number allocated by Central Office is taken from the statement of claim and the 'writ issued' line is omitted.

2 The description of the pleading required by RSC Ord 18 r6(1)(d). Since this is a composite pleading the description refers to both pleadings.

3 The description of the first pleading must follow the description of the composite pleading.

4 The body of the pleading must be divided into consecutively numbered paragraphs each containing, so far as is convenient, a single allegation: RSC Ord 18 r6(2).

5 The description of the second pleading must be included: SCP 18/18/1.

6 See note 4. Note that the numbering of the paragraphs in a composite pleading is continuous.

7 The counterclaim must plead specifically the relief or remedy sought by the defendant: RSC Ord 18 r18(a). The practice is, as with the statement of claim, to end the counterclaim with a prayer setting out each head of relief or remedy claimed in separate numbered paragraphs.

8 Signature of the barrister, solicitor or defendant acting in person who drafted the pleading.

9 The indorsement required by RSC Ord 18 r6(4)(a) and (b) and the date of service as required by RSC Ord 18 r6(1)(e). See note 6 at sample pleading (1).

Note: If the action were brought in the county court, the lay-out of the heading and the indorsements following the signature would be as in sample pleading (3) with the case number allocated by the court office being taken from the particulars of claim. The description and the lay-out of the pleading would be as in sample pleading (4).

Sample pleading
(5) Reply and defence to counterclaim

IN THE HIGH COURT OF JUSTICE   1995 F No 56678
QUEEN'S BENCH DIVISION
[DISTRICT REGISTRY]
BETWEEN

JAMES ROBERT FOSTER   <u>Plaintiff</u>   1

and

ALICE ROSE CARTWRIGHT   <u>Defendant</u>

REPLY AND DEFENCE TO COUNTERCLAIM ²

REPLY ³

1. Save insofar as it contains admissions, and save as is expressly
    admitted hereinafter, the Plaintiff joins issue with the Defence.
2.
3.

DEFENCE TO COUNTERCLAIM ⁵

4.
5. } 6
6.

                  (signed)_____ 7

Served the   day of   199
by Messrs _____ & Co of _____
Solicitors for the Plaintiff. 8

Notes

1 Heading as in previous pleadings.
2 The description of the pleading as required by RSC Ord 18 r6(1)(d).
   Since this is a composite pleading the description refers to both
   pleadings.

3   The description of the first pleading must follow the description of the composite pleading.

4   The body of the pleading must be divided into consecutively numbered paragraphs, each containing, so far as is convenient, a separate allegation: RSC Ord 18 r6(2). The content of para 1 is explained at p 61 below.

5   The description of the second pleading must be included.

6   See note 4. Note that the numbering of the paragraphs in a composite pleading is continuous.

7   Signature of the barrister, solicitor or plaintiff acting in person who drafted the pleading.

8   The indorsement required by RSC Ord 18 r6(4)(a) and (b) and the date of service required by RSC Ord 18 r6(1)(e). See note 10 at sample pleading (1).

Part 3: Content

To understand how to draft pleadings you must first know what a pleading should contain. We shall therefore devote a substantial section of this chapter to considering what matters should be included in pleadings. In doing so we shall look firstly at the subject matter of specific types of pleading, and secondly at those matters which must or may or must not be included in pleadings generally. Finally we shall consider the nature of the information which must be pleaded in respect of such matters.

Types of pleadings

The matters which must be included in any pleading are determined by its purpose. Consequently, in order to understand what a specific type of pleading should contain you must understand its purpose. In considering the content of specific types of pleading we shall therefore begin, in each case, by describing the purpose of that pleading.

The statement of claim/particulars of claim

Purpose

As the description, statement of claim or particulars of claim suggests, the purpose of the first pleading in any action is to set out the plaintiff's case. To put this another way, its purpose is to set out in writing the facts which the plaintiff intends to and must prove at trial in order to establish a cause, or causes, of action and so demonstrate the plaintiff's entitlement to the relief or remedy claimed in the pleading.

At the same time, sufficient facts must be pleaded to ensure that the pleading fulfils its further function of informing the defendant of the nature of the case which he or she has to meet. These purposes shape the rules which determine the content of the statement/particulars of claim, and must always be kept in mind when drafting.

Content

The purpose described above might be listed as follows:

(1) disclose cause(s) of action
(2) state relief or remedy claimed
(3) show nexus between (1) and (2)

show sufficient facts to inform a defendant of case to be met

This list provides a framework within which the content of the statement/particulars of claim and the rules relating to content can be examined.

CAUSE OF ACTION

The statement/particulars of claim that you draft must disclose a cause of action: this is the primary purpose of the pleading, as indicated, and is required by the rules.[12] If no cause of action is disclosed, the court may order that the pleading is to be amended or struck out and that the action is to be stayed or dismissed.[13] It should be noted, however, that no cause of action may be pleaded which has not been mentioned specifically in the writ or arises from the same facts as a cause of action which is mentioned in the writ.[14]

A cause of action has been succinctly defined as, 'simply a factual situation the existence of which entitles one person to obtain from the court a remedy against another person'.[15] The factual situations which enable plaintiffs to obtain remedies from the court are, of course, extremely varied, even if restricted to the field of tort. However, within each such situation can be detected a number of linked facts which together constitute the cause of action. These are, then, the essential facts which must be shown to exist for the cause of action to be established. They are, in short, the elements of the action.

---

[12] *Ibid* r19(1)(a); CCR Ord 6 r1(1).
[13] RSC Ord 18 r19(1)(a); CCR Ord 13 r5(1)(a).
[14] RSC Ord 18 r15(2).
[15] *Letang v Cooper* [1915] 1 QB 232, *per* Diplock LJ, at 242 quoted at SCP 15/1/3.

To illustrate this, let us consider the important tort of negligence. Many different factual situations may give rise to successful claims in negligence. However in every case the plaintiff succeeds because within each of the diverse factual situations, certain essential facts common to all actions in negligence, that is the elements of negligence, can be detected. These essential facts or elements are:

- that the person accused of wrongdoing owes a *duty of care* to the person claiming to have suffered as a result of that wrongdoing;
- that the alleged wrongdoing constitutes *breach of that duty of care;*
- that the *alleged breach of duty has caused injury or loss* to the person claiming to have suffered as a result of the wrongdoing.

This can be further illustrated by looking at several different factual situations in which negligence might be established. Thus, for example, successful claims in negligence might be brought by a pedestrian injured as a result of a collision with a motor vehicle, an employee injured when operating a defective machine at her workplace, a person tripping over an uneven paving stone and breaking his ankle, or a person whose house is flooded as the result of work undertaken by a builder who owns and is developing a site adjacent to the house.

In each case, however, to succeed at trial the plaintiff would have to prove that the defendant driver/employer/council/builder owed the plaintiff a duty of care, was in breach of that duty, and as a result has caused the plaintiff to suffer damage. Thus at trial each plaintiff would have to utilise the distinctive facts of his or her case to prove that the elements of negligence were made out.

However, a plaintiff can only adduce evidence at trial to prove a material fact that has been pleaded. Since no cause of action will be disclosed if any element of that cause of action is omitted, the material facts pleaded in the statement/particulars of claim must establish the existence of every element of the cause or causes of action relied upon by the plaintiff. Omission of any essential element will cause the plaintiff's claim to fail if it proceeds to trial.[16]

Approaches to pleading the elements of particular torts will be considered in the chapters dealing with those torts. One element which is common to many torts and will therefore be discussed more generally here is the element of damage.

---

[16] *Galoo Ltd v Bright Grahame Murray* (1994) *The Times*, 14 January, CA.

DAMAGE

Actions in which the plaintiff is not required to prove damage

In some tortious actions, such as trespass to land and certain kinds of nuisance,[17] the plaintiff is not required to prove that he or she has suffered damage. Consequently, in drafting the statement/particulars of claim it is not necessary to allege specific damage, but is sufficient to allege a claim in general terms, for example, 'the Plaintiff has thereby suffered damage'.

Actions in which damage must be proved

In actions in which damage must be proved a distinction is drawn between pleading general and special damage.

General damage

This means damage of a kind the law presumes to result from the wrong alleged. Such damage need not be particularised, that is, pleaded in detail. It is sufficient to plead that the plaintiff has suffered damage. An example of general damages is pain, suffering and loss of amenity in a personal injury action.[18]

You should note, however, that where the damage alleged is not the necessary and immediate consequence of the defendant's wrongful conduct, the plaintiff must plead full particulars so as to make clear to the defendant the nature and extent of the claim.

Thus a plaintiff who claims higher damages on the ground that the loss of amenity that she has suffered is greater than might be presumed to result from the injuries she has suffered must plead sufficient details to make clear the basis of such a claim. This might, for example, be the fact that she is an accomplished pianist who is no longer able to play because of her injuries.

It should be noted that some types of loss categorised as general damage are capable of calculation, for example, loss of future earning capacity in a personal injury case. When pleading such loss, details must be given to assist the court in calculating the amount the plaintiff is to receive if substantial damages are sought.

Special damage

This means damage not presumed to result from the wrong complained of, and such damage must always be pleaded and particularised.[19] An example of special damage is the financial loss

---

[17] See below, at p 300.
[18] See below, at p 187.
[19] SCP 18/12/19; *Green Book*, notes at p 160.

suffered when a plaintiff's property is damaged or destroyed as a result of the defendant's negligence. In practice, the term special damage is also used to describe all financial loss incurred by a plaintiff between the date of the wrongful conduct which caused that loss and the date of trial. Such special damage must, of course, be pleaded and particularised.[20]

The paragraph pleading damage in an action in which damage must be proved might typically be set out as follows:

> By reason of the matters aforesaid the Plaintiff has suffered loss and damage.

PARTICULARS OF SPECIAL DAMAGE

> Cost of repairs to the shop   £

Personal injury actions

A number of rules apply specifically to pleading damage in a personal injury case. An example is the requirement that a plaintiff pursuing a personal injury claim in the county court must file with the particulars of claim a statement of the special damages claimed.[21] The drafting of this schedule of financial loss, and other matters relating to pleading damage in a personal injury case, is discussed in Chapter 8 below.[22]

RELIEF OR REMEDY CLAIMED

The primary objective in bringing a legal action is to obtain from the court some relief or remedy in respect of the alleged wrongdoing of the defendant. Indeed, the purpose of identifying and pleading the plaintiff's cause or causes of action is to establish the legal basis for the plaintiff's claim to be entitled to some relief or remedy.

Two requirements of pleading flow from this. Firstly, the relief or remedy claimed by the plaintiff must be specifically stated in the statement/particulars of claim.[23] Secondly, there must be a nexus between the cause or causes of action pleaded and the relief or remedy claimed. That is, the cause or causes of action relied upon must give rise to a right to obtain the relief or remedy sought.

---

[20] *Ilkiw Samuels* [1963] 1 WLR 991.
[21] CCR Ord 6 r1(5)(b).
[22] See below at p 191.
[23] RSC Ord 18 r15(1): CCR Ord 6 r1(1).

A single cause of action may, of course, enable a plaintiff to claim more than one kind of relief or remedy. If this is the case, every kind of relief or remedy claimed must be pleaded. For example, a plaintiff who brings an action in nuisance can claim monetary compensation in the form of damages to be paid by the defendant or an injunction ordering the defendant to do some act or refrain from doing some act, so as to prevent further nuisance to the plaintiff or both damages and an injunction.[24] It should be noted, however, that equitable remedies, such as an injunction, are discretionary, and may be refused by the court even if the plaintiff's cause of action is established.

The claim for relief or remedy is made in the form of a prayer which commences with the words 'AND the Plaintiff claims:' and sets out each head of relief or remedy claimed in a separate numbered paragraph. Logically the claim is made after pleading the cause or causes of action relied upon as giving rise to the right to claim such relief or remedy. It is the practice, therefore, for the prayer to come at the end of the pleading.[25]

Costs

As is well known, litigation is very expensive, and a plaintiff whose action is successful will normally seek an order that the defendant is to pay the costs the plaintiff has incurred in pursuing his or her claim.[26]

RSC Ord 18 r15(1) expressly provides that in the High Court a claim for costs need not be specifically pleaded, and it is the practice in the Queen's Bench Division, where most actions in tort are brought, to omit the claim for costs from the prayer. In the Chancery Division, however, the prayer should include a claim for costs.[27] The County Court Rules are silent on the matter of pleading costs, and in practice no claim for costs is included in the prayer.[28]

Interest

Where an action in tort succeeds and the unsuccessful defendant is ordered by the court to pay damages to the plaintiff, the defendant will also be liable to pay interest to the plaintiff on the damages awarded, as from the date on which the cause of action arose to the date of judgment.

---

[24] SCP 18/15/2.

[25] SCP 18/15/1.

[26] It should be noted that even a plaintiff whose claim is wholly successful is unlikely to recover all the costs incurred in bringing the action.

[27] Casson and Dennis, *Odgers' Principles of Pleading and Practice* (Stevens, London).

[28] See the precedent in *Butterworth's County Court Precedents and Pleadings* at B [472], cited in the Green Book at p 161.

This liability arises in the High Court under s 35A Supreme Court Act 1981 and in the county courts under s 69 County Courts Act 1984.[29] However, a claim for interest, whether under one of these statutes or otherwise[30] must be pleaded. Consequently a plaintiff's claim for interest must be made in the statement/particulars of claim.[31] If it is not so pleaded, no interest will be awarded unless the pleading is amended.[32]

The plaintiff's claim for interest should be pleaded in both the body of the pleading and in prayer.[33] The basis on which interest is claimed must be identified, and where interest is claimed under s 35A or s 69 the pleading must refer specifically to the appropriate Act since it is not sufficient to plead a claim for 'interest under the statute'.[34] The amount in relation to the period for which and the rate at which interest is claimed must also be stated. In many tort cases this can be done in general terms, the plaintiff claiming:

> Interest pursuant to section 35A of the Supreme Court Act 1981 (or section 69 of the County Courts Act 1984) on the amount found to be due to the Plaintiff at such rate and for such period as the Court thinks fit.

The practice with regard to pleading interest in personal injury and fatal accident cases is discussed in Chapters 8 and 9.[35]

---

[29] Sections 35A and 69 provide that in any proceedings for the recovery of debt or damages simple interest may be awarded on all or part of debt or damages irrespective of when judgment is given or payment is made before judgment. Interest may be awarded at the rate the court thinks fit for all or part of the period between the date when the cause of the action arose and either the date of judgment or the date of earlier payment as may be appropriate. Sections 35A(2) and 69(2) provide that where judgment is given for damages for personal injury or death, interest must be awarded unless the court is satisfied that there are special reasons to the contrary. Nevertheless, the requirement under RSC Ord 18 r8(4) and CCR Ord 6 r1A that a claim for interest must be pleaded applies to claims for damages for personal injury or death as it does to other classes of damage: SCP 5163; notes to s 69 in the *Green Book* at pp 1420-21.

[30] See further SCP 18/8/9(21).

[31] RSC Ord 18 r8(4): CCR Ord 6 r1A. This requirement applies to a statement of claim indorsed on the writ: SCP 18/8/9(21).

[32] *Ward v Chief Constable for Avon and Somerset* [1985] 129 Sol J; 606 (WB 161): 537 (GB 299).

[33] SCP 18/9/9(21). Nevertheless, in *McDonald's Hamburgers v Burger King (UK) Ltd* [1987] FSR 112 it was held to be sufficient if the claim for interest under s 35A Supreme Court Act 1981 was only made in the prayer and not also in the body of the pleading. The County Court Rules do not appear to require the claim to be pleaded in both the body of the particulars of the claim and the prayer, and the precedent cited by the *Green Book*, see note 28 above, does not do so. However, many lawyers follow High Court practice and include the claim in both the body of the pleading and the prayer.

[34] SCP 18/8/9(21).

[35] See below, pp 192, 228.

The defence

Purpose

The obvious purpose of this pleading is to set out in writing a defendant's response to the case pleaded by a plaintiff in the statement/particulars of claim. The best way to obtain the client's response is to invite him or her to read through the statement/particulars of claim and to note down his or her response to each allegation. These comments, together with the evidence before the lawyer, form the basis on which the defence is drafted.

The defence is therefore the defendant's opportunity to state in written form not merely whether he or she admits or contests each allegation made by the plaintiff, but also his or her own version of the matters alleged. Since, except in so far as it consists of admissions, a defence is deemed to be traversed, that is contested, by the plaintiff.[36] A corollary and fundamental purpose of the defence is that, when read in conjunction with the statement/particulars of claim, it should make clear those matters on which the parties are in agreement and those on which they are in dispute.

Content

As this suggests, a basic defence will consist of a series of paragraphs admitting or traversing, or partly admitting and partly traversing the various allegations made in the statement/particulars of claim. Each material allegation made by the plaintiff must be pleaded to unless there is an express provision to the contrary in the rules. This is because any allegation in the statement/particulars of claim which is not traversed is deemed to be admitted.[37] The best forms of traverse are non-admission and denial. We shall therefore begin by examining the practice with regard to admissions, non-admissions and denials.

ADMISSIONS

Any plain and uncontroversial fact which it is not in the defendant's interest or power to dispute ought to be admitted.[38] Thus, for example, a paragraph identifying the plaintiff and the defendant is usually uncontentious and consequently can usually be admitted. The relevant paragraphs in the statement/particulars of claim and the defence in a road traffic accident case might read:

---

[36]   RSC Ord 18 r14(1).

[37]   *Ibid* r13(1).

[38]   SCP 18/13/2.

Statement/Particulars of Claim:

1. At all material times the Plaintiff was the owner and driver of a Toyota Corolla motor car registration number F149 BPX and the Defendant was the driver of a Peugeot 106 motor car registration number J562 LRP.

Defence:

1. Paragraph 1 of the Statement of Claim [Particulars of Claim] is admitted.

The effect of an express or a deemed admission is that the facts admitted are not in issue between the plaintiff and the defendant and need not be proved at trial. Consequently no evidence can be adduced at trial in relation to these facts.[39]

It is therefore very important to be absolutely clear as to the extent to which a defendant client admits the allegations made by the plaintiff. Nothing which the plaintiff ought to be forced to prove at trial should be admitted either expressly or by default through failing to traverse the relevant allegation. On the other hand nothing which ought to be admitted should be traversed simply to put the plaintiff to the trouble and expense of proving it, since a refusal to admit facts which ought to be admitted may ultimately result in the defendant being ordered to pay costs incurred by the plaintiff because of the defendant's conduct.[40]

Occasionally a defendant does not merely admit but also avers some fact or facts alleged by the plaintiff. The purpose in doing so may simply be to give emphasis to the admission. However, a matter may be averred in order to emphasise that it is part of the defendant's case. Thus, a defendant may admit and aver some fact pleaded by the plaintiff because that fact must be proved by the defendant to establish some element of a counterclaim against the plaintiff.[41]

TRAVERSE BY NON-ADMISSION OR DENIAL

Whether an allegation made in the statement/particulars of claim is traversed by non-admission or denial the effect is to put the fact or facts alleged in issue between the plaintiff and the defendant. In either case the plaintiff will therefore be required to prove the fact or facts alleged at trial or to resile from the allegation. This is why it is

---

[39] *Ibid.*

[40] RSC Ord 62 r6(7).

[41] See below, p 69.

sometimes said that the effect upon the plaintiff of the defendant non-admitting or denying an allegation is the same.

There is however an important distinction between not admitting or denying an allegation. A traverse by denial is reserving to the defendant the right to adduce evidence contrary to the plaintiff's allegation. No such right is reserved when an allegation is traversed by non-admission. Since the inability to call evidence on a contested allegation in the statement/particulars of claim might prove fatal to the defendant's case this is, as the notes to the *Supreme Court Practice* point out, a potentially vital distinction, and one that must be kept in mind.[42]

In practice a further distinction is often drawn between a non-admission and a denial. This is that a party traverses by non-admission matters which are not within his or her knowledge, but denies matters which are. Thus, a defendant council might deny that a highway was in a dangerous condition at the time of an accident which occurred on it, since the condition of the highway is within the council's knowledge, but traverse by non-admission the plaintiff's claim to have suffered loss as a result of the accident on the basis that the council has no knowledge whether or not such loss was incurred.

These two distinctions are linked in that the denial of an allegation made by a plaintiff is often based on the defendant's knowledge of facts which he or she intends to plead and prove in order to undermine the plaintiff's allegation. Thus a defence which denies that a road traffic accident in which the plaintiff was injured was caused by negligent driving on the part of the defendant might go on to allege that the accident was caused by defective brakes on the plaintiff's car and/or the negligence of the plaintiff.

When an allegation is traversed the defendant may add emphasis to the non-admission or denial by putting the plaintiff to strict proof of the matter alleged. This is illustrated in a sample paragraph at p 44.

Some defences also include a general traverse. This is a paragraph which traverses every allegation in the statement/particulars of claim which has not been expressly admitted in the defence. The example below illustrates how a general traverse may be pleaded:

Save as hereinbefore expressly admitted, each and every allegation contained in the Statement [Particulars] of Claim is denied as if the same had been set out herein and specifically traversed herein.

---

[42] SCP 18/13/5.

The general traverse therefore operates to deny any allegation which has not been pleaded to and which, in the absence of such a paragraph, would be deemed to be admitted. A general traverse is only appropriate when drafting in response to a statement/particulars of claim, or a counterclaim, which sets out a particularly complex case. When used it appears at the end of the defence.

It should be noted that some matters pleaded in the statement/particulars of claim will be deemed to be in issue and need not be expressly traversed. These are the claim for interest in the body of the pleading, the prayer and any matters pleaded as particulars of an allegation. It is only where the defendant wishes to admit or plead an alternative case that it is necessary to plead to such matters.

Sample admissions, non-admissions and denials

The following paragraphs provide simple illustrations of the way in which admissions, non-admissions and denials can be pleaded. The relevant paragraph or paragraphs from the statement/particulars of claim are given in brackets.

ADMISSIONS

[1. At all material times the Defendant owned and operated a fleet of minicabs known as 'Anne's Cabs'.

2. On 21 January 1996 at about 10.30 pm the Plaintiff hired one of the Defendant's said minicabs to convey her to Heathrow Airport.]

1. Paragraphs 1 and 2 of the Statement [Particulars] of Claim are admitted.

NON-ADMISSIONS

[7. By reason of the matters aforesaid the Plaintiff has been and is being caused annoyance and discomfort and the Plaintiff has thereby suffered damage.]

8. No admissions are made as to the nature, cause and extent of the alleged or any annoyance, discomfort and damage suffered by the Plaintiff.

DENIALS

[5. The matters complained of were caused by the negligence of the Defendant.

PARTICULARS OF NEGLIGENCE

(1) Failing to repair the said fence.

(2) Failing to take any or any adequate precaution to prevent the said cows from straying into the Plaintiff's said garden.

(3 ....]

6. It is denied that the Defendant was negligent as alleged in paragraph 5 of the Statement [Particulars] of Claim or at all or that the matters complained of were caused as alleged or at all.

In this example the defendant has no alternative case to plead with regard to any of the allegations made in the particulars of negligence and consequently has not pleaded to these.

PLEADING TO A CLAIM FOR INTEREST

The following paragraph would be appropriate if the defendant admitted the plaintiff's claim for interest but disputed the rates and period pleaded in the statement/particulars of claim.

7. The Plaintiff's claim to interest on any damages that may be awarded to her is admitted. No admissions are made as to the rates or period claimed.

PUTTING THE PLAINTIFF TO STRICT PROOF

6. No admissions are made as to the loss and damage alleged and the Plaintiff is put to strict proof thereon.

PLEADING AN AFFIRMATIVE CASE

The most basic form of defence is to not admit the allegations made in the statement/particulars of claim. However even the simplest claim is likely to require the defendant to admit some allegations, not admit others and deny the remainder. Indeed, all three types of response may be made in one paragraph of the defence pleading to a single paragraph of the statement/particulars of claim.

Moreover, it is seldom sufficient merely to admit or traverse the allegations made by the plaintiff. The presentation of an effective defence will usually require the defendant to plead his or her version of part or all of the factual situation on which the plaintiff's claim is based, and/or to plead additional matters, so as to undermine the plaintiff's case. This is often described as pleading a positive or affirmative case.

At the simplest level, pleading the defendant's positive case may consist of admitting an allegation made by the plaintiff, but restating it so as to plead the defendant's version of the fact or facts alleged.

Another way of admitting an allegation made in the statement/particulars of claim while putting the defendant's affirmative case is called 'confession and avoidance'. In this case the defendant 'confesses' the truth of the plaintiff's allegation but pleads facts which undermine the legal consequences of the confession. Thus, for example, a defendant may admit that he assaulted the plaintiff but seek to escape liability for the assault by pleading the defence of self-defence.

A more complex example of pleading a defendant's affirmative case is where an allegation in the statement/particulars of claim is denied and the defence goes on to allege matters which, if proved at trial, will weaken or destroy the effect of the plaintiff's allegation.

One example of this approach is illustrated below, with the relevant paragraph of the statement/particulars of claim set out in brackets.

[3. The said dog was of an aggressive and abnormal nature and the Defendant kept the said dog knowing that he was of such an aggressive and abnormal nature.]

4. Paragraph 3 of the Statement [Particulars] of Claim is denied. The said dog was docile by nature and had never previously bitten any person or caused any form of injury, loss or damage.

It is worth noting that the plaintiff in this example has failed to plead details of the allegation that the dog is of an aggressive and abnormal nature, for example, details of previous attacks by the dog. He has therefore opened himself up to a request by the defendant for further and better particulars of the allegation.

A further common example, which has been mentioned earlier,[43] is where the defendant denies that his negligent conduct caused an accident in which the plaintiff was injured, and subsequently alleges that the accident was caused in some other way.

---

[43] See above, p 42.

A denial of the plaintiff's version of how an accident, or some other situation as a result of which the plaintiff suffered damage, was caused is often accompanied by the allegation that the plaintiff's own negligent conduct caused or contributed to the accident or the loss alleged. Proving the first allegation will enable the defendant to escape liability. However, greater reliance is in many cases placed on the second, for even if the defendant is held liable for the plaintiff's loss, it may be possible to prove contributory negligence by the plaintiff with the result that the damages payable by the defendant will be reduced in proportion to the extent to which the plaintiff is held to be liable for his or her own loss.

As this shows, pleading a defendant's affirmative case may involve pleading certain well-established defences. These may relate to a specific cause of action, for example the defence of fair comment which may be raised in a defamation action, or to a number of torts, for example, the partial defence of contributory negligence, or to any claim, for example, the limitation defence.[44] It is therefore crucial for the lawyer to know the range of defences available to a defendant client in relation to the cause of action pleaded by the plaintiff.[45] The way in which the defence of contributory negligence and limitation should be pleaded is discussed later in this chapter.[46] The pleading of other defences is considered in the chapters which deal with the individual tort to which they relate.

Pleading other additional facts

A final function of the defence is to plead additional facts which fill gaps or clarify or correct minor errors in the plaintiff's account of the events alleged to have given rise to a cause of action. Thus, for example, where the plaintiff has referred to a third party whose name is known only to the defendant, such as the defendant's employer, that name may for clarity be inserted by the defendant when referring to the third party in the defence. Similarly an incorrect address, given by the plaintiff as part of a preliminary averment,[47] may be corrected in the defence.

---

[44] See below, pp 49-50. It should be noted that the defence of limitation does not apply to an action brought by a minor or a mental patient, s 28 Limitation Act 1980.

[45] See below, p 64ff.

[46] See below, p 68.

[47] For the meaning of 'preliminary averment', see below, p 64.

The counterclaim

Since a counterclaim pleads a defendant's claim against a plaintiff its function is essentially that of the statement/particulars of claim. Consequently it must disclose a cause of action, state the relief or remedy claimed by the defendant and show the nexus between the cause or causes of action relied upon and the relief or remedy claimed. The section dealing with the contents of the statement/particulars of claim should therefore be consulted when drafting a counterclaim.

The reply

A reply sets out a plaintiff's response to the defence. However if no reply is served all the allegations in a defence are deemed to be denied.[48] Consequently a reply should only be drafted if the plaintiff wishes to plead an alternative case in respect of one or more allegations made in the defence. It should be noted that this deemed joinder of issue no longer arises if a reply is served, and the reply must therefore deal with every allegation contained in the defence: RSC Ord 18 r13(1). Any allegation which is not pleaded to will be deemed to be admitted. For this reason the reply invariably commences with a paragraph taking issue with the defence except in so far as it consists of admissions or is admitted in the reply. The wording of this paragraph is illustrated in sample pleading (5) on p 32 above.

The defence to counterclaim

Since as we have seen a counterclaim performs for a defendant the function that the statement/particulars of claim performs for a plaintiff, the function of a defence to counterclaim is to put the plaintiff's case with regard to the counterclaim in the same way as a defence puts a defendant's case with regard to the statement/particulars of claim. Guidance on the content of the defence to counterclaim may therefore be found in the section on the defence above.

Matters which must, may or must not be included in pleadings

In addition to defining the purpose and so the basic subject matter of specific types of pleading, the Rules of the Supreme Court and the County Court Rules, and in particular RSC Ord 18, give considerable guidance as to the matters which must, or may, or may not be pleaded.

Some of the provisions of RSC Ord 18 are duplicated in the County Court Rules 1981. Where this is not the case the provisions apply to county court proceedings to the extent that they embody general

---

[48] RSC Ord 18 r14(1) and (4).

principles of High Court practice which may be adopted or applied by virtue of s 76 County Courts Act 1984.[49]

Matters which must be pleaded

There is a general requirement that a party must plead any conviction which he or she intends to adduce in evidence at trial,[50] and some such matters must be pleaded irrespective of the type of pleading which is being drafted. Other requirements relate to specific pleadings. For example, in a personal injury action, a plaintiff seeking provisional damages must plead that claim specifically.[51] In pleadings subsequent to a statement of claim the following must be pleaded:[52]

- any allegation which, if proved, would render the other side's claim or defence unsustainable, for example, expiry of the limitation period;[53]
- a matter which, if not specifically pleaded, might take the other side by surprise;
- any matter raising issues of fact which do not arise out of a previous pleading.

A number of matters which must be pleaded and may be relevant when drafting in tort are considered below.

Convictions
Where a party intends at trial to adduce evidence that another party to the action has been convicted by a court in the United Kingdom, or by a court-martial, that party's pleading must contain a statement of that conviction. It must give particulars of the conviction, the court, or the court-martial which made it, and the issue to which the conviction is relevant.[54]

Contributory negligence
A defendant who alleges that negligence on the part of the plaintiff contributed to the injury or loss for which compensation is claimed must plead contributory negligence as part of his or her defence. Failure to do so will prevent the judge from making a finding of contributory negligence.[55]

---

[49] *Green Book*, p 448n.
[50] RSC Ord 18 r7A.
[51] *Ibid* r8(3); SCP 18/8/15 (41); CCR Ord 6 r1B.
[52] RSC Ord 18 r8(1)(a)–(c); see also the *Green Book* notes on pp 189–190.
[53] See below under Limitation Act 1980.
[54] RSC Ord 18 r7A. An example showing how a conviction is pleaded appears at p 153 below.
[55] SCP 18/8/5 citing *Fookes v Slaytor* [1978] 1 WLR 1293 CA.

Exemplary damages

The situations in which an award for exemplary or aggravated damages may be made are limited and the need to plead a claim for them may seldom arise. However, there are situations in which a claim for aggravated or exemplary damages may be made, for example, where a police officer uses unjustifiable force and is sued for assault. In such a case a court may properly award aggravated or exemplary damages provided that the claim is pleaded in the body of the statement/particulars of claim together with the facts in support of such a claim. It is not sufficient merely to include the claim for exemplary damages in the prayer.[56]

Fraud

It is not open to the court to infer fraud from the facts pleaded by a party. Consequently an allegation of fraud must be specifically pleaded as must the facts on which the allegation is based.[57]

Interest

A claim for interest under s 35A Supreme Court Act 1981 in the High Court, or under s 69 County Courts Act 1984 in the county court on any damages awarded in respect of a plaintiff's claim or a defendant's counterclaim must be specifically pleaded. The claim for interest must be included in the body of the statement of claim or counterclaim and should be repeated in the prayer. Interest will not be awarded if the claim is not pleaded.[58]

Libel and slander

In defamation actions the defences of justification and privilege must be specifically pleaded together with the facts in support.[59]

Limitation Act 1980

This Act prescribes the periods within which particular types of action should be brought. When a plaintiff institutes proceedings after the expiry of the relevant limitation period, the action is 'statute-barred' or 'time-barred' and this provides the defendant with a complete defence

---

[56] RSC Ord 18 r8(3); SCP 18/8/7(13): CCR Ord 6 r1B and the notes thereto referring the reader to a precedent for a claim for aggravated and exemplary damages at *Butterworths County Court Precedents and Pleadings*, B [473] and B [3561].

[57] RSC Ord 18 r8(1); SCP 18/8/8(16).

[58] RSC Ord 18 rr8(4) and 15(1); SCP 18/8/9(21). Information on pleading a claim of interest made under another statute, a contract or the equitable jurisdiction of the court is given at SCP 18/8/9(21).

[59] SCP 18/8/6(8).

to the plaintiff's claim. This defence must, however, be expressly pleaded,[60] and if it is not so raised the action may proceed. In tort the basic limitation period is six years, but special rules apply to particular types of action, for example personal injury claims.

Provisional damages

In a personal injury action it is open to a plaintiff, in some circumstances, to seek a provisional damages award. If this claim succeeds, the plaintiff receives a sum by way of immediate damages, but will be entitled to apply for further damages if he or she develops a specified disease or suffers physical or mental deterioration of a specified nature.

The claim for such an award, and the facts upon which it is based, must, however, be pleaded in the body of the plaintiff's statement of claim and the prayer must include the words 'An order for the award of provisional damages under s 32A of the Supreme Court Act 1981'.[61]

Relief or remedy claimed

A party must expressly plead any relief or remedy claimed. This requirement does not, however, extend to a claim for costs.[62]

Particulars which must be pleaded

Whether or not a party is required by the rules to plead a particular matter, he or she must ensure that any claim or allegation is pleaded in sufficient detail to enable the other side to fully understand the case being presented. The detail required will therefore depend on the case pleaded.[63] Failure to plead sufficient details is likely to result in the other side serving a request for further and better particulars.

However, RSC Ord 18 r12 specifies certain allegations of which particulars must be given, and the notes relating to this order should therefore be consulted when drafting.

These are the matters which must be fully particularised:

---

[60] RSC Ord 18 r8(1); SCP 18/8/11(27), (28); *Green Book* notes at pp 189–90.

[61] RSC Ord 18 r8(3); SCP 18/8/15(41); CCR Ord 6 r1B and notes thereto.

[62] See above, p 38.

[63] RSC Ord 18 r12(1) obliges parties to state in their pleadings 'the necessary particulars of any claim, defence or other matter pleaded'. See also CCR Ord 6 r1(1), Ord 9 r2 and the notes thereto; *Green Book* p 448n.

Contributory negligence

A defendant alleging contributory negligence must give details of the acts or omissions alleged to constitute negligence by the plaintiff.[64]

Damages

No particulars need be pleaded of general damage, but details must be given of special damage, in the sense of monetary loss incurred between the date on which the cause of action accrued and the date of trial.[65] In an action for personal injuries, the plaintiff must serve a statement of special damages claimed with the statement/particulars of claim. This statement must give full details of expenses or losses already incurred, and an estimate of anticipated future expenses and losses including loss of earnings and loss of pension rights.[66]

Fraud

An allegation of fraud must be fully particularised. If the acts alleged to constitute fraud are not pleaded, evidence at trial cannot be adduced to support them.[67]

Knowledge

Where knowledge, or absence of knowledge, is material to a party's case, it should be pleaded and particularised.[68] This may be illustrated by the example of a plaintiff claiming in respect of injuries suffered in an attack by the defendant's dog. If it is the plaintiff's case that the defendant knew of the dog's dangerous nature, he or she must allege this knowledge and must also plead the facts, such as previous attacks by the dog, which support the allegation.

Libel

A statement of claim pleading libel must give full particulars of the precise words used by the defendant,[69] the document in which the words were contained and the date on which the words were published. Where fair comment or justification is pleaded in defence to

---

[64] SCP 18/12/5(17).

[65] SCP 18/12/6(21); 18/12/19(68).

[66] RSC Ord 18 r12(1A)(b) and (1C); SCP 18/12/22(2); CCR Ord 6 r1(5)(b) and 1(7) and the notes thereto.

[67] RSC Ord 18 r12(1)(a); SCP 18/12/7(28).

[68] RSC Ord 18 r12(4); SCP 18/12/1 (42).

[69] SCP 18/12/13(43). Libel is an example of a claim in which the precise words used are material. For slander, see SCP 18/12/18(67).

such a claim, the defendant must set out the facts and matters relied upon in support.[70]

Misrepresentation

Where misrepresentation is alleged, the statement of claim must give particulars of each misrepresentation, identifying its nature and by whom and to whom the false statement was made. It is must also state whether it was made orally or in writing and if in writing identify the document in which it was made.[71]

Negligence

In an action for negligence, the statement of claim must plead the facts which are alleged to give rise to a duty of care. It must also give details of the acts or omissions alleged to constitute the breach of that duty, that is, the particulars of negligence, and the details of the injury and damage sustained.[72]

Personal injuries

Where a plaintiff claims for damages due to injuries sustained as a result of a defendant's tort, a medical report setting out particulars of the injuries suffered must be served with the statement of claim.[73] Nevertheless, the statement of claim must plead a brief resume of the injuries suffered.[74]

Statutory particulars

In an action brought under the Fatal Accidents Act 1976 a plaintiff is required to deliver with the statement of claim, details of the person for whom and on whose behalf the action is brought and of the nature of the claim.[75]

Matters which may be pleaded

A party's pleading may raise any claim or make any allegation of fact which is not specifically prohibited under the rules. This applies to matters arising both before the writ or summons is issued and after the date of issue.[76]

---

[70] SCP 18/12/7(26).

[71] RSC Ord 18 r12(1)(a); SCP 18/12/14(49).

[72] SCP 18/12/15(51).

[73] RSC Ord 18 r1(1A)(a), (1C); SCP 18/12/22; CCR Ord 6 rr5(a) and 7 and notes thereto.

[74] *B v Wyeth & Brother Ltd* [1991] Med Lr 34 cited at SCP 18/12/22.

[75] Section 2(4) Fatal Accidents Act 1976; SCP 18/12/19(69).

[76] RSC Ord 18 r9.

Matters which must not be pleaded

Calderbank offer
Where a party makes a written offer to settle 'without prejudice as to costs', the offer must not be brought to the court's attention until all questions relating to liability or to the amount of damages recoverable (the quantum) have been decided. Consequently a Calderbank offer must not be pleaded.

Interim payment
In some circumstances a plaintiff may seek from a defendant an interim payment on account of the damages which it is anticipated that the plaintiff will recover at trial. Whether such a payment is made voluntarily or under a court order, it must not be pleaded since the trial judge must not be told of the payment until all questions of liability are settled.[77]

Payment into court
One way in which a defendant can put pressure on a plaintiff to settle a case before trial is to make a payment into court. If the plaintiff rejects the sum offered in settlement in this way, but fails at trial to recover more than that sum, he or she may be required to pay both parties' costs from the date of payment into court. Neither the amount of payment into court nor the fact that it has been made may be communicated to the trial judge before all questions relating to liability or to the amount of damages recoverable (quantum) have been decided. Consequently the 'payment in' must not be pleaded.[78]

The nature of the information to be pleaded

It is not enough to know that, for example, a statement of claim must plead the elements of a cause of action, or that a defence must plead any matter which, if not specifically pleaded, might take the other side by surprise. In order to plead effectively, you also need to know what information must be included in respect of such matters. To find guidance on the nature of the information that must be pleaded, it is necessary to examine further the rules relating to pleading, and, in particular, what may be described as the principal rules of pleading which are set out in RSC Ord 18 r7.

---

[77] RSC Ord 29 r15; SCP 18/8/9(22); CCR Ord 13 r12(1) applying the provisions of RSC Ord 29.

[78] RSC Ord 22 r7; SCP 18/8/15(38); CCR Ord 11 r7(1).

The rules set out at RSC Ord 18 r7 can be summarised as follows:

- plead only material facts;
- plead all the material facts;
- plead material facts not evidence;
- plead material facts not law;
- plead the material facts in summary form.

In one sense these rules are of course primarily concerned with the content of pleadings. However the rules must also be understood as giving guidance on how the matters which must be included in a pleading should be pleaded. This is particularly true of the requirement that material facts must be pleaded in summary form and this rule is therefore considered in greater detail later in this chapter. At present our discussion will be limited to a consideration of the function of these rules generally and the operation of the first four rules listed above.

The function of the principal rules of pleading

In order to apply the principal rules properly it is important to understand why they take their present form, or, in other words, why the rules place such emphasis on pleading material facts in summary form and on the prohibition on pleading evidence and law. To explain this requires further consideration of the purpose of pleadings.

The initial function of a pleading is, as indicated earlier, to state, for the benefit of other parties, the facts upon which the party pleading intends to rely at trial in order to establish its claim, defence or counterclaim as the case may be. However, the content of the pleadings is also shaped by the role of the court in determining any case before it.

That role is, of course, twofold. The court must first determine which of the facts alleged by the parties have been proved to its satisfaction, and then decide what legal consequences flow from the facts proved.

It is therefore essential that the court should obtain, as quickly as practicable, a clear grasp of the factual issues which it must decide. A crucial purpose of pleadings is to facilitate this. Consequently, a good pleading must state as concisely as possible ('in summary form') the facts which a party intends to prove at trial.

If, for example, both the statement of claim and the defence to it are properly pleaded, reading these pleadings will quickly reveal the facts on which the parties agree and disagree, and so clarify the factual issues between the parties.

Sometimes, however, a plaintiff or defendant includes in his or her pleading evidence, that is subordinate facts which tend to prove a fact in issue, or law, that is, the legal inferences which the party pleading intends the court to draw from the facts pleaded. The result of including such matters is to lengthen the pleading and to lessen its clarity by obscuring the material facts. This in turn obscures the issues of fact between the parties.

In addition, pleading law is a waste of the pleader's time and effort and consequently the client's money. The court cannot know the facts alleged by the parties until these are put before it, and partly for the reasons discussed the rules require these facts to be presented in the form of pleadings. However, the court is perfectly capable of drawing inferences of law from the facts alleged, and these need not, therefore, be pleaded.

Nor is it necessary to plead law in order to assist the other side rather than the court. A litigant in person is unlikely to benefit from this, and any other litigant can rely on his or her legal advisers to draw any necessary legal inferences.

It is not, however, enough to understand the rationale for these principal rules of drafting. A closer analysis of the rules and the way in which they operate is essential to acquire drafting skills.

How the principal rules operate

Plead only material facts

The facts pleaded must be 'material facts'. In essence this means the facts which a party is entitled to prove at trial in order to establish a claim or a defence. Not all the facts which may be relevant at trial to prove a party's case will, however, be material facts for the purposes of pleading.

A fact is material if it is necessary, at the stage at which a pleading is drafted, to include that fact in the pleading in order to make out a cause of action or a defence. In other words, the pleader must include any facts which are required to establish the elements of a cause of action or a defence. No other fact need, or should, be pleaded unless, exceptionally, the rules require it.

The process of identifying material facts can be illustrated in the context of a straightforward personal injury claim resulting from a road traffic accident.

Case of *Jane Smith v Paul Jones*

In this case the accident occurred on 23 August 1994 at 4.30 pm when a pedestrian, Jane Smith, who was crossing the High Street in West

Millcot, Essex was hit by a car driven by Paul Jones. Jane was on her way to the supermarket in Bridge Street when the accident occurred and Paul, who is the manager of a hotel in West Millcot was driving towards his house which is located at the north end of High Street, West Millcot. As a result of the accident Jane suffered injuries to her right arm and shoulder and her watch was damaged, her dress torn and her handbag ruined. When questioned by her solicitor about how the accident happened, Jane maintains that it was entirely Paul's fault in that he was driving far too fast to notice her or to stop if he did so.

Jane has been advised by her lawyer to bring an action for damages for the injuries and loss which she alleges resulted from Paul's negligent driving. As we have noted earlier, the elements of an action in negligence are:

- duty of care;
- breach of duty;
- causation;
- damage.

Jane must therefore plead any fact which it is necessary to prove in order to establish each and every element.

Firstly, Jane must plead the location of the parties in order to establish that Paul owed her a duty of care as a fellow road user. Secondly, she must plead the date, place and nature of the accident, so as to make clear the alleged breach of duty, and the acts or omissions by Paul which she alleges constitute negligence that is breach of duty. Thirdly, Jane must plead the alleged fact that Paul's breach of duty caused the accident and so Jane's injury and loss. Finally she must plead the facts of that injury and loss.

The elements of the action and the material facts which must be pleaded to establish this might be listed as follows:

• Duty of care:	location of parties	Jane – crossing High Street.
		Paul – driving along High Street in a northerly direction.
• Breach of duty:	occasion of breach	
	– date of accident	23 August 1994.
	– site of accident	High Street, West Millcot, Essex.
	– nature of accident	Jane was hit and knocked over by Paul's car. [The make and registration number would be pleaded to identify the vehicle.]

	– acts/omissions constituting breach	Paul's conduct in driving to too fast and failing to keep a proper lookout for pedestrians.
• Causation:	the fact that Paul's conduct resulted in the accident and so in the damage suffered by Jane.	
• Damage:	injuries suffered	the injuries to Jane's right arm and shoulder.
	special damage	the damage to Jane's possessions, ie the facts that her dress was torn, her watch damaged and her handbag ruined.

The rule with regard to pleading only material facts is in part designed to prevent a party from pleading irrelevant matters. In this case, for example, it is not necessary to prove that Jane was crossing the road in order to go to a supermarket. This fact is not needed to establish any element of Jane's case, indeed it does not assist in doing so. It is irrelevant and should not therefore be pleaded.

Similarly while the fact that the dress Jane was wearing at the time of the accident was damaged is material since she is claiming compensation for its loss, the fact that the dress was blue is irrelevant to her loss and ought not be pleaded. If such irrelevant facts were to be included in pleadings they might be struck out by the court.

Materiality depends, however upon the circumstances of a particular case. In the case of Jane and Paul, the fact that Paul is employed by a local hotel is immaterial. There is no need for Jane to plead Paul's occupation since it is not relevant to proving any element of the action.

However, if Paul had been a commercial traveller and his journey had been undertaken as part of his employment, Jane might reasonably have decided to sue his employer as vicariously liable for Paul's acts and omissions in the course of his employment.

In that action, the employer would have been the defendant or a co-defendant with Paul. Jane would therefore have needed to plead Paul's employment, and the identity of his employer, as these facts together with the fact that Paul was acting in the course of his employment would have to be proven at trial in order to establish the additional element of vicarious liability.

It should be noted, however, that a fact is not material for the purposes of pleading merely because it will be relevant at trial to prove the case pleaded, as the prohibitions on pleading evidence and law show.

Plead all material facts

Once the facts material to a party's case have been identified, they must all be pleaded. The omission of any material fact is fatal to a cause of action or defence, since if an essential fact is not pleaded, no evidence may be presented at trial to prove that fact.

Moreover, if facts established at trial represent a significant departure from the facts pleaded by a plaintiff, the action should be dismissed. If the action is not dismissed and the plaintiff succeeds, the judgment could be set aside on appeal and the action dismissed or, if appropriate, a new trial could be ordered by the Court of Appeal.[79]

Once again it is important to emphasise that it is all the facts material at that stage in the proceedings which must be pleaded. No fact should be pleaded on the basis that it might become material at a later stage in the proceedings.

Thus a plaintiff alleging misrepresentation under s 2(1) Misrepresentation Act 1967 must plead all the facts necessary to establish that the defendant made a statement of fact on which the plaintiff relied and which induced the plaintiff to enter a contract, but which later proved false causing the plaintiff to suffer loss. The plaintiff may anticipate that the defendant will seek to rely on the statutory defence that he or she reasonably believed at the time of contracting that the statement was true. Nevertheless facts material to the plaintiff's case if such a defence is raised must not be pleaded in the statement of claim. A pleader should not anticipate his or her opponent's case.

Plead material facts not evidence

While a pleading must state the material facts which a party must establish to succeed at trial, it should not contain the evidence by which it is intended that these facts will be proved.

This is a distinction which is easily stated but is not always easy to draw. Moreover, evidence is sometimes pleaded for tactical reasons. Nevertheless the unintentional inclusion of evidence merely clutters a pleading with unnecessary facts, and the inexperienced pleader must, therefore, make some effort to differentiate between material facts and evidence. This is particularly important in the light of the Practice

---

[79] SCP 18/7/10.

Direction [1995] 1 WLR 262 which makes clear that pleading evidence may result in a penalty in costs.

One rough and ready way of distinguishing between material facts and evidence is to ask yourself if a particular fact is essential to prove an element of the case being pleaded or if it is rather a subordinate fact which helps to prove an essential fact.

This can be illustrated by reference to the case of *Jane Smith v Paul Jones* mentioned above. It is Jane's case that Paul was negligent, and her version of the events of 23 August 1994 alleges that he was driving too fast. Let us suppose that there is a witness to the accident, Helen Rawlings, who supports Jane's case in that she also says that Paul was driving too fast.

The allegation that Paul was driving too fast is a material fact. It must be proved if Jane is to establish the essential element of breach of duty of care. This fact is therefore pleaded as a particular of negligence so that Paul is given sufficient facts to understand the nature of the breach of duty alleged against him. However, the fact that Helen says that Paul was driving very fast is a subordinate fact. It is part of the evidence by which Jane hopes to prove to the court the material fact that Paul was driving too fast.

Plead material facts not law

While material facts must be pleaded, it is generally wrong to plead law. What this really means is that a pleading must contain all the facts which are necessary to make out the legal elements of a claim or a defence, but it is unnecessary, and usually incorrect, to plead those elements expressly.

This can be illustrated by considering a claim for damages in respect of damage to a plaintiff's premises caused by water escaping from the defendant's premises.

In such a case the plaintiff might seek to rely on the rule of law established in the case of *Rylands v Fletcher*. However, the statement/particulars of claim will not expressly refer to the rule. The plaintiff will simply plead such material facts as that (on a particular date) water escaped from the defendant's land to the plaintiff's land causing damage to the plaintiff's property, that as a result the plaintiff suffered loss and damage, and that the presence of that water on the defendant's land was a non-natural use of the land. It is left for the defendant, and the court, to infer, on the basis of these facts, that the rule applies enabling the plaintiff to recover damages if the facts pleaded are proved at trial.

It is nevertheless conventional to plead certain matters of law. For this reason, although a claim in negligence will not normally expressly plead that the defendant owes the plaintiff a duty of care, but merely the facts on which the existence of such a duty may be inferred, the plaintiff will plead that the defendant has been negligent, that he has breached the duty of care owed to the plaintiff. The facts which are alleged to constitute negligence are pleaded not as the basis on which breach of duty may be inferred, but as particulars, or details, of the negligence alleged. Other matters of law which must be pleaded include, for example, fraud and the expiry of a limitation period.

Finally it should be noted that it is always open to a party to plead a point of law where this is necessary to clarify the issues in a case. For example, a defence might raise the question as to whether the plaintiff has *locus standi* to bring the claim alleged in the statement/particulars of claim. While a point of law can be dealt with at trial even if not pleaded, raising it in a pleading may result in a primary hearing to decide the point of law prior to trial with a view to avoiding unnecessary litigation. For clarity a point of law should be pleaded in a separate paragraph following that setting out the relevant facts.

Part 4: Putting a pleading together

By now you should have some understanding of what must, or may, be included in a pleading and the sample paragraphs used as illustrations will have given you some idea of how such matters are pleaded. It is, therefore, appropriate now to move on to examine the way in which the relevant matters are organised and presented so as to create a coherent and effective pleading.

The importance of structure and style

The key to producing an effective pleading is to develop the client's case logically and to express with clarity the allegations made. This is not merely because a document which is clearly phrased and logically organised is likely to be easy for both the defendant and the court to understand. A further telling reason is that an effective pleading may result in litigation being avoided. Thus a statement/particulars of claim or a counterclaim which presents a strong case effectively may persuade the other side to settle, saving the costs of litigation, and for maximum effectiveness, that case must be logically reasoned and expressed clearly. Similarly an effectively pleaded defence may persuade a plaintiff to settle or even to withdraw his or her claim.

STRUCTURE

A well-structured pleading is, then, one in which the client's case is developed logically. In drafting a pleading it is, therefore, the pleader's task to set down a number of statements or premises from which, if they are accepted to be true, a particular conclusion must follow.

In the statement/particulars of claim the major premises are, in essence, the elements of the cause of action relied upon by the plaintiff as entitling him or her to some relief or remedy. Provided that the relief or remedy appropriate to that cause of action has been identified, then, if each element of the cause of action is properly alleged, the basic premises are pleaded which, if proved, lead to the conclusion that the plaintiff is entitled to the relief or remedy claimed.

This can be illustrated by reference to a claim in negligence. Here the major premises are the statements that the defendant owes the plaintiff a duty of care and is in breach of that duty and that as a result the plaintiff has suffered damage. If these statements are made expressly, or can be inferred from facts pleaded, as may be appropriate, then the basic premises are pleaded which, if the material facts alleged in support of these statements are proved at trial, will lead the court to conclude that the plaintiff is entitled to the damages claimed.

In pleading a defence two basic types of statement may be made. Firstly, the defendant may deny the validity of one or more of the premises on which the plaintiff's claim is based, by traversing the relevant allegation or allegations in the statement/particulars of claim. As we have seen, where the traverse takes the form of a denial, the defendant may also make some affirmative statement in support of the denial. An example of this would be where the defendant denied causation as alleged and averred that the damage alleged was caused by the plaintiff's own conduct.

Secondly, the defendant may make an affirmative statement which will, if proved true, render the plaintiff's case unsustainable even if the elements of a cause of action are made out. An example of this is where the defendant pleads that the plaintiff's claim is statute-barred. Such statements are the premises from which the court is asked to conclude that the plaintiff's claim must fail. Hence the concluding paragraph sometimes used in pleading a defence:

> In the premises, it is denied that the plaintiff is entitled to the relief claimed in the Statement of Claim [Particulars of Claim] and/or any relief.

A logically structured pleading will therefore plead firstly certain premises and secondly the conclusion which follows from these. Thus, as we have seen the prayer for relief or remedy comes at the end of the statement/particulars of claim or a counterclaim.

In addition a major premise will usually be the conclusion which follows from certain minor premises and these too must be logically pleaded. An illustration of this is where the statement/particulars of claim sets out in one or more paragraphs certain material facts, the minor premises, and on the basis of these concludes that:

In the premises, the Defendant owed the Plaintiff a duty of care.

This would be appropriate where, for example, a plaintiff had suffered loss as the result of the negligent conduct of a professional person such as an accountant or a solicitor with whom the plaintiff had no contractual relationship.

In some cases the minor premises from which a major premise follows are pleaded as the particulars of that major premise. Thus the plaintiff in the statement/particulars of claim who alleges that an accident in which he was injured was caused by the negligence of the defendant sets out as particulars of negligence the facts on which the primary allegation is based. The usual structure of the relevant paragraph of a statement/particulars of claim is illustrated below. In this case the plaintiff is claiming damages for injuries received when he tripped over a length of cable left on the pavement by a contractor.

3. The said accident was caused by the negligence of the Defendant, his servants or agents.

PARTICULARS OF NEGLIGENCE

(a) Leaving the cable in a position where they knew or ought to have known that it was likely to be a danger to persons using the pavement.

(b) Failing to remove the cable from the pavement.

(c) etc.

The importance of producing a pleading that is logically structured cannot be overemphasised. However, there are a number of other matters relating to structure which need to be considered.

Firstly, as you will recall, the basic layout of a pleading consists of the formal parts and the body of the pleading in which the party's case is set out. You will also recall that the body of the pleading is divided into numbered paragraphs.[80] Two points should be noted here. One is that in a composite pleading, such as a defence and counterclaim, the numbering of the paragraphs in the two pleadings is consecutive. The other point is that in the statement/particulars of claim, or a counterclaim, the number of the paragraphs in the prayer does not follow on from that in the main part of the pleading. Indeed to distinguish the two sections, while the paragraphs in the main part of the pleading are usually given plain numbers, that is 1, 2, 3, etc, those of the prayer are often identified by numbers in brackets, or by lower-case letters in brackets.

Secondly, it should be borne in mind that each paragraph of a pleading should, so far as is convenient, contain a single allegation. This aids clarity and makes it easier for the other side to draft its responses to the matters pleaded. Nevertheless, it is common practice to plead causation and breach of duty, or causation and loss in the same paragraph as in the example below:

5. The said accident was caused by breach of statutory duty and/or negligence on the part of the Defendants, their servants or agents.

PARTICULARS

(a) ......

(b) ......

A less common example of pleading several allegations in one paragraph is where in a road traffic accident case the statement/particulars of claim pleads the facts of the collision, the facts giving rise to a duty of care, and breach of that duty causing loss and damage, in a single paragraph.[81]

The principles discussed above apply to the drafting of pleadings generally,[82] but a number of observations should be made with regard to the structure of specific types of pleading.

The statement/particulars of claim

The division of the statement/particulars of claim into paragraphs pleading the cause or causes of action and the prayer has already been noted. However, the section which pleads the elements of a cause of

---

[80] See above at p 26 note 3.

[81] See the sample paragraph at p 156 below.

[82] The drafting of further and better particulars of a pleading is not covered in this book, and you should consult other works for advice on how these should be drafted.

action, the major premise on which the claim to relief is based, must itself be appropriately structured. The elements should therefore be set out in the logical order in which they are normally described. Thus for example, the material facts which establish a duty of care should be pleaded before those which are alleged to constitute breach of duty.

The cause of action relied upon and the relief or remedy claimed constitute, as we have seen earlier,[83] the essential content of the statement/particulars of claim. However, while in many tort actions this pleading opens with the material facts which establish one or more of the elements of a cause of action, in others the paragraphs pleading a cause of action are preceded by paragraphs pleading what are known as 'preliminary averments', or 'matters of inducement'. These allege facts which are not essential to establishing a cause of action but are material to the case pleaded.

An example of a preliminary averment is a statement which describes the relevant status of a party. Thus in the tripping case mentioned above the opening paragraph of the statement/particulars of claim might read:

1. At all material times the Defendant was a building contractor undertaking work at a site at No 14 Lancaster Road, Welford.

The occupation of the defendant is not essential to the plaintiff's action in negligence, but it is part of the background to the events described in the pleading and so helps to explain or clarify these events. It is worth bearing in mind that the statement/particulars of claim is in one sense telling the story of what happened to the plaintiff that gives him or her the right to pursue some relief or remedy at trial. Any fact which must be included if the story is to be properly understood is material and ought to be pleaded.

You should note, however, that a description of a party may plead an essential element of a cause of action. If an action alleged the defendant to be liable under the Occupiers' Liability Act 1957, for example, the statement/particulars of claim must plead that the defendant was at all material times the occupier of the relevant premises.[84]

The defence

Since the defence is the defendant's response to the statement/ particulars of claim its basic structure is normally determined by the

---

[83]   See above at pp 34, 37.

[84]   See below at p 256.

way in which the plaintiff has pleaded his or her case. This is because the defendant must deal with every allegation made in the statement/particulars of claim and will be deemed to admit any allegation which is neither expressly admitted nor traversed. The easiest way to ensure that nothing is admitted by default which ought to be traversed, or traversed which ought to be admitted, is to deal with each of the plaintiff's allegations in turn.

The defendant's response to the allegations made by the plaintiff determines not only the broad framework of the defence but also the structure of its individual paragraphs. A few examples will illustrate this point.

Where a single paragraph of the statement/particulars of claim contains only one allegation which is admitted or not admitted, as the case may be, by the defendant, the defendant's pleaded response takes the form of a simply structured single paragraph as in the following example:

> 4. Paragraph 3 of the Statement [Particulars] of Claim is not admitted.

When however, the allegation is denied, the defendant will often have a positive case that must be pleaded and, as discussed further below, this will result in a more complex paragraph structure or in the defendant's response being pleaded in more than one paragraph.

A single paragraph of the statement/particulars of claim may, of course, contain several allegations. Moreover, even what appears to be a single allegation may actually amount to two or more allegations. For example, the assertion that: 'The Plaintiff was bitten by the Defendant's dog' contains two allegations. These are (1) that the plaintiff was bitten by a dog and (2) that the dog belonged to the defendant.

Whenever a single paragraph contains more than one allegation, each must be specifically admitted or traversed.[85] It is not, however, essential to repeat each allegation in the defence when pleading to it, but is sufficient to plead as in the following example:[86]

> 4. Each of the allegations in paragraph 3 of the Statement [Particulars] of Claim is denied.

---

[85]   RSC Ord 18 r13(3); SCP 18/13/6.
[86]   SCP 18/13/6.

Nevertheless, a traverse that is more fully pleaded, as in the example below, may add clarity and emphasis.

> [3. The Defendant's said horse entered the field and trampled down all of the crop of hay growing therein.]
>
> 4. The Defendant denies that the said horse entered the field or trampled down the crop of hay growing therein as alleged or at all.

It should also be noted that where the statement/particulars of claim alleges that the plaintiff has suffered loss and damage, the proper approach in drafting the defence is to traverse both the fact of damage and its extent.[87] As noted earlier, the traverse of loss and damage usually takes the form of non-admission. The sample paragraph below illustrates both points:

> 5. No admissions are made as to the loss and damage alleged or the amount thereof.

In the examples given above the defendant's response has been to admit, not admit or deny every allegation in a paragraph of the statement/particulars of claim. However, where a single paragraph of the statement/particulars of claim contains multiple allegations, the appropriate response may be a combination of admissions, non-admissions and/or denials or to traverse the paragraph by a combination of non-admissions and denials.

Where for example the defendant admits one or more of several allegations made in a paragraph of the statement/particulars of claim, but denies the rest, a structure commonly adopted in drafting the paragraph of the defence setting out this response is to set out the allegations which are admitted, introducing these with the words 'save that' and to deny the remainder of the paragraph, or *vice versa*. In the example given below the defendant takes this approach a step further, admitting one allegation, not admitting another and denying the remainder.

> [2. On Tuesday 3 April 1993 the Defendant entered the Plaintiff's field at Four Acre and seized and removed 2 Arab horses kept therein.]
>
> 3. Save that it is admitted that the said field is owned by the Plaintiff and that no admissions are made as to the presence of

---

[87] SCP 18/13/8.

the said horses, each of the allegations in paragraph 2 of the
Statement [Particulars] of Claim is denied.

The defendant thereby denies the allegations that he entered the field
on the alleged date and that he seized and removed the horses.

In some cases a paragraph may appear to consist of one allegation
while in fact containing a central allegation and one or more
subordinate allegations. In dealing with a paragraph of the
statement/particulars of claim it is therefore essential to ensure that, in
pleading to an obvious allegation, subordinate allegations are not
overlooked.

This can be illustrated by considering the following sample
paragraph from a statement of claim.

3. The Plaintiff showed the Defendant a storeroom in which there
    were several containers filled with highly inflammable
    substances used in laboratory experiments.

The defendant may admit the central allegation that the plaintiff
showed him the storeroom in which there were several containers, but
her response to the subordinate or implied allegations contained in the
paragraph must also be pleaded. Suppose, for example, that the
defendant says that she had no knowledge of the contents of the
containers or the uses to which those containers might be put. Simply
admitting the paragraph would therefore admit subordinate
allegations which the defendant should traverse.

4. Save that no admissions are made as to the contents of the said
    containers or as to their use in laboratory experiments,
    paragraph 3 of the Statement of Claim is admitted.

You may feel that there is a further implied allegation in the plaintiff's
paragraphs that the defendant had knowledge of the contents of the
containers and the use to which they were put, and that the defence
ought therefore to deny that the defendant had such knowledge.
However, a distinction should be drawn between a subordinate and an
implied allegation. The defendant should not traverse any matters
which the plaintiff might have but has not raised in the
statement/particulars of claim.[88]

---

[88] SCP 18/13/6.

Into this basic framework of admissions, non-admissions and denials, it will usually be necessary to integrate additional facts which the defendant must plead in order to clarify or correct the plaintiff's version of events or to put an affirmative case.[89] As a general rule these additional facts should be pleaded as they arise in addition to a particular allegation in the statement/particulars of claim. So, for example, a defendant who intends to deny causation as alleged by the plaintiff and to put forward the affirmative case that the plaintiff caused or contributed to the accident alleged might plead as follows:

4. It is denied that the said accident was caused by the negligence of the Defendants as alleged in the Statement [Particulars] of Claim or at all.

5. Further or alternatively the said accident was caused wholly or was contributed to by the Plaintiff's own negligence.

PARTICULARS

(a) ....
(b) ....

However, it should be noted that some lawyers plead the defence of limitation at the beginning of the pleading on the grounds that if the plaintiff's cause of action is proved to be statute-barred, it cannot be proceeded with even if every element of that action could be established. If this approach is adopted, the relevant paragraphs of the defence might read:

1. The Plaintiff's cause of action occurred more than 3 years before the commencement of proceedings herein by the Plaintiff and accordingly his action is statute-barred by reason of the provisions of section 11 of the Limitation Act 1980.

2. Without prejudice to the Defendant's contention that the Plaintiff's claim(s) herein are statute-barred, the Defendant pleads to the Statement [Particulars] of Claim as follows:

If, alternatively, the defence of limitation is pleaded as it arises in relation to facts pleaded by the plaintiff, it should be raised when the defence deals with the plaintiff's allegations as to breach of duty. An appropriate paragraph might read:

---

[89] See above at pp 44-46.

4. If, which is denied, the Defendant was negligent as alleged in paragraph 3 of the Statement [Particulars] of Claim or at all, the Defendant will say that any negligence on the part of the Defendant which the Plaintiff may prove occurred more than ... years before the beginning of proceedings herein by the Plaintiff and that, accordingly, his action was statute-barred by reason of the provisions of section 11 of the Limitation Act 1980.

For completeness it should also be noted that the defence of set-off is always the last defence as it leads directly into the defendant's counterclaim. An example of the final paragraph of the defence pleading set-off is given below:

Further or alternatively, if, which is denied, the Defendant is found liable as alleged, the Defendant will rely on his counterclaim herein by way of set-off in extinction or diminution of the Plaintiff's claim.

It is sensible to plead reliance on the counterclaim not merely to reduce but also, alternatively, to extinguish the plaintiff's claim if there is any chance that the court may award the defendant on his counterclaim a sum equal to or exceeding that awarded to the plaintiff.

While the structure of a defence should be logical, there is no objection to a defendant pleading two or more inconsistent defences. Thus a defendant may plead that he did not assult the plaintiff, but allege that if he did so he acted in self-defence.

The counterclaim

Since a counterclaim sets out a claim by the defendant in an action against the plaintiff, this pleading is in essence the defendant's statement/particulars of claim.

Consequently, a counterclaim is structured in basically the same way as the statement/particulars of claim. There is, however, one crucial difference in that where the facts which establish some element of the defendant's cause of action have already been pleaded in the defence, the relevant paragraph or paragraphs of the defence are simply incorporated into the counterclaim by using the phrase, 'Paragraph ... of the Defence is repeated'.

A more detailed discussion of how to plead a counterclaim together with a sample counterclaim is included in Chapter 7.

The reply

Since the primary purpose of a reply is to deal with those allegations in the defence in relation to which the plaintiff wishes to plead an affirmative case, its structure is simple. As we have seen, it invariably commences with a paragraph taking issue with the defence except so far as it consists of admissions or is admitted in the reply. The wording of this paragraph is given at p 32 (in sample pleading (5)) above. This is followed by one or more paragraphs pleading the plaintiff's affirmative case in relation to one or more allegations made by the defence.

The defence to counterclaim

Since a counterclaim is a defendant's claim against a plaintiff, a defence to counterclaim is structured in the same way as a defence to the statement/particulars of claim, and the section at pp 47 and 40ff above should be consulted.

STYLE

Even if a pleading is well-structured, its effectiveness may be lessened by poor presentation of the matters pleaded. It is therefore necessary to consider what features distinguish good drafting style. These may be grouped under three basic rules of style: write clear, plain grammatical English; write precisely; write concisely.

Clear, plain grammatical English

Since the purpose of a pleading is to communicate a party's case, it is obvious that the matters pleaded should be easily assimilated by the reader. Consequently, the pleader should adopt clear, plain English. It will of course be necessary, for reasons of precision and conciseness, to use some legal terminology, for example, duty of care. However, legal jargon should be kept to a minimum.

At the same time the pleader's use of language should be grammatically sound and the rules of punctuation should be observed. Grammatical errors, like errors of punctuation, may render the meaning of a sentence obscure. At best, ill-constructed sentences are likely to slow the pace at which the meaning of what is written is assimilated, and are aesthetically displeasing. It is worth noting, too, that a judge may be irritated by common grammatical errors such as split infinitives.

Precision

In drafting a pleading it is essential to present the client's case with precision. Lack of clarity, vagueness and ambiguity are likely to result in a request from the other side for further and better particulars asking questions which focus on and also expose the weakness of the pleading. Moreover, drafting replies to such requests causes expense which could have been avoided.

There is, of course, no place for invention or exaggeration in a pleading, which must reflect accurately the client's instructions and the evidence before the lawyer. The importance placed on this by the judiciary is reflected in the recommendation in the interim report of the Woolf Committee that a pleading should be signed by the party on whose behalf it is drafted.[90] All aspects of a client's case should, therefore, be accurately represented, but a few points should be noted in particular as indicated below.

Dates are very important since they give clarity to the framework of the events described. Moreover, the date of a particular event may be crucial in determining whether a claim or defence succeeds or fails. For example, in a personal injury case the date on which a plaintiff is injured or acquires certain prescribed knowledge about his or her injury determines when the relevant limitation period commences and so the date upon which an action for damages in respect of that injury will become statute-barred.

Dates, like **sums** and other **numbers** must be expressed in figures and not in words.[91] For clarity dates should be pleaded as follows:

On 3rd January 1996 ...

or

On 3 January 1996 ...

If a client is uncertain as to the precise date on which an event occurred, a few days leeway either way may be achieved by using the phrase 'on or about' as in:

On or about 3 January 1996 ...

It is unlikely, however, that this will allow the party pleading to lead evidence that the event occurred more than a few days before or after the date given. Where even the month in which an event occurred is

---

90 'Access to Justice; Interim Report to the Lord Chancellor on the civil justice system in England and Wales' (June 1995).

91 RSC Ord 18 r6(3).

uncertain the analogous phrase, 'In or about January 1995', may be adopted.

The **time** at which an event occurred may be material and, if so, should be pleaded as precisely as possible. In road traffic accident cases, for example, the time at which a collision occurred is often pleaded for clarity and may be crucial in determining liability. Where there is uncertainty as to the precise time of some occurrence the phrase 'at about' may be used as follows:

At about 9 pm on 3 January 1996 ...

It is also important to be precise in defining **property** referred to in a pleading. Thus, for example, a residential property or business premises should be defined by giving its full address, or the site at which it is alleged that some event or events occurred should be clearly and accurately described. This is so even if, as is sometimes recommended, a map or plan is attached to the pleading. Similarly, for example, equipment used at a workplace must be carefully defined, using technical terminology where this is necessary to ensure clarity and accuracy.

Some thought must also be given to the description of people mentioned in pleadings. As a general rule the parties are referred to as plaintiffs, defendants or third parties as the case may be. In rare cases, however, where there is a multiplicity of plaintiffs or defendants it may be clearer to refer to the parties by name. Where a person who is not a party is mentioned in a pleading their name should be given if known.

Where a **document** is mentioned in a pleading, it should be defined by giving the date on which it was created and, if material, the name of the person by whom or for whom it was created. In the case of a letter it should be stated by whom, to whom, on what date and by what means the letter was sent.

In pleading **conversation** the date of the conversation and the persons taking part should be stated. Where either a document or a conversation is referred to in a pleading, only the effect of the document or the purport of the conversation should be pleaded. The precise words should not be stated except in so far as the words themselves are material.[92] In an action in defamation, for example, the precise words used by the defendant are material and should be pleaded.[93]

Finally, it is important that the terminology adopted in a pleading should be used consistently. This does not, however, require lengthy

[92] Ibid r7(2).
[93] SCP 18/6/2.

repetition of descriptions, as we shall see by considering the third basic rule of style that a pleading should be drafted concisely. The importance of this is shown by the inclusion in RSC Ord 18 r7 of the rule mentioned earlier that the material facts must be pleaded in summary form.

Pleading the material facts in summary form

The requirement that the material facts should be pleaded in summary form, or concisely, is intended to prevent the inclusion of unnecessary matters which lengthen the draft and may obscure the essential facts of a party's case. Indeed, the lawyer's ability to write concisely is most tested in drafting pleadings; to achieve brevity while maximising clarity means that the matters pleaded must be stripped to their bare bones. In a properly drafted pleading every word earns its keep – there should not be a surplus word.

Few people write so concisely as a matter of course. When learning to draft you must therefore analyse each phrase without sacrificing accuracy or clarity. Economy of words is a matter of practice.

There are, however, a number of words and phrases which are commonly used in pleadings to assist in making them concise, and you should become familiar with these.

One commonly employed method of reducing words is to use what might be called an abbreviated description of a place or thing which will be referred to several times in a pleading. Once the place or object has been fully described in the pleading the abbreviated description may be used whenever it is referred to subsequently. So, for example, 'the premises' may be substituted for 'the premises known as 19 Picton Street, Bangor, Gwynedd' or 'the site' for 'a site at 20 Picton Street, Bangor, Gwynedd'.

The shortened form may be identified as such by describing the place or thing in full when it is first mentioned in a pleading and then introducing the abbreviated description by adding the words 'hereinafter called ...' as in the following example:

> The Plaintiff is the freehold owner of premises known as 219 Victoria Street, Bangor, Gwynedd, hereinafter called 'the premises'.

Alternatively, and in keeping with the current emphasis on lawyers to use plain English, the pleader might simply introduce the shortened form by adding it as in the example below:

> The Plaintiff is the freehold owner of premises known as 219 Victoria Street, Bangor, Gwynedd ('the premises').

A further alternative is to use the word 'said'. In this case the pleader would describe the premises at '219 Victoria Street' in full when it was first mentioned, and any subsequent reference would be to 'the said premises' or 'the Plaintiff's said premises'.

The word 'said' has indeed proved extremely useful to pleaders seeking to describe a place, thing, matter or occurrence concisely and precisely, as the following examples illustrate:

> During the course of the said work ...

> The Plaintiff in the course of her employment at the said premises ...

> The said accident was caused by the negligence of the Defendant.

> The Plaintiff's said injuries were caused by ...

> An injunction to restrain the Defendant by their servants or agents or otherwise howsoever from continuing the said nuisance.

Given its usefulness, the word 'said' is unlikely to disappear from pleadings. Nevertheless, and in the interests of achieving a simpler, less legalistic style of pleading, the view that its use often adds little to a pleading and may safely be omitted should be noted.[94]

The final example given in the preceding paragraph introduces another word which may appear in pleadings. Though seldom used in everyday language, the word 'howsoever' remains a useful tool in drafting to avoid longer phrases such as 'in whatever manner' or 'to whatever extent'. Similarly the words 'whosoever' and 'whatsoever' frequently appear in pleadings.

The tactics and ethics of pleading

While the procedure for bringing a claim or presenting a defence is set out in the Rules of Court, the process of litigation inevitably requires the parties to make decisions as to the best way to serve their objectives.

For example, the choice of a defendant may itself be a tactical decision. Thus, a plaintiff may choose to pursue the employer of a tortfeasor, rather than the tortfeasor himself, because the former is likely to have greater financial resources and so to be in a better position to pay any damages awarded to the plaintiff.

As this suggests, tactical decisions may influence the way in which pleadings are drafted. This is the more so because the way in which parties plead their cases is inevitably influenced by the adversarial

---

[94] Kessler, *Drafting Trusts and Will Trusts: a modern approach*, pp 18ff.

character of litigation. As a result pleadings are not merely statements of the parties' cases. Each side, in its pleadings, seeks to demonstrate the strength, or hide the weaknesses, of its case so as to persuade the other to abandon part or all of its claim or defence, as the case may be. So, for example, a plaintiff whose chances of succeeding at trial are in doubt may hope by means of a strongly drafted claim to achieve an early settlement avoiding the risks and potential expense of litigation. Similarly a defendant may hope that a strongly pleaded defence will persuade the plaintiff to avoid the risks of litigation and abandon a weak claim or, at least, settle for less than might be awarded if the claim succeeded at trial.

An illustration of such tactical pleading is where evidence is pleaded deliberately in order to indicate the strength of the client's case and so put pressure on the other side to settle.

Clearly such objectives are entirely legitimate, and it is the lawyer's task to plead a client's case as strongly as possible. However, the court's views of what ought to be contained in a pleading should be kept in mind. So, for example, while pleading evidence may have tactical advantages it will be necessary, in future, to bear in mind the strong warning against doing so contained in a 1995 Practice Direction.[95]

Moreover, concern to achieve the best possible result for a client must be tempered by ethical considerations. A lawyer must plead only the case he or she is instructed to plead. Nothing may be invented by the pleader. No allegation may be made for which there is no basis in the client's instructions or the lawyer's brief, nor any for which there is no supporting evidence. No allegation of fraud may be pleaded in the absence of apparently reliable corroborative evidence which would, if accepted by the court, be sufficient to establish a *prima facie* case of fraud.[96] No contention may be pleaded which the lawyer does not consider to be properly arguable. This does not include one which, though very weak, is arguable and seems, rather, to mean a contention which is unsustainable.

The potential content of a pleading is therefore determined by the pleader's instructions and the evidence before him or her. The actual content of the pleading may, however, be a tactical decision. Thus, for example, where a plaintiff has the option of pursuing several causes of action, the decision as to which should be pleaded may be a tactical

---

95 Practice Direction (Civil Litigation: Case Management) [1995] 1 WLR 262.

96 Counsel is under a duty not to plead fraud 'unless he had clear and sufficient evidence to support it'. See Lord Denning in *Associated Leisure Ltd v Associated Newspapers Ltd* [1970] 2 QB 450, 456 cited at SCP 18/8/8(16).

one. The plaintiff and his legal advisers must consider which, if any, is the stronger cause of action and what, if any, are the relative advantages and disadvantages of each in terms of the relief or remedies available.

Aside from such general considerations, there may be tactical decisions to be made concerning the pleadings of details with regard to a particular case. Thus it may be necessary to consider whether pleading a particular fact will strengthen or weaken that case, or may alert the other side to some weakness in the pleader's own case.

Finally, the pleader must always remember that flaws in a pleading may result in it having to be amended and that this may require the leave of the court, with costs being incurred. More serious flaws may result in the other side applying to have the pleading set aside and, perhaps, the client's case dismissed. Here, too, tactical considerations may influence decisions taken by the parties.

As these brief comments on tactics and ethics are intended to indicate, it is important to be aware of tactical considerations when drafting pleadings. Nevertheless, the pleader must never lose sight of the basic function of a pleading, nor of the ethical considerations which flow from this. Nor must a lawyer become so caught up in the pleading of a particular case or in the procedural aspects of pleading that the client's real interests are forgotten. As Lord Justice Saville was reported as commenting in a 1994 case:[97]

> Pleadings were not a game to be played at the expense of litigants and nor were they an end in themselves but the means to the end of giving the parties a fair hearing.

---

[97] *Trust Securities Holdings Ltd v Sir Robert McAlpine and Sons Ltd* (1994) *The Times*, 21 December.

Chapter 4

Drafting Injunctions

Scope of chapter

In addition to pleadings there are, as we noted in our introductory chapter, other types of document created for court use which a lawyer who handles tort cases must be able to draft. In the present chapter we shall discuss how to draft several such documents which may be required when a client makes an application to court for an interlocutory injunction. The circumstances in which particular documents will be required are also explained. For completeness we shall also consider how to plead the claim for a final or perpetual injunction in the statement/particulars of claim.

When an interlocutory injunction is granted, the party obtaining the order is normally required to give to the court one or more promises which are known as undertakings. The most important of these is the undertaking in damages. Other promises relating to procedural requirements may be required according to the nature of the application made. Undertakings which relate to the facts of the case in which an injunction is sought may also be given by either party. In some cases undertakings are accepted by the court in lieu of making an injunction order. The drafting of undertakings is therefore also considered in this chapter.

Checklist of type of documents discussed in this chapter

The checklist below sets out the types of documents covered in this chapter and gives the page references for sample documents.

- Interlocutory order on *ex parte* application, High Court, Chancery Division, p 89.
- Notice of motion for interlocutory injunction, High Court, Chancery Division, p 85.
- Summons for interlocutory injunction, High Court, Queen's Bench Division, p 86.
- Draft interlocutory injunction order on *inter partes* application, High Court, Queen's Bench Division, p 92.
- Final injunction order, High Court, Queen's Bench Division, p 94.

- Undertakings in lieu of injunction, High Court, Queen's Bench Division, p 105.
- Application for injunction order, county court, Form N16A, p 101.
- Draft interlocutory injunction order, county court, Form N16, p 102.
- Document containing undertakings, county court, Form N117, p 104.

Relationship between Chapter 4 and Chapter 5

In tort cases it is generally only necessary to draft affidavits in relation to certain interlocutory applications made to the courts once proceedings have been commenced but before trial. A common application of the kind is for an interlocutory injunction. In both the High Court and the county court the rules require that an application for an interlocutory injunction must be supported by affidavit evidence: RSC Ord 38 r2(3); CCR Ord 13 r6(3)(b). Consequently whenever a client seeks such an injunction you will need to prepare one or more affidavits containing the evidence in support of the application. When a client opposes such an application, affidavit evidence will again be required. Consequently in examining in Chapter 5 how to draft an affidavit, we have focused on the type of affidavit required to support an application for an interlocutory injunction. Chapters 4 and 5 should, therefore, be read in conjunction with each other. However, the basic skills required in drafting an affidavit of this type are relevant to the drafting of affidavits generally.

Injunctions and undertakings

What is an injunction?

An injunction is an equitable remedy in the form of an order of the court requiring a party to do, or to refrain from doing, specified acts. Its purpose is to put an end to some existing interference, or to prevent some anticipated future interference, with some legal right or rights of the party applying for the order.

Where the court requires a party to do specified acts, the order made is a **mandatory injunction**. Suppose, for example, that Mr White wrongfully creates a wall on land belonging to his neighbour, Mrs Black. In these circumstances Mrs Black might apply to the court for a mandatory injunction requiring Mr White to demolish the wall.

Where the court requires a party to refrain from doing certain acts the order made is a **prohibitory injunction**. If, for example, Mrs Black trespasses on Mr White's land by walking across it without his permission in order to go to and from her own property, Mr White might apply to the court for a prohibitory injunction restraining her from doing so.

In some cases, even though there has been no actual interference with the applicant's legal rights, an injunction is obtained *quia timet*, that is, 'because he (or she) fears' that such interference is threatened and the court, accepting that such fears are justified, considers an injunction necessary to prevent the threatened interference. An injunction obtained in these circumstances is therefore known as a *quia timet* **injunction** and may be mandatory or prohibitory.

Where an injunction is granted as a permanent remedy in respect of the infringement of some legal right or rights, the order obtained is known as a **final injunction**. Such an order will only be made after the applicant's case has been established at trial. However, once proceedings have been issued, an **interlocutory injunction** may be sought to give relief from the conduct complained of in the period before trial of the action. Indeed, in urgent cases an application for an interlocutory injunction may be made before proceedings are issued and the order made on the basis that the applicant undertakes to issue proceedings forthwith.[1] The hearing of an interlocutory application for an injunction is normally on the basis of affidavit evidence only with no opportunity for cross-examination of witnesses. Consequently interlocutory injunctions are normally prohibitory in form as the courts are reluctant to make orders requiring a party to do specified acts prior to the full hearing of the matters in dispute.

An application for an interlocutory injunction may be made *ex parte* or *inter partes*. An application is *ex parte* when only the party applying for the order is to be present, or represented, at the hearing. Since the courts are understandably reluctant to make an injunction order requiring the conduct of a party who has not been given an opportunity to address the court, an *ex parte* application is appropriate only when the matter is of such urgency that it is impossible for the plaintiff to give the defendant[2] formal notice of the hearing as required by the rules of the court, or giving such notice would defeat the

---

[1] An interlocutory injunction may be sought to regulate the defendant's conduct pending trial whether or not the plaintiff is seeking a final injunction at trial: RSC Ord 29 r1(1).

[2] RSC Ord 29 r1(2) authorises the making of an *ex parte* application for an injunction by a plaintiff, but the rules do not provide for the making of such an application by a defendant: SCP 29/1/8. An *inter partes* application for an injunction may be made by a plaintiff or a defendant, but a discussion of the circumstances in which a defendant might seek an injunction and the procedure in relation to such an application is outside the scope of this book. In the examples given in this chapter the application for an injunction is made by the plaintiff. Consequently no further reference will be made to the defendant as an applicant for an injunction.

purpose of the application.[3] An *inter partes* application is attended by both parties or their legal representatives.

The fact that an injunction is an equitable remedy means that even if a plaintiff[4] can establish that one or more of his legal rights have been infringed, an injunction cannot be obtained as of right but is within the discretion of the court.

One final point to be borne in mind is that an injunction may only be granted if the court has jurisdiction to make such an order. Although this seems obvious, injunction orders which the court has no power to make have occasionally in the past been both sought and granted. However, it should also be remembered that even an injunction which is not properly made is binding on the defendant, if properly served upon him or her, until varied or discharged.

Injunction orders in tort cases

In tort actions the main remedy available to a plaintiff who can establish that he or she has suffered harm as a result of a defendant's tort is an award of damages, that is, monetary compensation. This is, indeed, the only remedy where an action is brought in negligence.

An injunction may, however, be sought wherever the nature of the defendant's wrongdoing makes such an order an appropriate remedy. In some cases damages may be sought and awarded in addition to an injunction. This is usually the case where a plaintiff brings a successful action in defamation. In other cases the victim of tortious conduct may have little or no interest in obtaining financial compensation, and the sole object of bringing proceedings may be to obtain an injunction to prevent any continuation or repetition of the wrongdoing alleged. This might be so, for example, where the plaintiff alleges that the defendant's conduct constitutes nuisance.

A claim for assault is a further example of an action in which an injunction is often the primary remedy sought, though damages may also be claimed, as is illustrated in the sample pleadings set out later in this chapter.

In tort cases in which an injunction is an appropriate remedy, an application is often made for an interlocutory injunction to restrain the alleged wrongdoing until trial. It should be noted that such an application may be made even if no claim for a final injunction has been included in the writ.

---

[3]   As, for example, where the plaintiff seeks a Mareva injunction to restrain a defendant from dissipating his or her assets or removing them from the jurisdiction before trial in order to defeat any judgment the plaintiff might obtain.

[4]   See note 1 above.

What is an undertaking?

An undertaking is a promise given by a party to the court to do or to refrain from doing some act or acts specified in the undertaking. When an injunction is granted, the plaintiff is usually required to give one or more undertakings. Whether the application is made *ex parte* or *inter partes* an undertaking in damages is essential.[5] This is in effect a promise that if the defendant establishes at trial that the injunction was wrongly granted the plaintiff will compensate him or her for any loss which the court accepts was incurred as a result of the injunction. When the application is made *ex parte*, further undertakings will be required, eg an undertaking to notify the defendant of the terms of the order made. When an injunction is sought before an action has been commenced, the plaintiff must also undertake to issue proceedings forthwith. It is on the basis of its acceptance of such promises that the court makes the order sought by the plaintiff.

Where the hearing of the application is *inter partes* the defendant may also give undertakings, and, on the basis of the defendant's willingness to do so, the court may be prepared to modify the terms of the injunction sought by the plaintiff or even to accept the undertakings in lieu of making an injunction order.[6]

It must, however, be emphasised that while a plaintiff must be prepared to give an undertaking in damages on obtaining an injunction, and that in some circumstances additional undertakings may be required by the court, neither a plaintiff nor a defendant can be forced to give any undertaking. However, no order will be made in the absence of appropriate undertakings by the plaintiff, while the defendant's ability to persuade the court not to make the order contended for may, in some cases, depend on his or her willingness to give undertakings which render the making of the order unnecessary.

It should be noted that an undertaking is given to the court, not to the other party, and is enforceable in the same way as an injunction. Thus breach of an undertaking constitutes contempt and is punishable by committal.

Drafting the claim for a final or perpetual injunction

In the High Court, most actions in tort are commenced by writ, and actions in which permanent injunctive relief is sought invariably so. In

---

5   A legally-aided plaintiff may be granted an injunction even though his undertaking in damages may be of little value: *Allen v Jambo Holdings* [1980] 1 WLR 1252.

6   See below at p 105.

the county courts all tort actions are commenced by summons.[7] As you will recall, in an action begun by writ in the High Court or by summons in the county court, the relief or remedy claimed by the plaintiff must be pleaded in the statement of claim or particulars of claim respectively and is set out in the prayer.[8] In addition, the material facts on which the claim for some relief or remedy is based must be pleaded in the body of the statement/particulars of claim.[9]

Consequently, where the remedy of an injunction is to be sought at trial, the claim for an injunction must be indorsed on the writ or county court summons and in drafting the statement/particulars of claim the plaintiff must set out in the body of the pleading the facts on which the claim for injunctive relief is based and plead the claim itself in the prayer.

The plaintiff must therefore plead in the body of the statement/particulars of claim those facts which establish that he or she has been the victim of wrongful conduct on the part of the defendant which gives rise to a cause of action in tort entitling the plaintiff to seek injunctive relief. Since, however, an injunction is an equitable remedy, the plaintiff must plead additional facts which will persuade the court to exercise its discretion to grant the relief sought, that is to say facts which will convince the court that, unless an injunction is granted, the wrongful conduct alleged will, on the balance of probabilities, continue.

To establish this future risk, it is common to plead in the statement/particulars of claim details of attempts by the plaintiff to persuade the defendant to cease the wrongful conduct alleged and to plead expressly the plaintiff's fear that, in spite of these attempts, the wrongful conduct alleged will continue unless an injunction is granted.

Two paragraphs taken from the particulars of claim in a trespass case[10] will illustrate these points. In the first of these paragraphs the material facts of the defendant's wrongful conduct are set out as follows:

> 3. From about 5 November 1995 the Defendant has wrongfully parked motor vehicles on the Plaintiff's said forecourt so as to

---

[7]   See above at p 13.

[8]   See above at p 37.

[9]   This follows from the requirement in RSC Ord 18 r12(1) that a party must plead any claim in sufficient detail to enable the other side to understand fully the case presented and from CCR Ord 6 r1(1) which provides that the particulars of claim must state briefly the material facts on which the plaintiff's claim to some relief or remedy is based.

[10] For pleading in a trespass case, see Chapter 12.

obstruct and interfere with access to the Plaintiff's said premises by the Plaintiff and his clients.

The second paragraph pleads the plaintiff's unsuccessful attempts to persuade the defendant to cease parking vehicles on the plaintiff's forecourt, and the plaintiff's belief that the defendant will continue to do so unless restrained by an order of the court:

4. Since about 10 November 1995 the Plaintiff has on numerous occasions orally and by solicitor's letters dated 15 December 1995 and 5 January 1996 requested the Defendant not to park vehicles on the Plaintiff's said forecourt but the Defendant threatens and intends to continue to do so unless restrained by injunction of this court.

Drafting the claim for an injunction in the prayer is straightforward. The example below relates to the same county court action in trespass:

AND the Plaintiff claims:

(1) an injunction forbidding the Defendant whether by himself or by instructing or encouraging any other person from in any manner trespassing on the land belonging to the Plaintiff referred to in Paragraph 1 of the Particulars of Claim;

(2) damages;

(3) interest pursuant to section 69 of the County Courts Act 1984 as aforesaid.

In the further example given below the claim for an injunction is made in a nuisance action brought in the High Court:[11]

AND the Plaintiff claims:

(1) damages;

(2) an injunction to restrain the Defendant whether by himself or by his servants or agents or otherwise from continuing or repeating the said nuisance;

(3) interest pursuant to section 35A of the Supreme Court Act 1981 as aforesaid.

---

[11] For drafting in a nuisance case, see Chapter 11.

Drafting the application for an interlocutory injunction

While the drafting required when seeking a perpetual injunction is broadly the same in the High Court and county courts, the procedure for obtaining an interlocutory injunction and the nature of the documents which must be drafted differs according to the court in which the application is made. In this section, therefore, High Court and county court proceedings will be considered separately.

High Court proceedings

DECIDING WHAT DOCUMENTS MUST BE DRAFTED

Where a client seeks an interlocutory injunction in High Court proceedings, the drafting which must be undertaken depends partly on the decision as to the division in which the proceedings have been or are to be commenced and partly on the nature of the application. Whether or not any claim has been made for a final injunction, the plaintiff must normally notify the other side of the application. When the hearing is to be *inter partes* this is done by preparing a notice of motion if the application is made in the Chancery Division or a summons if it is made in the Queen's Bench Division.[12] An affidavit in support of the application must also be drafted. Where, exceptionally, the application is made *ex parte*, the notice of motion or summons is dispensed with, the defendant being given notice of the proceedings informally, unless notification is inappropriate,[13] but a draft of the order to be sought must be prepared in addition to the supporting affidavit. If the application is made before proceedings have been issued, a draft writ must be prepared.[14]

DRAFTING A NOTICE OF MOTION OR SUMMONS

The basic format of a notice of motion and a summons is as set out in sample documents (1) and (2) below. The terms of the order sought must be inserted as indicated. For guidance on drafting the injunction order see below at p 95.

---

[12] The application for an interlocutory injunction must be brought in the division in which the action is proceeding or, in the case of an intending action, will be brought.

[13] Notice should not be given where doing so is likely to defeat the purpose of the application.

[14] As to drafting the indorsement on a writ, see Chapter 2.

Sample document
(1) High Court – Chancery Division
Notice of motion for interlocutory injunction

IN THE HIGH COURT OF JUSTICE [a]   **CH 199 –L No** [b]

CHANCERY DIVISION [c]

BETWEEN [d]

JENNIFER LAWTON   <u>Plaintiff</u>

and

PAULINE HAMMOND   <u>Defendant</u>

[1]

TAKE NOTICE [2] that this Honourable Court will be moved before Mr Justice _____ [3] sitting at the Royal Courts of Justice, Strand, London, WC2A 2LL on [Monday] the _____ day of _____199_ at ____ o'clock [4] or so soon thereafter as Counsel can be heard, by Counsel for the above-named Plaintiff for an order that the Defendant be restrained whether by herself or her servants or agents or otherwise[5] howsoever until judgment in this action or further order from [*set out the terms of injunction sought*].

AND that provision may be made for the costs of this application. [6]

[AND FURTHER TAKE NOTICE that leave to serve short notice of motion has today been granted by the Honourable Mr Justice ____ .[3]] [7]

DATED the ___ day of _____199_.

To the Defendant [and to

_____   _____

_____ [8] his Solicitors]   Solicitors for the Plaintiff [9]

| Notes |

1 Heading
   a The court in which the application is made.
   b The year in which the writ was issued, and the letter and number of the action.
   c The division of the High Court in which the application is made.
   d The names of the parties.
2 The opening two words of the notice are in upper case.
3 Insert name of judge.
4 Insert full date, giving day of week, together with time.
5 See below, p 99.

6   A sentence setting out the costs order sought may be substituted, for example:

AND that the costs of this application be the Plaintiff's costs in the cause.

The sentence referring to costs may be set out as a separate paragraph. As to appropriate costs orders see RSC Ord 62 and David Bean, *Injunctions* (Longman, London: 1994 edn) pp 85–88. The various types of costs orders available in the High Court are defined at RSC Ord 62 r3(6).

7   This paragraph should be included if the plaintiff has applied to the court for leave to serve the notice of the *inter partes* hearing without giving the defendant the two working days required by the rules.

8   Insert name and address of the defendant's solicitors.

9   Insert name and address of the plaintiff's solicitors.

Sample document
(2) High Court – Queen's Bench Division
Summons for interlocutory injunction

IN THE HIGH COURT OF JUSTICE   **199_ P No**
QUEEN'S BENCH DIVISION

BETWEEN

IQBAL PATEL   <u>Plaintiff</u>

and

WINSTON SMITH   <u>Defendant</u>

1

LET ALL PARTIES [2] attend the Judge in Chambers of Room No , Royal Courts of Justice, Strand, London WS2A 2LL on [Monday] the ____ day of _____ 199_ at _____ o'clock [3] on the hearing of an application by the Plaintiff for an order that the Defendant be restrained, whether by himself or his servant or agents or otherwise [4] from [*set out terms of order sought*].

AND that provision may be made for the costs of the application. [5]

This summons will be attended by Counsel.

DATED the ____ day of _____ 199_.

Notes

1   Heading. See further sample document (1) and note 1 a–d.

2   The opening three words of the summons are capitalised.

3   Insert full date giving day of week together with the time of hearing.

4 See below, p 99.
5 See sample document (1) note 6.

Preparing a draft order

As indicated, a draft order is essential when making an *ex parte* application for an injunction. Moreover, where the parties reach an agreement as to the terms of an injunction during the course of last minute negotiations, it may be necessary to draft an injunction at the door of the court. It is therefore very important to be able to draft an appropriate order even when pressed for time. The content and structure of an injunction are therefore considered in detail below.

Content and structure generally

The contents of a High Court injunction may be divided into four categories as follows.

Firstly, there are the formal parts at the beginning and end of the order. Secondly, there are a number of introductory paragraphs setting out the circumstances in which the order was made. These might also be described as formalities in the sense that the wording of such paragraphs is standard in form with only minor variations reflecting the style of the person drafting the document. Thirdly, the undertakings given by either or both parties must be included in the injunction. Fourthly, there are the orders made by the court.

The order in which these categories have been given is, if the closing formalities are excepted, the order in which they appear in the injunction. The structure of the document is, therefore, as set out below:

(1) formal parts: heading, title of draft injunction (optional);

(2) standard introductory paragraphs;

(3) undertakings;

(4) orders;

(5) formal parts: date, warning of consequences of disobeying order.

Each of these categories will now be considered in greater detail.

FORMAL PARTS

The formal parts at the beginning of an injunction take the form of a heading. This is the same in content and structure as the heading on a pleading and therefore sets out the court in which the application is made, the case number and the names of the parties. The final order will include the name of the judge who made the order and the draft order should include the name of the judge who is to hear the application if this is known. A draft order may also include the title of the document, for example, 'Draft Minutes of Order', but this is optional.

The closing formal parts of an injunction consist of the date of the order, which must be left blank on a draft order, and a warning to the defendant of the consequences of disobeying the order.

The content and lay-out of the formal parts of injunctions are illustrated in the sample injunctions set out at pp 89, 92 and 94 below.

STANDARD INTRODUCTORY PARAGRAPHS

It is conventional to include in the injunction, immediately after the heading, or title, if any, a number of paragraphs setting out the circumstances in which the order was made. These record, in a largely standard format, who addressed the court and what affidavits and other documents were before the court at the hearing of the application, and so indicate the nature of the evidence on the basis of which the order was made. Examples of such introductory paragraphs are given in the sample injunctions set out at pp 89, 92 and 94 below.

UNDERTAKINGS

As indicated at p 81 above, an injunction must contain an undertaking in damages and may include a number of other standard undertakings depending upon the circumstances in which it is made. You should, therefore, become familiar with the way in which such standard undertakings are worded, and examples illustrating this are included in the sample injunction at p 89 below. Where undertakings relate the specific facts of the case, the choice of wording is a matter for the person preparing the draft order, but any undertaking should be clearly, precisely and concisely drafted. This is discussed below at p 105.

SAMPLE INJUNCTION ORDERS

The sample injunctions set out below illustrate how to draft the formal parts, introductory paragraphs and standard undertakings in injunctions in High Court proceedings. Standard orders as to costs, which are discussed below at p 91 note 9, are also illustrated. The drafting of the other orders and non-standard undertakings which vary according to the facts of individual cases is discussed with sample paragraphs at p 95 below.

Sample document
(3) High Court – Chancery Division
Interlocutory injunction order
on *ex parte* application

IN THE HIGH COURT OF JUSTICE a   CH 199_ M Nob

CHANCERY DIVISION c

    Mr Justice _____ d

    In the matter of an intended action e

    [Thursday] the ___ day of _____ 199_ f

                                             1

BETWEEN g

               MORE MUSIC LIMITED   Plaintiff

                     and

               FREDERICK RICE   Defendant

UPON MOTION [2] for an injunction this day made unto this Court by Counsel for the intended Plaintiff (hereinafter called 'the Plaintiff') [3]

AND UPON READING a draft writ of Summons in the above mentioned intended action and a draft affidavit of Anne Fischer [4]

AND the Plaintiff by his Counsel undertaking [5]

(1) To issue forthwith a Writ of Summons in the form of the said draft Writ of Summons

(2) To procure the said Anne Fischer to swear an affidavit in or substantially in the terms of the said draft affidavit and to file the same forthwith

(3) To notify the intended Defendant (hereinafter called 'the Defendant') forthwith of the terms of this Order and thereafter to serve upon him the Writ of Summons, this Order and the affidavit aforementioned

(4) To abide by any Order this Court may make as to damages in case this Court shall hereafter be of the opinion that the Defendant shall have sustained any by reason of this Order which the Plaintiff ought to pay.

                                             6

THIS COURT DOTH ORDER that the Defendant be restrained until after [Monday] the ___ day of _____ 199_ or until further order in the meantime from:- [7] [*set out terms of the order sought*]

AND the Defendant is to be at liberty to apply to the Court to discharge or vary this injunction on [___ hours] previous notice to the Plaintiff.[8]

AND IT IS ORDERED that the costs of this motion are to be costs reserved. [9]

TAKE NOTICE that if you, the within-named Frederick Rice, disobey this order you will be liable to process of execution for the purpose of compelling you to obey the same. [10]

Notes

1   Heading

     a   The court in which the application is made is stated in capital letters in the top left-hand corner of the document. This must be the court in which the action has been or is to be brought. Exceptions to this rule are where a party to an action proceeding in a county court seeks a Mareva injunction or an Anton Piller order, since an application for the former order must usually, and an application for the latter order must always, be made in the High Court. These orders are outside the scope of this work, and for further information you should consult a practitioner's textbook such as Bean, *op cit.*

     b   As in a pleading this shows the year in which the writ was issued, and the letter and number of the action. See further sample document (1), note 1b at p 25. Note that in the Chancery Division the letters CH precede the case number.

     c   This shows the division of the High Court in which the application is made, which will be the division in which the action has been or is to be brought.

     d   The name of the judge before whom the application is to be made should be given if known.

     e   Where the application is made before the writ is issued, these words should be included.

     f   The date on which the order was made, including the day of the week should be set out as illustrated.

     g   The names of the parties to the action should be set out as in a pleading. See further sample document (1)note 1f at p 26.

2   In the Chancery Division an application for an interlocutory injunction, whether *ex parte* or *inter partes* is made by motion to a judge in open court. The judge may, in a proper case, exclude the public so that the hearing is *in camera.*

3   This paragraph records the fact that counsel for the plaintiff addressed the court. Note the use of the phrase 'hereinafter called "the Plaintiff"' to avoid repetition of the word 'intended'. The first two words of the paragraph are capitalised.

4   This paragraph records what documents were placed before the court at the hearing. The first three words are conventionally

capitalised. Note that where the matter is urgent, the documents may be in draft form. In cases of extreme urgency evidence may be given orally by counsel who must undertake to procure the swearing of an affidavit in or substantially in the same terms as the evidence given.

5   The phrase 'AND the Plaintiff [or Defendant] by his [or her] Counsel undertaking', adapted as indicated in brackets when appropriate, is conventionally used to introduce an undertaking. The plaintiff or defendant, as the case may be, addresses the court through his or her barrister, hence 'by his [or her] Counsel undertaking'. Where a party gives several undertakings, these may be set out below the introductory phrase, in logical order in numbered paragraphs, as illustrated here. Note that only the first word of the introductory phrase is capitalised.

6   Undertakings given to the court. See further, p 105 for guidance on drafting undertakings.

7   This wording is conventionally used to introduce the orders made. In both the Chancery Division and the Queen's Bench Division the usual practice on an *ex parte* application is to grant an injunction on an interim basis until a date specified in the order on which the matter is returned to court: Gee, *op cit*, 75. Nevertheless, in an appropriate case, the injunction need not specify a return date: *East Hampshire DC v Scott* ((1993) *The Times*, 6 September, CA).

8   This paragraph informs the defendant of his or her right to apply to the court on short notice, as specified in the order, to have the order varied or discharged. Where there is any doubt as to whether the defendant will fully understand the meaning of this paragraph an undertaking should be given by the plaintiff to explain the nature of this right to the defendant. This might be worded as follows:

AND the Plaintiff by his Counsel undertaking

(3) To notify the Defendant of his right to apply upon notice to this Court to vary or discharge this order.

9   An injunction must include an order dealing with costs. On an *ex parte* application the normal order is 'costs reserved' which enables the court to consider the question of costs at the *inter partes* hearing. For the precise meaning of 'costs reserved' see RSC Ord 62 r3(6).

10 This standard paragraph warns the defendant of the consequences of disobeying the injunction.

IN THE HIGH COURT OF JUSTICE   **199_ W No**
QUEEN'S BENCH DIVISION
    The Hon Mr Justice _____ (Judge in Chambers)

BETWEEN

                EDWARD TERENCE WILSON   <u>Plaintiff</u>
                        and
                CREAMERY SUPPLIES PLC   <u>Defendants</u>

[1]

    UPON HEARING Counsel for the Plaintiff and the Defendants and upon reading the affidavit of the Plaintiff filed _____199_ and the affidavit of James Parry filed _____ 199_ and the exhibits thereto [2]

    AND the Plaintiff by his Counsel undertaking to abide by any Order this Court may make as to damages in case this Court shall hereafter be of the opinion that the Defendants by reason of this Order shall have sustained any which the Plaintiff ought to pay [3]

    IT IS ORDERED that [4] [*set out terms of the order sought*].

    AND IT IS ORDERED that the costs of this application be costs in the cause. [5]

    DATED this ____ day of _____ 199_. [6]

    TAKE NOTICE, etc. [7]

Notes

1   Heading. See further sample document (3), note 1 a–d, g. Note that the wording used to identify the judge hearing the application differs slightly from that adopted in the Chancery Division. The phrase 'Judge in Chambers' indicates that in the Queen's Bench Division the application is heard by a judge sitting in private rather than in open court as is the practice in the Chancery Division. Note also that in this case the writ has been issued and that the words 'In the matter of an intended action' are therefore omitted.

2   This paragraph records the fact that counsel for both parties addressed the court and identifies the affidavit evidence put before the court at the hearing of the application. Where the application

for an injunction is made on notice in the Queen's Bench Division each party must lodge at court in advance of the hearing, a bundle containing specified documents including copies of any affidavits to be used at the hearing: SCP 32/1–6/7. The parties will therefore have complied, in advance of the hearing, with the requirement in RSC Ord 41 r9 that an affidavit used in court proceedings should be filed in the appropriate court office. The date of filing is therefore given in this paragraph. In the Chancery Division there is no need to lodge or file affidavits in advance of the hearing, but two copies of the writ and notice of motion should be lodged in advance. Note that this paragraph should not only identify the affidavits before the court but should also indicate whether any documents were used in conjunction with each affidavit. This is done by stating if there were exhibits to the affidavit, since any document used in conjunction with an affidavit must be exhibited to it. See further RSC Ord 41 r11 and below p 119. It is standard practice to capitalise the first two words of this paragraph. The affidavits could be referred to in a separate paragraph. If so, the opening words of that paragraph would be capitalised as follows: 'UPON READING the affidavit ...' etc.

3   The plaintiff's undertaking in damages.

4   This is the phrase conventionally used to introduce the orders made by the court. The first three words should be capitalised. A variant is the phrase 'IT IS ORDERED AND DIRECTED that ...' with the first five words being capitalised. If several orders are made they may be set out in separate numbered paragraphs under the introductory phrase.

5   This costs order is commonly made when an injunction is granted on an *inter partes* application as it provides that the party who is finally successful in the action is entitled to the costs of the injunction hearing.

6   The date on which the order was made. It is not necessary in the Queen's Bench Division to give the day of the week.

7   This paragraph is standard. See sample document (3), note 10, at p 91.

```
Sample document
(5) High Court – Chancery Division
    Final injunction order
```

IN THE HIGH COURT OF JUSTICE   CH 199_ M No
CHANCERY DIVISION
    Mr Justice _____
    [Tuesday] the ____ day of _____199_

1

BETWEEN

          THE MELLOW MUSIC COMPANY   <u>Plaintiff</u>
                 and
          GOLDEN TUNES LIMITED   <u>Defendant</u>

UPON THE TRIAL of this action [2]

AND UPON READING the documents recorded in the Court File as having been read [3]

AND UPON HEARING Counsel for the Plaintiff and the Defendant [4]

THIS COURT DOTH ORDER that the Defendant Golden Tunes Limited by their directors, officers, servants, workmen and agents or any of them or otherwise howsoever be restrained from doing the following acts or any of them that is to say: [*set out acts which are prohibited by the order, using numbered sub-paragraphs if necessary for clarity ie if several and distinct acts are prohibited*] [5]

AND IT IS ORDERED that the Defendant do pay to the Plaintiff his costs of this action (including therein the costs of the motion for an injunction made on _____ 199_) such costs to be taxed by the Taxing Master. [6]

```
Notes
```

1   Heading. See further sample document (3), note 1 a–e, g. Note that where the plaintiff is a limited company, the first letter of the company's name, omitting 'the' is used in the case number.

2   This introductory line records that the injunction has been made at the trial of the action and indicates that the order is final (ie not interlocutory). The first three words of the phrase are capitalised.

3   This records that the court has read the documentary evidence put before it at trial. Again, the first three words are capitalised

4   This records that counsel for both parties addressed the court. The first three words are also capitalised.

5   These words are conventionally used to introduce the order or
    orders made by the court. The first four words are capitalised. Note
    the wording used in the case of a defendant who is a limited
    company to ensure that all persons who might act on behalf of the
    company are restrained from doing the prohibited acts.

6   Provision must be made for costs. This is a standard order. The
    words in brackets should be included where the plaintiff is entitled
    to the costs of an application for an interlocutory injunction and the
    date of that application must be inserted as indicated.

Note

- If the defendant is to be given liberty to apply to vary or discharge
  the order, liberty to apply must be specifically included in the order.

- In trespass cases it is sometimes necessary to obtain a declaration as
  to the existence of the plaintiff's legal right or rights which are
  alleged to be infringed in order for an injunction restraining
  infringement of those rights to be granted. See below, p 306.

Orders

The heart of a draft injunction is the orders which the court is to be
asked to make, and this section considers the skills required in drafting
these. The wording of the orders will, of course, reflect the distinctive
facts of individual cases, but certain general principles apply. These
may be listed as follows:

- draft clearly and precisely (avoid vagueness and ambiguity);
- use plain language whenever possible;
- deal comprehensively with the conduct complained of;
- avoid oppressive orders.

The discussion that follows is a detailed examination of these principles.

Draft clearly and precisely

The essence of a well-drafted order is that it explains to the defendant
using clear, plain language, precisely what it is that the court says he or
she must, or must not, do. This is of crucial importance because if there
is any vagueness or lack of clarity or ambiguity in the wording of an
order, it is likely to be unenforceable. In other words, even were the
court to grant such an order, it might be difficult, if not impossible, to
establish that a specific act or omission on the part of the defendant
constituted breach of the order. Even if the court took the view that,

properly interpreted, the order had been breached, it might be difficult to establish that the defendant had understood the effect of the order as intended by the plaintiff and that the act or omission complained of was an intentional breach by the defendant.

Consequently, as with a pleading, and to an even greater extent, every word of an injunction order must be chosen with care in order to ensure that it achieves the effect intended. The two examples given below illustrate this and the need to avoid vagueness and ambiguity.

EXAMPLE 1: AVOIDING VAGUENESS

In this case the plaintiff owns several farms in the Shrewsbury area. The defendant persistently enters the plaintiff's land at Pyke Farm, Ditton, without the plaintiff's permission, and the plaintiff is seeking an interlocutory injunction to prevent him from doing so pending the hearing of the plaintiff's claim for a perpetual injunction.

An order that the defendant be restrained 'from entering the Plaintiff's land' is obviously too vaguely worded. If such an order were to be made, the defendant might be in breach of the order simply because he enters land at another farm without realising it belongs to the plaintiff. A precisely worded order might read as follows:

That the Defendant be restrained from entering the Plaintiff's land at Pyke Farm, Ditton, near Shrewsbury.

EXAMPLE 2: AVOIDING AMBIGUITY

In this case the plaintiff and defendant own adjoining properties and the northern boundary between their properties is marked by a wooden fence located on the plaintiff's land. There is a similar fence located on the defendant's land which marks the eastern boundary between the two properties. If the defendant is threatening to remove the fence on the plaintiff's land, an order that he be restrained 'from trespassing on the plaintiff's land and removing his fence' is not only vague in that it fails to identify clearly the land in question but also ambiguous in that 'his fence' may refer either to the fence located on the plaintiff's land or that on the defendant's land. Similarly an order restraining the defendant 'from removing the Plaintiff's fence' would be ambiguous if there were more than one fence on the plaintiff's land, and even more so if the plaintiff owned a number of other fenced properties.

Precision in defining the land or building or chattels or other things, such as machinery, to which an injunction order relates is therefore essential. Often a brief description will be adequate, eg, 'the Plaintiff's land at 50 High Street, Wilcot'. In other cases a longer description will be necessary to ensure absolute clarity as to the property or thing, or part of it, covered by the injunction. This is illustrated by the following mandatory order:

> IT IS ORDERED that the Defendant do forthwith demolish and remove so much of the garage recently erected at the rear of his premises of The Lodge, Farlow Lane, Beckham as is erected upon any part of the Plaintiff's land at 9 Farlow Lane, Beckham.

This example also illustrates the need to define precisely the way in which a required act is to be performed. It would not be sufficient in this case to draft an order requiring the defendant simply to demolish the part of the garage which has been erected on the plaintiff's land, since this would leave the defendant free to retaliate by refusing to remove the resulting debris.

Similarly, in drafting a prohibitory injunction care must be taken to define precisely the ways in which the defendant is forbidden to act. Thus where the plaintiff alleges that she has been defamed in a pamphlet published by the defendant, the injunction sought might seek to restrain the defendant 'from further printing, circulating, distributing or otherwise publishing' the pamphlet.

Use plain language

Achieving precision may in some cases require the use of specialised or technical terminology. Thus it might in a particular case be necessary to describe in language that is technical in character a machine alleged to be causing nuisance by noise. Generally, however, in drafting an injunction it is important to use plain language so that the contents of the document can be easily understood by the person to whom it is addressed.

The importance that the judiciary attaches to the use of plain language is reflected in the simplified wording adopted in the new forms issued for injunctions in county court proceedings, which are discussed below, and in the plain modern English used in the judicially approved draft Anton Piller order issued by the Chancery Division for use by practitioners. Compare, for example, the wording used in the undertaking in damages in county court Form N16 (General form of injunction on p 103) and the Chancery Division draft Anton Piller order, illustrated below, and the technical wording used in the same undertaking in the sample High Court injunction set out at p 92 above.

FORM N16 (GENERAL FORM APPLICATION)

The Plaintiff (Applicant/Petitioner) gave an undertaking (through his counsel or solicitor) promising to pay any damages ordered by the court if it later decides that the Defendant/Respondent has suffered loss or damage as a result of this order.

CHANCERY DIVISION DRAFT ANTON PILLER ORDER

If the Court later finds that this Order has caused loss to the Defendant and decides that the Defendant should be compensated for their loss the Plaintiff will comply with any Order the Court may make.

Be comprehensive

An injunction must be comprehensive in two ways. Firstly, it must cover every act which the defendant is required to do or refrain from doing. As we have shown, this is part of what is meant by drafting with precision.[15] Secondly, an injunction must be carefully worded so as to prevent the defendant from evading, wholly or in part, the effect of the order.

In the case of a mandatory order we have already discussed the importance of defining precisely the way in which an act is to be performed in order to deal comprehensively with the wrongdoing alleged.[16] In drafting a prohibitory order it is particularly important to bear in mind the two key ways in which a defendant may be able to escape the effect of an order and to eliminate any loopholes which would make this possible.

Firstly, a defendant may evade the effect of a poorly drafted order by doing some act which, while not prohibited under the terms of the order, has the same effect for the plaintiff as an act which is proscribed. A well-drafted order will therefore avoid this potential loophole by prohibiting any variations of the allegedly wrongful conduct. Typically this is done by identifying and expressly prohibiting the most obvious ways in which the wrongful act or acts may be committed and covering any other ways which might occur to the defendant by using a catch-all phrase such as 'or otherwise howsoever'.

---

[15] See above, p 97.

[16] *Ibid.*

Thus in the example given earlier, the defendant accused of libel is to be restrained 'from further printing, circulating, distributing *or otherwise publishing*' the allegedly defamatory pamphlet. The italicised words are the catch-all phrase inserted to prevent the defendant from publishing the alleged libel in some way not covered by words 'printing', 'circulating' or 'distributing'. This example focuses upon the processes by which a libel may be promulgated.

In a different case it might be more appropriate to focus upon the equipment used to commit a wrongful act. So, for example, an order might prohibit a defendant 'from trespassing on the plaintiff's land at [address] by entering or remaining or causing or permitting tractors or other agricultural vehicles to be placed or remain thereon'. In yet another case it might be necessary to focus on the places at which an wrongful act might be committed. An appropriate order in such a case might restrain the defendant from causing a nuisance to the plaintiff by playing a stereo radio set loudly 'in the hallways, stairways or any other part of the premises at [address]'.

Secondly, it may be possible in some cases, unless preventative measures are taken, for a defendant to evade the effect of an order either by actively inciting or encouraging or by merely permitting some other person to do the prohibited act or acts. Certain phrases are therefore inserted into orders to prevent this from occurring.

In the High Court, where an order is directed against a single defendant the approved wording is as follows:

... the Defendant whether by himself his servants or agents or otherwise howsoever ...

Where several defendants are restrained, the phrase used is:

The Defendants (and each of them) either by themselves, their servants or agents or otherwise howsoever ...

If the defendant is a limited company or a corporate body the wording used is:

... the Defendant [name of company] Limited by their directors, officers, servants, workmen or agents or any of them or otherwise howsoever ...

The use, where several defendants are restrained, of the phrase 'and each of them' is a further example of drafting comprehensively. It is included to make clear that the defendants are restrained individually as well as collectively.

Don't draft an oppressive order

While the need to deal comprehensively with the conduct complained
of is crucial, it is also very important to avoid drafting an order which
the court might consider oppressive in the extent to which it seeks to
restrain the defendant. An order will be oppressive if it goes further
than the court considers is necessary to protect those legal rights of the
plaintiff which the defendant is infringing or threatening to infringe.
Thus an injunction prohibiting a builder from using noisy building
equipment at any time would be likely to be viewed as imposing
unreasonable restraints on the defendant and so refused as being
oppressive. In such a case it would be more realistic to seek an order
restraining the defendant from using the equipment except during
specified hours, such as 9 am to 1 pm and 2 pm to 6 pm, Monday to
Friday.

County court proceedings

DECIDING WHICH DOCUMENTS MUST BE DRAFTED

In the county court an application for an interlocutory injunction must
normally be made by completing Form N16A and drafting a
supporting affidavit. Except in an urgent case, a draft of the operative
terms of the order sought must be prepared for submission to the
judge for approval if the order is granted.

When the application is made *ex parte*, Form N16A must be
prepared for service on the defendant after the order has been
obtained. If the application is made before proceedings have been
issued, a summons should be prepared as the plaintiff will be required
to undertake to issue one forthwith if the injunction is granted. When
an application is successful, the order is made in Form N16 which may
also be used for any draft order.

If there are any undertakings given other than the plaintiff's
undertaking in damages, which is printed on Form N16, these must be
recorded in a document and served on the defendant. The relevant
prescribed form is Form N117. Sample forms are set out below.

The notes to the prescribed forms give guidance on completing
them, and the only drafting required is in respect of the orders and any
undertakings to be inserted on the appropriate forms. The principles
that apply to drafting these are as discussed in relation to drafting
injunctions and undertakings in High Court proceedings and reference
should be made to the relevant parts of this chapter at pp 95ff and 105.

N. 16A
General form of application for injunction
Order 13, rule 6(3), Order 47, rule 8(2)
[*Introduced* 1991]
[*Title – Form* N. 16]

Seal

Notes on completion	☐ By application in pending proceedings
Tick whichever box applies	☐ In the matter of the Domestic Violence and Matrimonial Proceedings Act 1976

(1) Enter the full name of the person making the application

The Plaintiff (Applicant/Petitioner)(1)

applies to the court for an injunction order in the following terms:

(2) Enter the full name of the person the injunction is to be directed to

That the Defendant (Respondent)(2)

be forbidden (whether by himself or by instructing or encouraging any other person)(3)

(3) Set out here the proposed restraining orders (If the defendant is a limited company delete the wording in brackets and insert "Whether by its servants, agents, officers or otherwise"

(4) Set out here any proposed mandatory orders requiring acts to be done

And that the Defendant (Respondent)(4)

(5) Set out here any further terms asked for including provision for costs

And that(5)

(6) Enter the names of all persons who have sworn affidavits in support of this application.

The grounds of this application are set out as in the sworn statement(s) of (6)

This (these) sworn statement(s) is (are) served with this application.

(7) Enter the names and addresses of all persons upon whom it is intended to serve this application

This application is to be served upon(7)

(8) Enter the full name and address for service and delete as required

This application is filed by(8)

(the Solicitors for) the Plaintiff (Applicant/Petitioner) whose address for service is

Signed   **Dated**

This section to be completed by the court

* Name and address of the person application is directed to

To *
of

This application will be heard by the (District)Judge at

on   the   day of   199   at   o'clock
If you do not attend at the time shown the court may make an injunction order in your absence.
If you do not fully understand this application you should go to a Solicitor, Legal Advice Centre or a Citizens' Advice Bureau

---

The Court Office at
is open from 10 am to 4 pm. When corresponding with the court, address all forms and letters to the Chief Clerk and quote the case

N. 16
General form of injunction
Order 13, rule 6
[Amended 1991]

Injunction Order	**In the**	
		County Court
Between......... Plaintiff / Applicant / Petitioner	**Case Number**	*Always quote this*
and .... Defendant / Respondent	**Plaintiff's Ref**	
To [The name of the person the order is directed to	**Defendant's Ref**	
of [The address of the person the order is directed to]	*For completion by the court* **Issued on** **199**	

Seal

If you do not obey this order you will be guilty of contempt of court and you may be sent to prison

On the   of   199   the court considered an application for an injunction

The Court ordered that [*The name of the person the order is directed to*]

is forbidden (whether by himself or by instructing or encouraging any other person) [*The terms of the restraining order. If the defendant is a limited company, delete the words in brackets and insert 'whether by its servants, agents, officers or otherwise'*]

This order shall remain in force until (the   of
199   at   o'clock
unless before then it is revoked by a further order of the court

And it is ordered that [*The name of the person the order is directed to*]

shall [*The terms of any orders requiring acts to be done*]
on or before [*Enter time (and place) as ordered*]

It is further ordered that [*The terms of any other orders, costs etc*]

Notice of further hearing [*Use when the order is temporary or ex parte otherwise delete*]
The court will re-consider the application and whether the order should continue at a further hearing at

on   the   day of   199   at   o'clock
If you do not attend at the time shown the court may make an injunction order in your absence.
You are entitled to apply to the court to re-consider the order before that day [*Delete if order made on notice*]

If you do not understand anything in this order you should go to a Solicitor, Legal Advice Centre or a Citizens' Advice Bureau

The Court Office at
is open from 10 am to 4 pm, Mon-Fri. When corresponding with the court, address all forms and letters to the Chief Clerk and quote the case number

Injunction Order – Record of Hearing   Case No _____

On _____ the_____ day of _____ 199_
Before H__ Honour (District) Judge_____
The court was sitting at _____
_____

The ☐ Plaintiff ☐ Applicant ☐ Petitioner (Name) _____
was ☐ represented by Counsel
     ☐ represented by a Solicitor
     ☐ in person
The ☐ Defendant ☐ Respondent   (Name) _____
was ☐ represented by Counsel
     ☐ represented by a Solicitor
     ☐ in person
     ☐ did not appear having been given notice of this hearing
     ☐ not given notice of this hearing

The court read the affidavit(s) of
     ☐ the Plaintiff/Applicant/Petitioner   sworn on _____
     ☐ the Defendant/Respondent   sworn on _____
And of _____ sworn on _____
_____

The court heard spoken evidence on oath from
_____
_____

The Plaintiff (Applicant/Petitioner) gave an undertaking (through his counsel or solicitor) promising to pay any damages ordered by the court if it later
decides that the Defendant/Respondent has suffered loss or damage as a
result of this order. *

* Delete this paragraph if the court does not require the undertaking

Signed _____ **Dated** _____
                    (Judge's Clerk)

N. 117
General Form of Undertaking
Order 29, rule 1A
[As amended 1991]

General Form of Undertaking	In the	
		County Court
Between......... **Plaintiff** **Applicant** **Petitioner**	**Case Number**	*Always quote this*
and .... **Defendant** **Respondent**	**Plaintiff's Ref**	
	Defendant's Ref	

This form is to be used only for an undertaking not for an injunction

On the   day of   199   (Seal)

[Name of the person giving undertaking]
[appeared in person] [was represented by Solicitor/Counsel]
and gave an undertaking to the Court promising [*Set out terms of undertaking*]

And to be bound by these promises until [*Give the date and time or event when the undertaking will expire*]
The Court explained to [*Name of the person giving undertaking*] the meaning of his undertaking and the consequences of failing to keep his promises
And the Court accepted his undertaking [*The judge may direct that the party who gives the undertaking shall personally sign the statement overleaf*] [and *if so ordered* directed that [*Name of the person giving undertaking*] should sign the statement overleaf].
And the Court ordered that [*Set out any other directions given by the court*]

Dated

Important Notice
To [*Name of the person giving undertaking*]
of [*Address of the person giving undertaking*]

- You may be sent to prison for contempt of court if you break the promises that you have given to the Court.
- If you do not understand anything in this document you should go to a Solicitor, Legal Advice Centre or a Citizens' Advice Bureau.

The Court Office at
is open from 10 am to 4 pm, Mon-Fri. When corresponding with the Court, address all forms and letters to the Chief Clerk and quote the case number

Undertakings in lieu of an injunction

In both the High Court and the county court undertakings may be offered by the defendant as an alternative to the making of an injunction order either in interlocutory proceedings or at trial. For example, a defendant may offer to give an undertaking before an *inter partes* interlocutory hearing, so as to avoid the necessity for that hearing or may do so when the court has found in favour of the plaintiff at such a hearing or after a full trial of the case.

As you will remember, a defendant cannot be compelled to give an undertaking, but in some cases defendants prefer to do so rather than have a court order made against them. You will also recollect that an undertaking is given to the court and is enforceable in the same way as an injunction.

A plaintiff who has established his or her case at trial is not obliged to accept the defendant's offer of an undertaking or undertakings in lieu of injunction. If such an offer is accepted, however, care must be taken to ensure that the undertaking or undertakings given to the court give him protection equivalent to that which would have been obtained by means of the injunction order sought. This is particularly important because, unlike an injunction, an undertaking cannot be varied if the protection given proves insufficient.

The annotated sample document set out below illustrates how an undertaking in lieu of an injunction is drafted in proceedings in the Chancery Division of the High Court.

```
Sample document
(6) High Court – Chancery Division
Undertaking in lieu of injunction
```

IN THE HIGH COURT OF JUSTICE   CH 199_ P No
CHANCERY DIVISION

    Mr Justice _____

    [Monday] the ____ day of _____199_

BETWEEN

PATRICIA PARRY   <u>Plaintiff</u>

and

GWYNETH WILLIAMS   <u>Defendant</u>

    UPON MOTION this day made unto this Court by Counsel for the Plaintiff [2]

    AND UPON HEARING Counsel for the Defendant [3]

    AND UPON READING the Writ of Summons issued on the ___ day of _____ 199_ and the Plaintiff's Affidavit filed the same day [4]

    AND the Plaintiff undertaking by her Counsel to abide by any Order this Court may make as to damages in case this Court shall hereafter be of the opinion that the Defendant shall have suffered only by reason of the Defendant's undertaking hereinafter contained which the Plaintiff ought to pay [5]

    AND the Defendant undertaking by her Counsel that until after judgment of this action or further order she will not whether by herself her servants or agents or otherwise howsoever [*set out the acts which the defendant undertakes not to do; eg 'trespass on the Plaintiff's land at [address]'*] [6]

    THIS COURT doth not think fit to make any Order on the said Motion save that the costs thereof be costs in the cause. [7]

```
Notes
```

1   Heading. See further sample document (3) note 1 a–c, g at p 90.
2   This paragraph records the fact that the plaintiff's barrister addressed the court. Note that the first two words are capitalised.
3   This paragraph records the fact that the defendant's barrister addressed the court. Note that the first three words are capitalised.

4   This paragraph records what documents were placed before the court at the hearing, and commonly refers to the writ and to any affidavit evidence filed by the parties. The dates on which the writ was issued and any affidavits filed are given. Note that the first three words of the paragraph are capitalised.

5   The plaintiff's undertaking in damages. This is an appropriately modified form of the undertaking which must be given when an injunction is obtained. The opening word is capitalised.

6   The terms of the undertaking. The opening word is capitalised.

7   Taken together paras 6 and 7 record that, on the basis that the defendant gave the undertaking recorded in para 6, the court decided to make no order other than the order for costs recorded in para 7.

Practising drafting injunctions

We hope that this chapter has given you a basic understanding of how to approach drafting an injunction order. If you wish to practise doing so, there is an opportunity in Chapter 13 to test your skills by drafting an application for an injunction in a case of trespass to the person. Please read the entire chapter before beginning to draft. The annotated version which we have included at p 333 should enable you to check whether you have included all the necessary matters.

Chapter 5

Drafting Affidavits

What is an affidavit?

An affidavit is a sworn written statement of the evidence which the person making it can give which is relevant to some cause or matter on which the court must adjudicate. The rules of court require that evidence is given by affidavit in certain types of proceedings, for example, High Court actions begun by originating summons[1] and some interlocutory applications in the High Court or county court. In other proceedings, such as actions begun by writ in the High Court or by summons in the county court, affidavit evidence may be given with the leave of the court.[2]

The use of affidavits in tort cases

The frequency with which a lawyer is called upon to draft affidavits will depend to a large extent on the types of cases which he or she handles. Thus a family practitioner is likely to draft affidavits regularly, while a specialist in personal injury may do so only occasionally. Nevertheless, every lawyer handling tort cases must be capable of drafting an effective affidavit when necessary, particularly since in many interlocutory applications affidavit evidence is required and is the basis on which an order is granted or refused. One such application is that made for an interlocutory injunction, which was discussed in Chapter 4. As you will recall, interlocutory injunctions are commonly sought in certain actions in tort, such as defamation, trespass to land, trespass to the person and nuisance. It is very important, therefore, that a lawyer who handles such actions should acquire the skills needed to draft an affidavit.

Scope of the chapter

The present chapter therefore examines these skills by focusing on the sort of affidavit which must be put before the court in support of an application for an interlocutory injunction. At the same time, the

---

1   RSC Ord 28 r1A.
2   RSC Ord 38 r2(1); CCR Ord 20 r6. Affidavit evidence may also be admitted at trial by agreement of the parties: SCP 38/2/9; CCR Ord 20 r7(1).

comments made with regard to structure, style and the use of exhibits, as well as many of the points raised in discussing content, are relevant to the drafting of affidavits generally. The annotated sample affidavit in support of an application for an interlocutory injunction also illustrates some points of general application.[3]

Structure

The basic structure of an affidavit is in part determined by the formalities which it must contain. These consist of the heading, the commencement and the *jurat*. In addition, a description of the document may be included and following the commencement there is always what is basically a standard introductory paragraph leading into the body of the affidavit in which the deponent's evidence is set out. The basic lay-out of the affidavit is, then, as follows:

- heading;
- description of affidavit (optional);
- commencement;
- standard introductory paragraphs;
- body of affidavit;
- *jurat*.

The body of the affidavit should be divided into paragraphs each containing a distinct portion of the deponent's evidence. Paragraphs must be consecutively numbered[4] and sub-headings may be used if this is felt to add to the clarity of the document. The events described should be set out in chronological order so far as this is practicable so that the sequence of these events is easily grasped by the reader. However, the order in which the matters deposed to are presented is decided by the person who drafts the affidavit, and in some cases it may be more appropriate to structure the body of the affidavit on the basis of issues rather than to present a strictly chronological account. Whichever order is adopted it should be kept in mind that information is more easily absorbed if the document presenting it is clearly structured.

The way in which the information is presented in the other sections of the affidavit is shown by the sample document at p 120 below.

---

3   The general rules which relate to drafting affidavits in the High Court and the county court are contained in RSC Ord 41 and CCR Ord 20 r10 respectively.
4   RSC Ord 41 r1(6).

Content

The matters deposed to in an affidavit will, of course, vary according to the purpose for which it is to be used and the facts of individual cases, but a number of general comments can be made with regard to the content of the various sections of the affidavit set out above.

Heading

In both the High Court and the county courts the heading of an affidavit must include certain indorsements or 'markings' which are set out on the top right-hand corner of the first page of document. In the High Court the affidavit must be so indorsed to show the party on whose behalf it is filed, the initials and surname of the deponent, the number of the affidavit in relation to that deponent, the date on which the affidavit was sworn and the identifying initials and number of each exhibit to the affidavit. These markings should also appear on the backsheet and, where space allows, on the first page of every exhibit.[5] The markings may be set out in a single line, as below:

Dft: J. W. Smith: 1st: 15.6.95

Alternatively the information required may be presented in the tabular form as illustrated in sample affidavit below.[6] In the county courts the markings are expanded to include the date on which the affidavit was filed. Presentation is as in the High Court.

The content of the remainder of the heading is as in the pleading. The court in which the action is proceeding and, in the case of a High Court action, the relevant division of the court must be shown, together with the title of the action consisting of the names of the parties. The lay-out of the heading can be seen in the sample document on p 120.

Description of document

A description is optional. If included it may be very concise or very full. Examples are set out below:

---

5 *Practice Direction (Evidence: Documents)* [1983] 1 WLR 922, reproduced at SCP 41/11/1 as amended by *Practice Direction (Evidence: Documents)* [1995] 1 WLR 510. RSC Ord 41 r9(5) requires every affidavit to be indorsed to show not only on whose behalf the affidavit is filed and the date of swearing, but also the date of filing, as in the county courts. The rule states that an affidavit which is not so indorsed may not be filed or used without the leave of the court. The notes at 41/9/1 refer, however, to the solicitor's duty to file an affidavit after it is used. It appears that, at present, practitioners do not include the date of filing when drafting affidavits for use in High Court proceedings.

6 CCR Ord 20 r10(3).

AFFIDAVIT

AFFIDAVIT OF JOHN WILLIAM SMITH

AFFIDAVIT IN SUPPORT OF THE PLAINTIFF'S APPLICATION
FOR AN INTERLOCUTORY INJUNCTION

Commencement

The commencement is a brief paragraph which gives the deponent's
name, address and occupation and his or her declaration that the
evidence contained in the affidavit is given on oath.[7] The example
below gives the traditional wording.

> I, JOHN WILLIAM SMITH, of 52 High Street, Radley, Wiltshire,
> company director, MAKE OATH, and say as follows:

The deponent's name and the words 'make oath' are usually in upper
case, as in the example, but this is optional. The deponent's full name
should be given. The address stated is that at which the deponent
resides, or, if the deponent is acting in a professional, business or
occupational capacity, the address at which he or she works. In the
latter case the position held by the deponent and the name of his or her
firm or employer must also be stated. If the deponent has no
occupation, a description may be given, for example 'retired'. Where
the deponent is a party, the description 'the above-named plaintiff' or
'the above-named defendant' is sufficient, but the place of residence
must be stated.[8]

Standard introductory paragraph

The first substantive paragraph of an affidavit is, as indicated,
standard in content. First the status of the deponent in relation to the
proceedings must be identified. Where the deponent is a party this
may be done by commencing the paragraph as follows:

> 1. I am the Plaintiff [Defendant] in this action ...

This phrase may, however, be omitted if the deponent has already been
described as a party in the commencement. Where the deponent is not
a party, the paragraph should state that he or she is authorised to make

---

7   Any person who objects to giving evidence on oath may make an affirmation; see below at
    p 121 note 4.
8   SCP 41/1/7.

the affidavit by the person or party on whose behalf evidence is being given, and might commence as follows:

1. I am duly authorised to make this affidavit on behalf of the Defendant [Plaintiff] ...

An affidavit may be made by two or more deponents,[9] but this is uncommon. If an affidavit is made by a plaintiff on behalf of himself and a co-plaintiff, or by a defendant on behalf of himself and a co-defendant,[10] this may be indicated as in the following example:

1. I am the First Plaintiff in this action and am duly authorised to make this affidavit on behalf of myself and the Second Plaintiff.

Secondly, the purpose for which the affidavit is made should be indicated. Thus, for example, where a plaintiff seeks an interlocutory injunction in the county court the opening sentence of the first paragraph of his or her affidavit might read:

1. I am the Plaintiff in the above case, and make this affidavit in support of my application for an interlocutory injunction against the Defendant in the terms set out in the Notice of Application herein.

Thirdly, and finally, the introductory paragraph should contain a declaration that the matters deposed to are true and within the personal knowledge of the deponent. This might be phrased as in the following example:

The facts deposed to herein are true and (are) within my knowledge.

The inclusion of hearsay evidence,[11] where permitted, must be indicated by modifying the declaration. Examples of how to do so are set out below:

The matters to which I hereinafter depose are true to the best of my knowledge and belief and are within my personal knowledge unless expressly stated to the contrary.

---

9 RSC Ord 41 r2.

10 In such a case the other plaintiff, or defendant, may make a short sworn statement confirming the truth of the matters contained in the co-plaintiff's or co-defendant's affidavit.

11 See below, p 114.

The facts deposed to herein are true to the best of my knowledge and belief and are within my personal knowledge unless stated otherwise.

Body of affidavit

As indicated above, the content of the body of an affidavit will be determined by the purpose for which it is to be used and the facts of the case to which it relates. The following matters are, however, of general application.

RELEVANCE

An affidavit must contain only evidence which is relevant to a question or questions to be determined in the proceedings in which it is used. Any matter which is irrelevant may be struck out by order of the court.[12]

ADMISSIBILITY

Except in so far as hearsay is permitted, only admissible evidence should be included in an affidavit. The court will strike out facts or matters that are inadmissible.[13]

HEARSAY EVIDENCE

In the High Court an affidavit may not contain hearsay evidence unless it falls within one of the excepted categories listed in RSC Ord 41 r5. The exceptions which are relevant to actions in tort are where an affidavit is used in interlocutory proceedings, or in proceedings under RSC Ord 14 for summary judgment or pursuant to an order under RSC Ord 38 r3(2)(a).[14] In the county courts an affidavit which contains hearsay evidence may be used unless the court orders otherwise.[15]

ACCURACY

When drafting an affidavit is important to ensure that it represents accurately the evidence which the deponent can give. Nothing must be invented or exaggerated.

FULL AND FRANK DISCLOSURE

A plaintiff who applies *ex parte* for an injunction is under a duty to make full and frank disclosure to the court of all the material facts

---

12   RSC Ord 41 r6.
13   SCP 41/6/1.
14   RSC Ord 41 r5(1)(a),(d),(e) and (2); SCP 41/5/1.
15   CCR Ord 20 r10(4).

within his or her knowledge, including facts adverse to the plaintiff's case. The suppression of material facts may result in any injunction obtained being subsequently discharged by the court. Where an application is made *inter partes*, the duty of disclosure imposed on the applicant is less stringent, since the other side will be able to put its case at the hearing. Nevertheless, there is always a duty imposed on all parties not to mislead the court.

Legal Argument

The central purpose of an affidavit is to put before the court those material facts known to the deponent which support the case of the party on whose behalf the affidavit is to be used. The legal arguments which the party may advance on the basis of these facts should not be included in the affidavit.

With regard to the facts which will be material to an application for an interlocutory injunction some further general points should be noted.

Background Facts

The affidavit in support of an application for an interlocutory injunction should put before the court facts which explain the background to the matters complained of by the plaintiff. The parties should be described and their relationship explained and any relevant land or property clearly defined. Events leading up to the matters complained of should also be described.

Matters Complained of by the Plaintiff

The affidavit must describe clearly and accurately the acts or omissions of the defendant which are alleged to constitute wrongful conduct giving rise to a cause of action which entitles the plaintiff to claim injunctive relief. In general these are best set out in chronological order. The facts deposed to must show that there is a serious issue to be tried.[16]

Inadequacy of Damages for Plaintiff

An interim injunction will not be granted if the court is satisfied that damages would be a sufficient remedy for the plaintiff.[17] The affidavit must therefore include facts showing that damages would not be an adequate remedy with regard to the wrongdoing alleged.

---

[16] *American Cyanamid v Ethicon Ltd* [1975] 1 All ER 504, HL.
[17] *Ibid.*

ADEQUACY OF PLAINTIFF'S UNDERTAKING IN DAMAGES

The court is unlikely to grant an interim injunction if the potential damages to the defendant is unquantifiable and the plaintiff lacks the means to compensate the defendant if the injunction is held to have been wrongly granted.[18] The plaintiff's affidavit should therefore, where appropriate, include facts with regard to the plaintiff's financial status which establish the adequacy of his or her undertaking in damages.

BALANCE OF CONVENIENCE

The plaintiff's affidavit should demonstrate that the balance of convenience is in favour of granting an interlocutory injunction,[19] that is that the potential harm to the plaintiff if an injunction is refused is greater than the potential harm to the defendant if an injunction is granted. Determining whether or not damages provide an adequate remedy for either party is one stage in deciding the balance of convenience, and may settle the question.

FACTS JUSTIFYING *EX PARTE* APPLICATION

Where an injunction is sought *ex parte* the plaintiff must include in the supporting affidavit facts which justify making the application without giving the defendant the notice required by the rules. The facts relied upon will vary from case to case, but, for example, a plaintiff who seeks an injunction to restrain publication of an allegedly defamatory article might justify the application being made *ex parte* by deposing to the imminence of the publication date.

THE *JURAT*

The statement that the affidavit has been sworn by the deponent before a solicitor or other commissioner for oaths, which must be signed by both the deponent and the person administering the oath, must appear immediately following the text of the affidavit. Consequently an affidavit must not end on one page with the *jurat* following on the next sheet.[20] The *jurat* must state in full the address of the place where the affidavit was sworn, and the signature of the commissioner for oaths should be written immediately below the words 'Before me'. The signature of the deponent must appear opposite the *jurat*, as illustrated below:

---

[18]   *Ibid.*
[19]   *Ibid.*
[20]   SCP 41/1/11.

SWORN at 10 Porter Street, Westfield
WR3 1XA on the 15th day of June 1995   *Jennifer Hart*
Before me,   (signature)
(signature)
Solicitor

The example below shows the *jurat* where an affidavit is sworn at the county court.

SWORN at the Halifax County Court
at Prescott Street, Halifax, West Yorkshire
HX1 2JJ on the   day of   199   *Jennifer Hart*
Before me,   (signature)
(signature)
An Officer of the Court appointed by the Judges to take affidavits.

This should be noted as from time to time it is necessary to actually draft affidavits at court.

In an affirmation in writing, the word 'AFFIRMED' is substituted for the word 'SWORN'.

Style

In drafting an affidavit, as in drafting any legal document, the aim must be to communicate information accurately, clearly and concisely and in appropriate language. In addition, however, an affidavit must be written persuasively. We shall therefore examine these qualities more closely.

Accuracy

Accuracy is of crucial importance, since the maker of the affidavit is required to swear to the truth of the matters contained in it. Clearly, therefore, it is wholly inappropriate for the person drafting an affidavit to exaggerate or otherwise distort what the deponent says, or to invent matters, in order to strengthen the evidence given. One the other hand, it is neither necessary nor, in some cases, desirable to reproduce exactly the language of the witness, since the whole point of employing a lawyer to draft an affidavit is to ensure that the evidence which the witness can give is presented in the most appropriate and effective way.

It is for the lawyer drafting the affidavit to decide when it will be appropriate to incorporate into the document the precise language used by the witness. If a deponent expresses his or her views strongly, the affidavit may properly reflect this. Equally, where hearsay is permitted, it may be appropriate to quote strong language used by others. You should remember, however, that the inclusion of intemperate or unnecessary hostile language or allegations is likely to increase the tension between the parties and so may hinder resolution of the dispute.

Clarity

The ability to write clearly is very important. Ideally the affidavit should be so clearly expressed that a busy judge, reading quickly, can easily assimilate the information contained in it. In addition, it is obvious that the maker of the affidavit, who must swear to the truth of its contents, must be able to understand the language used by the lawyer who drafts the document.

Conciseness

Provided that it is not achieved by omitting relevant information, conciseness is also a virtue likely to be appreciated by the judge. Certainly there is no requirement, as there is in drafting pleadings, to present the relevant facts in summary form, but the temptation to become discursive should nevertheless be resisted. Sufficient words must be used to produce an account that flows in a way that makes it easy for the reader to assimilate the information given. However, a wordy affidavit is likely to be dense and confusing.

Appropriate language

Appropriate language must be used in drafting an affidavit. The wording which should be used in drafting the formal paragraphs has already been indicated. In the body of the affidavit what is appropriate language will vary according to the evidence being given. Where a witness deals with complex and highly specialised matters, his or her affidavit may properly include technical terms. In general, however, plain English is to be preferred, and complicated phrasing or legalistic terminology should be avoided.

Two rules relating to the wording of affidavits should be noted. Firstly, an affidavit must be written in the first person singular throughout or, in those rare cases where an affidavit is made by two people, in the first person plural. Secondly, numbers should be expressed in figures and not in words.

Persuasiveness

Persuasiveness is an essential quality of an effective affidavit. In part, of course, persuasiveness will depend on the strength of the evidence being given but, as with evidence given orally, persuasion may be a significant factor in its effectiveness.

Doubtless the ability to write persuasively, to present information in a way the reader will find both attractive and convincing, is a talent which some people have in greater measure than others. However, an affidavit that is well-structured and uses appropriate language to present relevant information accurately and concisely is more likely to be persuasive than one which is woolly and discursive.

It is, however, important to be aware of the impact on the reader of the words selected. Thus, for example, while emotive language should generally be avoided, the emotional or other connotations of particular words or phrases should be kept in mind. Note, for example, the difference in meaning conveyed by the words 'job' and 'career'. Deciding when it is appropriate to use a neutral word and when it would be more effective to employ one carrying particular connotations is part of the skill of producing a persuasive affidavit.

Finally, as indicated earlier, in some cases the effectiveness of a witness's testimony may be enhanced by quoting the precise words used. For example, the persuasiveness of an affidavit in support of a application for an interlocutory injunction to restrain trespass to the person may be increased by quoting *verbatim* threats made to the plaintiff by the defendant.

Exhibits

In drafting an affidavit it is often necessary to refer to one or more documents which support the evidence being given. A typical example is where the deponent claims to be the tenant of a property and refers to the lease conveying the tenancy into his or her name. Other items, for example, cassettes, may be referred to in the same way. In each case the item mentioned should be exhibited with the affidavit.

The practice with regard to exhibits is set out in *Practice Direction (Evidence: Documents)* (1983) and *Practice Direction (Evidence: Documents)* (1995) cited at p 111 above. In particular it should be noted that where a number of letters are referred to in an affidavit, these should not be exhibited singly, but should be collected together and exhibited in one or more bundles. Every item exhibited must be identified by markings made up of the deponent's initials and a number relating to the order in which exhibits are mentioned in the affidavit. Thus the first item exhibited in an affidavit made by Margaret Richards will be marked 'MR1'.

When an item which is to be exhibited is first mentioned in an affidavit it must be introduced as an exhibit. The words conventionally used are as follows:

> There is now produced and shown to me and exhibited herewith (or hereto) marked 'MR1' a plan ...

The markings are then given followed by a description of the item exhibited as shown below.

It is also necessary for the exhibit to an affidavit to be identified by a certificate made by the person before whom the affidavit was sworn or affirmed. This is usually done by attaching a front sheet to the exhibit. The front sheet will bear the same indorsement as the affidavit, described at p 111. Under this the words:

> This is exhibit 'MR1' referred to in the affidavit of ...

appear together with the solicitor or commissioner for oaths who has administered the oath.

Sample affidavit

Deponent: PA Parfit
1st Affidavit
For: Plaintiff
Sworn: 9.10.95
Filed: 10.10.95
Exhibits: PAF [1]

IN THE CAERNARFON COUNTY COURT   Case No: [2]

BETWEEN

ANN PARFIT   Plaintiff
and
WILLIAM MORRIS   Defendant

AFFIDAVIT [3]

I, PAULA ANN PARFIT, of 106 Victoria Street, Bangor, Gwynedd, librarian, MAKE OATH and say as follows: [4]

1. I am the Plaintiff in the above case, [5] and make this affidavit in support of my application for injunction relief against the Defendant as set out in my Notice of Application herein. [6] The matters deposed to herein are true to the best of my knowledge and belief. [7]

2. I [8] am the owner and occupier of the premises known as 108 Victoria Street, Bangor, Gwynedd.

3. ...

4. There is now produced and shown to me and exhibited herewith marked 'PAF 1' [9] ...

5. etc

6. Accordingly, I believe that the Defendant threatens and intends, unless restrained by this Court to [insert conduct complained of] and I respectfully ask the Court to grant the order in the form requested. [10]

Notes [11]

1 *Markings.* These should appear at the top right-hand corner of the first page and give the initials of the forenames, and the surnames in full of the deponent, the number of the affidavit in relation to the deponent, the party on whose behalf the affidavit is sworn, the date of swearing, the identifying initals and number of each exhibit to the affidavit and, in the county court, the date of filing.
2 *Heading.* As in pleadings to show the court, the names of the parties and the case number.
3 *Title.* A short title is sufficient. For further examples see p 112.
4 *Commencement.* State full name, occupation, or if none, 'unemployed' or 'retired', and address of deponent. The deponent's name need not be in capital letters, and the address may be the deponent's workplace if the affidavit is made in a professional or business capacity. The declaration of oath or affirmation, need not be in capital letters. The wording of the affirmation is, 'I, [name] of [address], do solemnly and sincerely affirm'. See further at p 112 note 7.
5 Indicate the status of the deponent in the proceedings.
6 State the purpose for which the affidavit is sworn.

7   Where hearsay is included in an affidavit, the following words should be added: '... and are within my personal knowledge unless expressly stated to the contrary.'

8   The deponent must use the first person singular throughout: RSC Ord 41 r1(4).

9   *Exhibits*. These can be written documents, cassettes, videos, photographs, deeds or any object which are relevant to the affidavit. They are exhibited to the affidavit by the words used here. Each exhibit must be marked with the same initials and number as in the affidavit. The swearing or affirmation of the exhibit must be recorded by a solicitor or officer of the court on the exhibit and the affidavit. See further at p 119.

10 In the final paragraph it is usual to summarise the reasons the deponent gives in the affidavit for the terms of the order sought.

11 *Jurat*. This must be properly completed for the affidavit to be valid. It must be signed by the deponent in the presence of a commissioner for oaths or an authorised person: SCP 41/1/11, 41/1/14. It consists of the names and signatures of the deponent and the commissioner of oaths together with the place and date when the affidavit was sworn.

Practising drafting an affidavit

As the preceding discussion suggests, drafting an affidavit is not to be undertaken without a clear grasp of the evidence the deponent can give in relation to the case, an understanding of the function of an affidavit, and a knowledge of the principles of drafting outlined above. With experience, however, you should find drafting an enjoyable and relatively straightforward task.

If you wish to practise drafting a simple affidavit, there is an opportunity to do so in Chapter 13. You should read the entire chapter before beginning to draft. Our annotated version, included at p 334, should enable you to check that you have dealt with the appropriate matters.

In drafting the affidavit you will need to reorganise the information supplied in the plaintiff's account at p 330. The extent to which this will be necessary in drafting other affidavits will vary from witness to witness. Generally, however, you should try to preserve the deponent's individual style as far as this is compatible with the function of the affidavit in question and with clarity of presentation. The document should be one which the deponent can recognise as his or her testimony. It is after all, as the use of the first person singular reminds the reader, a document made by the deponent.

Chapter 6

Writing an Opinion or Advice

What is an opinion or advice?

An opinion or advice may broadly be defined as a barrister's written professional views on some matter or matters which he or she has been instructed to consider by a solicitor acting on behalf of a client or clients. The solicitor who instructs the barrister, the instructing solicitor, is the barrister's professional client to whom the opinion or advice is delivered. The person on whose behalf the opinion or advice is commissioned is the barrister's lay client.

When a barrister is so instructed, what is being sought is advice based upon that barrister's professional expertise and experience. In some cases this will be because the barrister approached is known to be a specialist in a particular field of law. A barrister whose practice is of a more general character may be instructed to advise on a variety of matters in relation to which he or she is able to offer legal expertise and litigation experience. The services of a barrister may also be sought when a lay client's problem requires legal research which the solicitor handling the matter lacks the time to undertake or lies in an area with which that solicitor is unfamiliar.

The terms 'opinion' and 'advice' are broadly interchangeable. However, many barristers select one term or the other to describe what they write according to the nature of the advice sought. This is discussed further at p 130.

Instructions to advise

The brief

Instructions to advise are sent to a barrister in the form of a brief. This consists of written instructions as to the kind of advice required together with copies of relevant documents. A backsheet which gives details of the client's name, the other parties (if any) and, if appropriate, the court in which the matter is proceeding, plus the barrister's fee and the names and business address of the instructing solicitor and the barrister instructed is also included. By convention the brief is tied up with red (actually pink) cotton ribbon.

The instructions

While the factual situations upon which lay clients seek advice are diverse, the client's problems generally require a legal adviser to address one or more fundamental questions common to most cases. Thus, whether a client has entered an agreement on the basis of false information supplied by the other party to the contract, or has lost money because someone has defaulted on a debt, or has been injured due to the careless behaviour of another person, the fundamental questions to be considered by the legal adviser will be whether or not the client has a cause of action at law against the alleged wrongdoer and, if so, whether the case is likely to succeed at trial. These questions in turn raise further questions, common to all cases, as to whether the available evidence is sufficiently strong to prove the client's claim at trial and whether or not the potential defendant has any defence to that claim. Where the client is the alleged wrongdoer the same questions must be addressed from the viewpoint of a potential defendant.

Consequently, instructions to advise commonly request the barrister instructed to consider one or more of the following matters:

Liability

Does the lay client have a cause of action? If so, what are the chances of this succeeding at trial? What legal defences could a potential defendant raise? Would these succeed at trial enabling the defendant to escape liability or (as with the partial defence of contributory negligence) reducing the amount of any damages which the defendant might be ordered to pay if liability is established? If more than one cause of action is available to the client, which cause or causes of action ought to be pursued? If there is more than one potential defendant, which defendant or defendants should be sued?

Remedies

If the lay client is successful at trial, what are the legal remedies and are these available to a successful plaintiff as of right or only at the discretion of the court? If a particular cause of action enables a plaintiff to choose between different types of remedy, which should be pursued? If more than one cause of action is open to a client, which offers the best solution to the client's problem in terms of the remedies available? Should the client seek any interim remedy, such as an injunction, pending trial?

Quantum

What sum of money is the client likely to receive if he or she succeeds at trial and the court requires the unsuccessful defendant to pay damages as compensation for loss caused by the defendant's wrongdoing?

Evidence

What evidence is there which could be put before the court to establish those facts which the lay client must prove in order to succeed at trial? How strong is the available admissible evidence? What further evidence is needed and how could it be obtained?

Merits

What are the strengths and weaknesses of the client's case?

Settlement

What are the prospects of solving the client's problem and so avoiding the expense of litigation by negotiating a settlement with the other side? Is a settlement which is being negotiated in the client's interest?

Thus a barrister may be instructed to advise on liability and/or quantum or on the evidence and/or merits with regard to a particular case. Sometimes the instructions will consist of or include specific, precisely drafted, questions reflecting the distinctive facts of a client's problem. In relatively straightforward cases a barrister may simply be instructed to 'advise generally' and must therefore exercise his or her own judgment in determining what questions arise from the facts revealed by the brief which require answers and upon what matters advice must be given. In any case, whatever the nature of the instructions received, a barrister must always consider whether or not there are any further matters or questions, not specifically raised in the instructions, which need to be considered by the client and should advise upon these.

In addition to stating the nature of the advice sought, instructions normally include a list of the documents contained in the brief, and a synopsis of the client's problem. The solicitor may also include his or her own views of the problem and possible solutions.

Writing an opinion

We have outlined above the circumstances in which a solicitor might seek counsel's advice and the broad types of advice that might be sought. The central purpose of this chapter is, however, to explain how to write an advice or an opinion. The remainder of this chapter deals with this subject, examining firstly how a barrister prepares to write an opinion or advice and secondly the writing process itself in the context of an opinion as to liability and quantum.

Preparation

Reading the brief

A barrister's first task on receiving a brief to advise upon some matter is to ensure that it contains all the documents listed in the instructions. Once satisfied on this point, the barrister reads the instructions with care. The next step is to read the documents contained in the brief, putting them into some appropriate order if necessary. If there are pleadings, these may usefully be read first, since they should, if well drafted, give a clear and concise synopsis of the facts of the case.

Analysing the facts

While reading the brief for the first time, the barrister will already have begun the process of analysing the facts of the situation as revealed by the documents in the brief. During this process the barrister will have consistently in mind the nature of the advice sought and any questions explicitly raised by the instructions. At the same time he or she will be noting any questions implicitly raised either by the instructions or by documents within the brief.

A common flaw in student opinions is to draw an inference which cannot be supported by the facts on which the writer relies. It is very important to check that every inference that has been drawn can be sustained by facts contained in the barrister's instructions.

Identifying relevant areas of law

While analysing the factual situation underlying the client's problem as this is disclosed by the brief, a barrister will consider what area or areas of law are relevant to such a problem so as to determine what legal solutions may be available to the client. Thus where a lay client has been injured in an accident at work and forced to give up his or her employment as a result, the barrister will immediately consider an action for damages in tort. He or she will therefore scrutinise the facts of the accident as revealed in the brief in order to determine whether these will support a claim based on negligence on the part of the employer or a fellow employee, breach of the employer's duty of care to provide, for example, a safe system of work, or breach of statutory duty by the employer.

Undertaking legal research

In some cases a barrister's existing legal knowledge will be sufficient to enable him or her to advise immediately on the law relating to the client's problems. In others it will be necessary to undertake legal research. Since for the barrister, as for the instructing solicitor, time is at a premium, the ability to research quickly and effectively is a vital subskill involved in producing written advice and one that must be cultivated by the trainee barrister.[1]

Providing an answer to the client's problem

The process of analysing the facts of a lay client's situation in the light of relevant law should enable a barrister to arrive at answers to the questions raised explicitly or implicitly in the brief. This in turn means that advice can be given as to whether or not there is any solution to the lay client's problem.

From time to time the advice given will be that the client has no claim in law, or, in the case of a defendant client, that there is no valid defence to a plaintiff's claim. Where legal steps can be taken in pursuance of a claim or defence, the nature of these will be explained. Often the desirability of reaching a settlement with the other side will be emphasised and advice may be given on steps which may be taken to promote settlement. Sometimes a non-legal solution to a client's problem will be suggested.

As this suggests, while a barrister's opinion is sought because of his or her legal expertise, the law is, for the barrister, essentially a means to an end. In the process of analysing the facts of the case he or she will seek to identify a legal framework within which these facts can be interpreted so as to establish that a client is entitled to claim some legal remedy or can resist the claim brought by another party. If this can be achieved, the client's problem can be solved by taking or defending legal proceedings. If, however, there is some solution which avoids recourse to law, or will put an end to ongoing litigation, the barrister will point this out. The task is to solve the lay client's problem, whether by utilising the law or through some other means, and to explain to the professional client, the solicitor, what can be done to achieve a solution.

Planning the advice

Once the barrister knows what is to be included in the advice, some thought must be given to how that information is to be presented. If this stage is omitted, the resulting advice may lack clear organisation, omit key points and be further flawed by repetition. Of course such flaws can be eliminated by re-writing sections of the opinion, but it is far easier and less time-consuming to plan what is to be written in advance. The way in which the opinion is to be structured[2] should therefore be decided before beginning to write the opinion.

---

[1]   Lack of space precludes our discussing legal research in detail. Students should consult Holborn, *Butterworth's Legal Research Guide* (1993) and Stott, *Legal Research* (1993).

[2]   See further below.

Writing the opinion or advice

The way in which an opinion or advice is written is not regulated by any formal rules. While the content is necessarily determined by the barrister's understanding of the nature of the client's problem and the relevant law, once he or she has decided what advice is to be given, presentation is largely a matter of individual choice.

Nevertheless, it is possible to outline an approach to opinion writing which may assist the student barrister and which represents what many barristers would agree to be good practice. We shall now examine this approach by focusing on structure, content and style.

Structure

A clear structure is an essential feature of a well-written opinion. Its function is to provide a framework for the development of the barrister's advice so that this can easily be followed and assimilated by the reader. While the way in which an opinion is structured is to a large extent a matter of choice, certain key elements can be identified which appear in and give shape to most opinions. These are:

- a heading;
- a title;
- introductory paragraphs;
- paragraphs setting out the advice given;
- conclusions.

Some thought must be given to the structure of the section which sets out the advice given and which forms the major part of the opinion. The aim must be to adopt a clear and logical structure which enables the reader to assimilate easily the advice given.

To some extent the structure of this section is likely to be shaped by the nature of the advice sought. This is particularly so with regard to an opinion dealing with liability and quantum and an advice on evidence, as indicated below.

OPINION ON LIABILITY AND QUANTUM

This should be structured so as to deal with all issues of liability before quantum is discussed. Such an approach is logical since liability must normally be established before quantum will be assessed.[3] Consequently, if there is more than one potential cause of action, each should be discussed before addressing quantum. However, if the

---

[3] An exception is where quantum is agreed and only liability is in issue.

quantum of damages for each cause of action is different, as may be the case if, for example, an action lies in both tort and contract, it may be appropriate to advise on quantum in relation to the first cause of action before dealing with liability in the second.

ADVICE ON EVIDENCE

An advice on evidence in a civil case may be given a logical structure by focusing on the issues of the case. The matters in issue between the parties should be listed, indicating with regard to each the paragraph or paragraphs of the statement/particulars of claim, the defence and any other pleading in the case in which that matter appears. The advice should then deal with each issue in turn, indicating the witnesses who may be called and the documents which can be used to prove the client's case. Any gaps in the available evidence or problems with existing evidence should be identified and advice given on obtaining any further evidence which is needed.

Where instructions to advise generally are received, the barrister must decide the nature of the problems on which advice must be given, and this decision will influence structure as well as content. However, the following basic structure may be appropriate in these, and other, circumstances:

- causes of action;
- remedies (eg damages, injunction);
- any other points (eg evidential points, points of procedure).

Where specific questions are asked, the answers should be incorporated in the advice at an appropriate point. This will depend on the nature and importance of the question. However, points of importance, whether discussed in response to specific questions or not, should be prominently located. Where, for example, the barrister advises that there is a limitation problem, this advice may sensibly be given at the beginning of the opinion.

Finally, the structure of an opinion can be improved by sensible use of paragraphs, sub-headings and tables.

PARAGRAPHS

The conventional paragraph is basic to the structure of an opinion or advice, and the way in which paragraphs are used can assist or hinder the assimilation of information by the reader. In particular, a series of very short paragraphs can be irritating to a reader, whereas very long paragraphs are hard to digest. The occasional very short paragraph may be useful to emphasise a point. In general, however, the paragraphs in an opinion should be moderate in length.

SUB-HEADINGS

A well-chosen sub-heading, which summarises the character of the subject matter of the paragraph or paragraphs which follow, is a structural aid which helps the reader to follow the development of the advice being given. Brevity is important, however. A very long sub-heading lacks visual clarity and does not serve as an aid to comprehension.

If no sub-headings are used it is essential to make it clear to the reader when a new paragraph is dealing with a different topic from that discussed in the preceding paragraph. It is intensely irritating to discover, only when half-way through a paragraph, that the subject matter has changed.

TABLES

From time to time you may find that information can be presented more clearly in tabular form. For example, the list of issues together with paragraph references to pleadings which is included in an advice on evidence may conveniently be presented as a table.

Content

HEADING

The heading of an opinion or advice consists of the name of the case. How the case is named will depend on whether or not proceedings have been issued. If advice is sought concerning a potential claim by the client, the name of the case will be that of the client preceded by 're', as in the examples below.

or   Re TESSA LARSON

Re MRS TESSA LARSON

If proceedings have been issued the name of the case will include both parties, and may be presented as follows:

LARSON v PORTER

Alternatively, the full court heading as used in pleadings may be adopted, and this may become increasingly common with the use of computers to store and generate documents. An example is given below at p 131.

TITLE

The title follows immediately after the heading. 'Advice' or 'Opinion' should be used. 'Opinion' is often used when advising on liability, or liability and quantum, and 'Advice' when advising on evidence or on quantum only. An example showing a full court heading and appropriate title is set out below:

IN THE WORCESTER COUNTY COURT   Case No

BETWEEN

TESSA LARSON   <u>Plaintiff</u>

and

ROBERT PORTER   <u>Defendant</u>

<u>ADVICE ON EVIDENCE</u>

INTRODUCTORY PARAGRAPHS

Every opinion or advice should at the outset indicate the instructions which the barrister has been given. The phrase conventionally used to introduce this information is 'I am asked to advise ...'. As you will remember it is the lay client who is receiving the advice, and the summary of the barrister's instructions often indicates this, as in the following example: 'I am asked to advise Mrs Larson in connection with an accident which occurred ...'

Two other matters may also appear in the introductory paragraphs. Firstly, some barristers include a summary of the key facts of the case. Providing it is very concise, such a synopsis of the facts can be useful. It may help a busy solicitor handling a large number of cases to remember the case in question more easily. It can also be helpful to a barrister to whom a case is returned several months after he or she advised on it to have a summary of the facts in his or her own words. In addition, some barristers feel that summarising the key facts protects them against any allegation that some crucial fact has not been considered when preparing the advice. A student barrister must be careful, however, not to write at length on the facts of the case. While some barristers do set out the facts at length, most consider this a waste of time and space. A few sentences is normally sufficient.

Secondly, a summary of the barrister's main conclusions may be included in the introductory paragraphs. Such a summary has value as a structural aid, indicating the matters which will be discussed in the advice. However, many barristers take the view that the appropriate place for conclusions is at the end of the advice. The inclusion of this at the start of the advice is therefore, as with a summary of the main facts, a matter of individual taste.

PARAGRAPHS CONTAINING BARRISTER'S ADVICE

The contents of these paragraphs will, of course, depend on the nature of the advice sought. However, in many instances one or more of the following matters will be considered.

Causes of action and potential defendants

Advice on the causes of action available to a client and on potential defendants must be included in the opinion when the barrister is instructed to advise on liability and, in many cases, where his or her instructions are to 'advise generally'.

The section of the opinion which deals with establishing liability must cover a number of matters. A key task is to consider all available causes of action which could potentially succeed, and show the extent to which the elements of each can be established on the basis of the facts contained in the brief. In addition the advice should indicate what further evidence, if any, is required to establish each element, and how this is to be obtained.

The client should also be advised which cause or causes of action to pursue, and the reasons for this advice must be given. A particular cause of action might be preferred because, for example, it could be proved more easily than any other available cause of action, or because, if established, it would enable the client to claim a particular remedy, such as, an injunction or exemplary damages, or would result in greater damages being awarded.

Finally, advice must also be given as to the appropriate defendant or defendants. Where there is more than one potential defendant, the barrister should state which of them should be sued and why. A common example is where a client is advised to sue the tortfeasor's employer, rather than the tortfeasor, because the employer is likely to have greater financial resources and so will be better able to meet an award of damages. Sometimes the advice will be to sue more than one defendant. This would be appropriate, for example, where it was not clear which potential defendant caused a road traffic accident in which the client was injured.

Potential defences

Any consideration of liability must include advice on the strength of any defences that the other side is likely to raise and on how these can be countered if necessary. The possibility of the defendant alleging contributory negligence should always be considered when the plaintiff's action is based on negligence, breach of statutory duty, nuisance, *Rylands v Fletcher* or the Occupiers' Liability Act 1957.[4] Where a defendant is likely to raise the defence of limitation, this is sufficiently serious to warrant separate treatment, possibly immediately after the introductory paragraphs.

---

4   Contributory negligence has been recognised by the Court of Appeal to be a possible defence to battery in *Barnes v Nayer* (1986) *The Times*, 19 December and by Brooke J as a defence to an action in negligent misstatement in *Edwards v Lee* (1991) *The Independent*, 1 November.

Remedies and the quantum of damages

Where a client has been advised as to the causes of action which may be pursued, information must normally also be provided with regard to the remedies available. If different causes of action give rise to different remedies, this must be made clear and any advantages or disadvantages of pursuing particular remedies discussed. When an equitable remedy, such as an injunction, may be claimed, the chances of the court granting the relief sought must be assessed and the factors which will be taken into account by the court should be indicated.

In tort cases the main remedy available is damages. It will therefore normally be appropriate to discuss the quantum of potential damages. This means that an attempt must be made to assess how much money the client is likely to receive from the defendant in the form of damages if the action succeeds. There is no set way in which to advise on quantum, but the following suggestions may be helpful.

The advice given might begin by stating the basis on which damages will be assessed by the court. This is likely to be particularly useful where the client has potential causes of action in both tort and contract, so that the basis of assessment will depend upon which cause of action is pursued.[5]

Advice may then be given on each potential head of loss, indicating if damages are recoverable in respect of that loss and, if so, the amount likely to be recovered. The advice must, therefore, consider any factors which might prevent recovery or limit the amount recoverable. Damages will not be recoverable if the loss alleged is too remote, that is, not a reasonably foreseeable consequence of the tortious conduct, or if an intervening cause breaks the chain of causation between the defendant's breach of duty and the plaintiff's loss.

An important factor which may limit the damages recoverable in actions based on negligence and certain other torts is contributory negligence.[6] A plaintiff's failure to mitigate may prevent recovery of damages or limit the amount awarded, since no damages can be obtained for avoidable loss. Breach of the duty to mitigate may consist of failing to take reasonable steps to mitigate the loss incurred or unreasonably incurring expense subsequent to the defendant's wrongful conduct.

In addition, it may be convenient when advising on heads of loss, to deal with special damage before general damage. The terms 'special' and 'general' damage are used here in the sense which relates to the

---

5   In tort, damages are intended to put the plaintiff in as good a position as if no tort had been committed. Contractual damages aim to put the plaintiff in as good a position as if the contract had been performed.

6   See further above at p 132.

pleading. Special damages is damage of a kind which the law will not presume to result from the wrongful act alleged and which must therefore be pleaded and proved. General damage is damage presumed by the law to result from the wrongful conduct. While the fact that such damage has been suffered must be pleaded, the question of quantification is left to the court. Special damages can normally be calculated with precision and should present few, if any, problems. Advising on general damages is more complicated. Since these are quantified by the court, only an approximate figure can safely be given. Such a figure may be obtained by comparison with earlier cases and this is the standard approach in, for example, personal injury cases or cases for trespass to the person brought against the police.

A number of other matters which affect the amount recovered in damages may need to be considered. On the one hand, interest on any damages recovered may be awarded by the court. On the other, the sum which the plaintiff receives may be reduced by the taxation procedure or by the requirement that any legal costs paid by the Legal Aid Board must be repaid to the Board.

Advice on quantum is frequently sought where a client has a potential claim for damages for personal injury. In such an action special damage consists of the financial loss incurred by the plaintiff up to the date of trial. This includes, for example, medical expenses, damage to property and loss of earnings. General damage includes compensation for pain, suffering and loss of amenity and for loss of future earning capacity. When advising on general damages the advice given must be reasoned, and supported if possible by reference to other, similar, cases. A precise figure should not be given, as it is impossible to predict the court's decision with such a degree of accuracy, especially as no two cases are identical. The anticipated award should be expressed as being 'in the region of £xx'.

The following approach may safely be adopted when advising on the quantum of damages for pain, suffering and loss of amenity in a personal injury case. Firstly, the Judicial Studies Board Guidelines figures for each type of injury suffered by the client should be quoted. Secondly, one or two cases should be cited in which the plaintiff's injuries were similar to those suffered by the client. The sums awarded in these cases should be updated using the inflation table in *Kemp and Kemp, The Quantum of Damages*, and both the original and the updated figures should be quoted.[7] Thirdly, by referring to any differences

---

7   This will enable instructing solicitors to update the sum when necessary by using the original figure awarded.

between the facts of these cases and that of the client, the advice should explain why the amount which is suggested that the client is likely to receive is more or less that the awards in the cases cited.

Further advice

Once quantum has been dealt with, it will often be necessary to include in the advice one or more paragraphs covering any further matters on which advice must be given. There may, for example, have been questions raised in the instructions which could not conveniently be dealt with in the main part of the advice. This may also be the appropriate point at which to advise on reaching a settlement with the other side or on procedural matters such as, for example, obtaining discovery or seeking an injunction. Any points with regard to obtaining further evidence which have not been made earlier could also be raised here.

CONCLUSIONS

Many barristers feel that conclusions must logically be presented at the end of the opinion. However, while the barrister's conclusions must be prominently located, it does not really matter whether they appear at the beginning or the end of the opinion. Certainly if the overall advice given is not summarised in the opening paragraphs it is **essential** that this should be done in the final paragraphs. However, where the introductory paragraphs include a summary of the advice given there is little point in repeating this word for word at the end of the opinion. In this case the final paragraph or paragraphs should be used to present a very concise summary of the conclusions reached or for some other purpose, for example, to remind instructing solicitors of any steps which must be taken, particularly urgent procedural steps. Where instructing solicitors have been asked to undertake a number of tasks these may be listed for clarity. Finally, it should be noted that a point should never be raised for the first time in the concluding paragraphs.

Signature

An opinion or advice must be signed by counsel.

SOME GENERAL POINTS ON CONTENT

A few general points on content are applicable to opinions and advice of every kind. These are discussed briefly below.

Avoid irrelevant matters

It is crucially important that everything in an opinion is relevant to the questions which arise explicitly or implicitly in the instructions received. A barrister who is unable to distinguish between relevant and irrelevant matters is unlikely to be instructed again.

Be accurate

An ability to present material accurately is essential. Mistakes as to the facts of the client's case are inexcusable, but do appear from time to time in opinions written by student barristers. It is also amazing how often students refer to their client by the wrong name, a mistake which is unlikely to recommend the barrister to either the lay client or the professional client. Mistakes may also easily be made when presenting figures. As these examples suggest, it is important to proofread an opinion.

Do not draw inferences not supported by facts

A related and common fault in student opinions is the tendency to draw inferences which are not supported by the facts on which they are based. It is very important to consider carefully whether any inference drawn can be sustained.

Give advice

A barrister writing an opinion must give advice. This is what he or she is being paid to do. An opinion is not simply an excercise in analysing the issues raised. Conclusions must be drawn. Thus, for example, when considering the options open to a client, advice must be given as to which option, in the barrister's opinion, the client ought to pursue.

Give reasoned advice

Any advice given must be reasoned so that the professional and lay clients can understand how the conclusions presented in the opinion were reached.

Cite cases with moderation

Some of the advice given in an opinion may be reasoned on the basis of case law. It is, however, unnecessary to cite every case which has helped to shape the conclusions drawn. Indeed, doing so is likely to irritate the reader rather than illuminate the matters discussed. It is usually appropriate to draw to the attention of instructing solicitors any recent case which changes the law or court practice in a way which will affect the client's case. Cases in which the facts are very similar to those of the client's case should also be cited. When assessing quantum it may, as indicated previously, be appropriate to cite, and refer briefly to relevant facts in, similar cases. In general, however, it is unnecessary to set out in detail the facts of any case cited, and often no reference at all need be made to those facts.

Use cases properly

In students' opinions, cases are occasionally cited as if they are deciding points on the basis of the facts of the client's case rather than those of the case cited. The correct approach is to cite the relevant case in support of a general principle which is applicable to the client's case.

Be practical

Finally, and this is a very important point, the advice given must be practical in character. An opinion is not an academic essay and there is no place in it for analysis of academic interest only. The barrister's aim must be to identify the most practical solution to the client's problem, whether or not this involves taking legal steps. The emphasis must be on the facts of the case and these are interpreted by applying legal knowledge, experience, legal or otherwise, and, not least, common sense. It is sometimes difficult for a student barrister to achieve this emphasis on facts rather than law, and a common fault is to set out relevant law in some detail and then apply that law to the facts of the case. A better approach is to integrate relevant law into an analysis of the facts of the case, and this may assist in avoiding an unnecessarily detailed exposition of the law. Indeed, the law is only relevant in so far as it relates to particular facts of the case, so a detailed abstract statement of the law is always undesirable.

Style

Every barrister develops his or her own style of writing an opinion or advice. However, a number of points concerning style need to be kept in mind by the student barrister, and these are discussed below.

WRITE SOUND ENGLISH

A well-written opinion will use English that is grammatically sound and properly punctuated. Words should be spelled correctly and, if necessary, the spellcheck facility of a word processor should be used. An opinion is always written in the first person singular.

WRITE PLAIN ENGLISH

A well-written opinion will consist largely of plain standard English which can be understood by a lay reader. Unnecessarily complicated language is unlikely to impress anyone other than the writer. However, where clarity of meaning requires the use of legal or other specialist terminology, this may properly be included since, if necessary, this can be explained to the lay client by the instructing solicitor.

WRITE CONCISELY

Few readers, least of all busy solicitors, wish to struggle to grasp the gist of a wordy opinion. A student who has a tendency to write verbosely should seek constructive criticism from a lecturer or a fellow student who writes concisely.

WRITE CLEARLY

As indicated a wordy opinion will usually lack clarity. However, it is possible to write so concisely that the meaning of what is written is not easily followed. An opinion should be written in a style that makes it possible for a reader to assimilate easily the advice given.

WRITE COURTEOUSLY

Student opinions are occasionally unintentionally discourteous. An example is where a client is referred to by his or her surname only. It may be salutary to remember that the lay client is the source of the barrister's fees, whether these are paid privately or through the Legal Aid Fund. However it is acceptable to refer to the lay client as 'our client' or, if proceedings are under way, 'the plaintiff' or 'the defendant'.

WRITE TACTFULLY

Instructing solicitors sometimes make errors and clients sometimes act foolishly. If it is essential to refer to such matters it is only prudent to do so tactfully.

WRITE POSITIVELY

As mentioned above, the function of an opinion is to give advice, and the style of writing should therefore be positive. This does not mean that an opinion cannot give negative advice, merely that the tone should not be vague or ambivalent. However, it is important not to be dogmatic. What is being offered to the client is simply the opinion of the barrister instructed. Another barrister may take a different view. However, the student barrister should note that declaring that what has been written is one's own opinion is no defence if that opinion is ill-informed.

An outline of an opinion on liability and quantum: notes on structure and content

Heading

Traditionally the names of the parties, or the client if proceedings have not been commenced, in capitals.

Examples:

LARSON v PORTER

Re TESSA LARSON

Alternatively a full court heading could be used.

Title

OPINION or ADVICE or ADVICE ON EVIDENCE as appropriate. May be underlined or put in tramlines as follows:

OPINION

Opening paragraph(s)

Should always include a concise statement of the barrister's instructions. Conventionally phrased: 'I am asked to advise on ... '

May also include (optional):

- *a brief statement of what the case is about*
  (1) must be **very concise** (usually a few lines is sufficient unless the case is very complicated)
  (2) include only key facts
  (3) don't simply restate or copy out instructions
- *a summary of the main conclusions*
  (1) must be concise
  (2) must not include new points

Paragraphs containing advice

Should deal with the following matters, advising on liability before discussing remedies and the quantum of damages:

- *causes of action and potential defendants*
  (1) explain how each cause of action considered can be made out against a defendant or defendants on the basis of the facts contained in the brief
  (2) indicate if **further evidence** is necessary to establish any element of a cause of action and how this should be obtained
  (3) advise which cause or causes of action should be pursued, explaining why (eg can be proved more easily; will result in more substantial damages being awarded)

  (4) advise as to which potential defendant or defendants should be sued and why (eg employer rather than employee because former has greater financial resources)
- *potential defences*

  (1) advise as to the strength of any defences the other side may raise

  (2) beware of a limitation defence, see p 49
- *remedies and quantum of damages*

  advise on

  (1) remedies available

  (2) amount of any potential award of damages

  (3) factors affecting amount likely to be recovered
     - remoteness, intervening action, contributory negligence, failure to mitigate
     - taxation, legal aid charge, interest
     - in a personal injury case do not give a precise figure; a phrase commonly used is 'in the region of £xx'
- *further advice*

  It is usually necessary to include one or more paragraphs giving further advice, for example, advice on reaching a settlement or on procedural matters.

Conclusions

If the introductory paragraphs contained a summary of the advice given in the opinion there is little point in repeating this in detail. Either have a very concise summary of the overall conclusions or use the final paragraph(s) for some other purpose, eg reminding instructing solicitors of any steps which must be taken, especially urgent procedural steps. If the conclusions were not summarised at the beginning of the opinion it is **essential** to present the overall conclusions in the final paragraph(s). Note:

- **never** raise a point for the first time in the concluding paragraph(s)
- some barristers close the opinion with a list of the steps which instructing solicitors need to take (eg obtaining further advice; procedural steps).

Signature

Counsel must sign the opinion or advice.

Chapter 7

Drafting in Relation to Property Claims
in Negligence

Scope of chapter

In Chapter 3 the basic rules of drafting pleadings were illustrated in the context of a simple personal injury claim arising out of a road traffic accident. In that case, a pedestrian, Jane Brown, alleged that a car driver, Paul Smith, had breached the duty of care he owed her as a fellow road user by driving in a way which caused the accident in which she was injured. The claim that was pleaded was therefore framed in negligence.

Breach of a duty of care may also result in damage to or the loss of property. This too was illustrated in the context of Jane Brown's claim since she sought damages to compensate her for a dress, watch and handbag ruined in the accident. In non-personal injury cases, damage to or loss of property may be the sole cause of complaint. The present chapter looks at how to draft pleadings in such a case.

Negligence

The nature of the action

As we have seen negligence may be defined as an act or omission which constitutes a breach of a duty of care owed to another person by the person who acts or fails to act and which causes that other person to suffer harm.

Consequently, as you will remember from Chapter 3, the elements of negligence which must be established if the plaintiff's action is to succeed are as follows:

- duty of care (owed by defendant to plaintiff);
- breach of duty of care;
- causing;
- loss and damage.

To understand what must be pleaded in order to establish these elements it is necessary to look at each of them in greater detail.

Elements of negligence

DUTY OF CARE

To succeed in negligence a plaintiff must prove that at the time of the alleged wrongful conduct the defendant was under a duty to take such care as would ensure that his or her act(s) or omission(s) would not cause the plaintiff loss and damage of the type suffered by the plaintiff.

It is well established that a duty of care will only arise if the plaintiff is a person whom it was reasonably foreseeable was likely to be harmed by the defendant's wrongful conduct. What this means is that the court must be satisfied that there existed between the plaintiff and the defendant a relationship of such proximity (or neighbourhood) that it was in the reasonable contemplation of the defendant that carelessness on his or her part might be likely to cause damage to the plaintiff.[1]

It seems clear that if the court is so satisfied it must also be satisfied that it is just and reasonable to impose such a duty.[2]

The law recognises many situations in which such a duty of care arises. Thus, for example, it is well established that the driver of a motor vehicle owes a duty of care to other road users. In determining whether, on the facts of a particular case, a duty of care exists, the court will be guided by previous case law. A plaintiff seeking to establish a duty of care in a novel situation must do so by analogy with established categories of situations in which a duty of care has been found to exist.[3]

It should be noted that there are only limited circumstances in which the court will find that a defendant was under a duty not to cause the plaintiff pure economic loss. Thus a plaintiff who suffers financial loss which is not connected with, and does not result from, damage to his or her person or property will have no action in negligence unless on the facts the claim falls within the limited categories of negligence which give rise to liability for pure economic loss. Such loss could be recovered, for example, if the facts of the case enabled the plaintiff to rely on the principles of negligent misstatement.

BREACH OF DUTY OF CARE

Once a plaintiff has satisfied the court that the defendant owes him or her a duty of care, it must be proved that the defendant has breached

---

[1] For a detailed analysis of the concept of duty of care, see *Charlesworth on Negligence*.
[2] *Caparo Industries plc v Dickman* [1990] 1 All ER 568, 573–74 HL, *per* Lord Bridge.
[3] *Murphy v Brentwood District Council* [1990] 2 All ER 908, 915, HL, *per* Lord Keith.

that duty. This means that it is for the plaintiff to convince the court that the alleged wrongful conduct of the defendant failed to meet the standard which, given the circumstance in which the act(s) or omission(s) occurred, a reasonable person would have expected. If a judge decides that the defendant took reasonable care in all the circumstances, the plaintiff's case will fail.

CAUSATION

Even though a plaintiff is able to prove both duty of care and breach of that duty, the claim will fail at trial unless it can be established that any loss the plaintiff is alleged to have suffered was caused by the defendant's breach of duty. It is for the plaintiff, therefore, to prove a factual causal connection between the defendant's wrongful conduct and the loss alleged.

The test applied by the courts to establish factual causation is the 'but for' test. If, on the balance of probabilities, the harm suffered by the plaintiff would not have occurred but for the defendant's wrongful conduct, that conduct was a factual cause of the harm suffered. This will not necessarily mean that it was the sole cause. If on the facts of the case the defendant's conduct is one of several causes of the harm suffered, the court must determine which of these causes was or were in law the effective cause or causes. The defendant will be liable in damages to the extent that he or she is held to have caused the harm suffered.[4]

It should be noted that one cause of the harm suffered may be the plaintiff's own carelessness. Where there is such contributory negligence by the plaintiff, the defendant's liability may be reduced accordingly. Thus if the harm was caused equally by the defendant's wrongful conduct and the plaintiff's carelessness, in a case where the defence of contributory negligence is available, the defendant would be liable only for 50% of the plaintiff's damage. This defence does not however apply to an action in deceit.

LOSS AND DAMAGE

Once liability in tort is established a plaintiff can recover from the defendant any loss or damage which has been claimed provided that it can be proved and is not held to be too remote. If in the view of the court the loss or damage claimed was not a reasonably foreseeable consequence of the defendant's wrongful conduct, it will be too remote and cannot be recovered.[5]

---

4   As to where two or more tortfeasors cause the same harm, see below at p 146.
5   For a full discussion of remoteness in tort, see *Clerk and Lindsell* (17th edn, 1995).

Remedies

An award of damages is the principal remedy in tort and the only remedy open to a plaintiff claiming in negligence. The primary aim of damages in tort is to put the plaintiff in the position he or she would have been in if the tort had not been committed.

Interest

A claim may be made under s 35A Supreme Court Act 1981 in the High Court or s 69 County Courts Act 1984 for interest on any damages awarded.[6]

Defences

Limitation

Where a plaintiff fails to bring an action within the time limit laid down by the Limitation Act 1980, the action is time-barred and this gives the defendant a complete defence to the action. The limitation period for actions in tort is normally six years, but it should be noted that the primary limitation period in respect of a personal injury claim or a claim under the Fatal Accidents Act 1976 is three years.[7]

Volenti non fit injuria

To succeed with this defence, the defendant must prove that the plaintiff, having full knowledge of the nature and extent of a particular risk created by the defendant's conduct, agreed to run that risk and so waived his right to take legal action in respect of any harm he suffered as a result of the defendant's conduct.[8]

Novus actus interveniens

A defendant relying upon this defence must persuade the court that the act of another person intervened between the defendant's wrongful conduct and the harm suffered by the plaintiff so as to

---

[6] See above, p 38.

[7] See further the Limitation Act 1980, ss 11, 14 and 33, and the notes thereto in SCP, vol 2, 6144-52, 6155-59.

[8] The concept of *volenti non fit injuria* is a complex one, and should be researched more fully before advising a defendant to rely on this defence.

constitute a new cause, which breaks the chain of causation between the defendant's negligence and the damage.[9]

Contributory negligence

Where a defendant who is held liable to the plaintiff in tort can prove that the plaintiff's own negligent conduct was also a cause of the loss he or she suffered, the Law Reform (Contributory Negligence) Act 1945 applies to give the defendant a partial defence. The defendant's liability to compensate the plaintiff is consequently reduced to the extent that the plaintiff is held liable.

Remoteness

The defendant may allege that part or all of the damage alleged by the plaintiff is too remote to be recovered.[10]

Drafting in a negligence case

Drafting on behalf of the plaintiff

Who should be sued?

In most cases the only potential defendant is the person whose wrongful conduct has caused the plaintiff to suffer harm. In some circumstances, however, the plaintiff has a choice of defendants.

This is so where the person whose act(s) or omissions(s) caused the harm complained of by the plaintiff was at the time of those act(s) or omission(s) an employee acting in the course of his or her duties on behalf of his or her employer. In these circumstances, the employer is vicariously liable for the employer's wrongful conduct, and the plaintiff may sue either the employee or the employer or both of them.[11]

An employer who can be shown to be vicariously liable for an employee's wrongful conduct will usually be the preferred defendant. This is because the employer is likely to have greater financial resources than the employee and will therefore be in a better position to pay any damages awarded to the plaintiff. However if, for example, there is doubt as to the financial status of the employer or as to

---

[9] See further *Clerk and Lindsell on Torts, op cit.*
[10] See above, p 149.
[11] See below, p 152.

whether the employee was acting in the course of his employment, it would be prudent to join the employee as defendant.

Where two or more persons are jointly responsible for a tort, they are joint tortfeasors, and the plaintiff may sue any one of them for the full extent of the damage suffered. On being found liable such a defendant may claim a contribution from the fellow tortfeasor towards any damages which he is ordered to pay to the plaintiff.

Again the choice of whether to sue one or more joint tortfeasors rests with the plaintiff and may be determined by the financial status of the potential defendants.

Where it is alleged that two or more persons caused different harm to the plaintiff, it may be appropriate to join such persons as defendants in one action. This can be done without the leave of the court where, if separate actions were brought, some common questions of law or fact would arise in all the actions and all rights to relief claimed in the action arise out of the same set of circumstances.

If these conditions do not apply the leave of the court must be sought before commencing a single action against both defendants.[12]

Which court?

The High Court and the county courts have concurrent jurisdiction in matters of tort. In general, therefore, an action in negligence may be commenced in either court. However, the rules applying to the allocation of a case for trial should be kept in mind when deciding in which court to commence an action.

Where the value of the claim is less than £25,000 the case will be tried in the county court; where the value is more than £50,000 the claim must be tried in the High Court, and where the value is between £25,000 and £50,000 allocation is determined on the basis of prescribed criteria relating to such matters as the complexity of the facts or legal issues involved in the case.

Cases may also be transferred from the High Court to the county court and *vice versa*, if the court to which the case is allocated decides, having regard to the criteria, that the case ought to be so transferred.[13]

It should be borne in mind that where an action includes a claim for personal injury the action must be commenced in the county court if the personal injury claim is for less that £50,000.[14]

---

[12]   RSC Ord 15 r4(1).

[13]   Article 7 High Court and County Courts Jurisdiction Order 1991.

[14]   County Courts Act 1984, s 15.

The Statement/ Particulars of Claim

As we explained in Chapter 3, the basic framework of a statement of claim or particulars of claim is provided by the essential elements of the cause of action. In negligence these elements, which are discussed in detail above, are:

- duty of care (owed by the defendant to the plaintiff);
- breach of duty;
- causation;
- damage.

The Supreme Court Practice Notes to Ord 18 r12 state that particulars of negligence must be given in the pleading.[15] This is because the defendant must be given sufficient facts to enable him or her to understand the case that must be met. What this means in practice is that the statement/particulars of claim must plead the material facts which the plaintiff alleges establish the elements of negligence. These are:

- the facts giving rise to a duty of care owed by the defendant to the plaintiff;
- the facts constituting breach of that duty;
- the facts which show a causal link between the defendant's breach of duty and the harm suffered by the plaintiff;
- the facts identifying the injury and/or damage sustained.

These requirements are now considered in greater detail.

THE FACTS GIVING RISE TO A DUTY OF CARE

Duty of care is a legal concept. Since a pleading must contain material facts not law,[16] it is not the duty of care that must be pleaded but the material facts from which the court can infer that such a duty existed at the time of the wrongful conduct alleged.

This may be illustrated by considering the common situation where the rider of a motorcycle alleges that a collision in which his motorcycle was damaged was caused by the carelessness of the driver of the motor car involved in the collision.

In this case the duty of care owed by the driver to the motorcyclist arises from the fact that they are fellow road users travelling in such proximity that a reasonable person would have concluded that carelessness on the part of the driver might cause the motorcyclist harm.

---

[15] SCP 18/12/15.
[16] See above, p 59.

The material facts from which the court can infer such a duty, and which must therefore be pleaded, are as follows:

- plaintiff riding motorcycle along road;
- location of plaintiff immediately prior to collision;
- defendant driving car along road;
- location of defendant immediately prior to collision.

Sorting out these facts will usually be done in the paragraph of the statement/particulars of claim which pleads the collision. The relevant paragraph (italicised to indicate the material facts from which the defendant driver's duty of care may be inferred) might read:

1. On 1 May 1995 at about 9 pm *the Plaintiff was riding his motorcycle,* registration number [   ] *along Bristol Road towards* [ ] when *as he passed the junction with Albert Road* he was struck by a *Lada motor car* registration number [   ] *driven out of Albert Road by the Defendant.*

In most cases it will be unnecessary, and wrong, to plead duty of care explicitly. However, there are some circumstances when it is appropriate to do so.

One example of this is where the duty of care alleged is novel in character and likely to be contested. In such a situation the relevant paragraph of the statement/particulars of claim might, after pleading the material facts from which the alleged duty is to be inferred, add for clarity:

In the premises the Defendant owed the plaintiff a duty of care.

A further example is where a plaintiff alleges that, on the particular facts of the case, a higher standard of duty of care is owed by the defendant. Thus it might be alleged that a solicitor specialising in a particular field of law owes a client not merely the duty of care to be expected of a competent and experienced solicitor, but that to be expected of a solicitor specialising in that field of law.

To illustrate this, let us suppose that an architect who advertised himself as a specialist in planning and supervising the repair and renovation of early 18th century buildings was employed by the owner to supervise the repair and renovation of a Georgian house. Let us also suppose that, due to the negligence of the architect, work was done which was likely to damage that type of building and did so damage it.

In such circumstances, the plaintiff owner could sue the architect in contract and for professional negligence. The duty of care alleged by the plaintiff would go beyond that to be expected of a competent and experienced architect. The plaintiff could claim that the duty owed was that to be expected of an architect specialising in planning and supervising the repair and renovation of early 18th century buildings.

This might be pleaded as follows:

2. At all material times, the Defendant held himself out to be competent and experienced in the planning and supervision of repair and renovation work to early 18th century buildings.

3. In the premises, it was the duty of the Defendant to act with the skill care and diligence to be expected of an architect specialising in planning and supervising repair and renovation work to such buildings.

Note that para 2 pleads the material facts from which a duty of care can be inferred, and para 3 states the duty explicitly. The phrase 'at all material times' is used here to allege that the defendant so held himself out both when he contracted to perform and when he performed his duties as the architect employed by the builder.[17]

THE FACTS CONSTITUTING BREACH OF DUTY OF CARE

While the term negligence is used to define a particular tort, lawyers also use this word to describe one element of that tort, namely breach of duty. In this sense negligence means that act or omission which constitutes breach of a defendant's duty of care, and it is in this sense that the term is used in a pleading.

When pleading breach of duty, therefore, the statement/particulars of claim will allege that the event or events which occasioned the harm suffered by the plaintiff was or were caused by the negligence of the defendant. Thus in the simple road traffic accident case considered above the relevant paragraph of the statement/particulars of claim might commence:

The said accident was caused by the negligence of the Defendant.

However, to plead breach of duty properly the plaintiff must set out the material facts which will be relied upon at trial to establish breach. This is sometimes referred to as particularising breach of duty, and the relevant facts may be pleaded under a sub-heading, such as 'Particulars' or 'Particulars of Negligence'.

---

[17]   See also p 189.

If in the example given above, the plaintiff claimed that the accident happened because the defendant was driving too fast, failed to warn the plaintiff of his approach and was not keeping a proper watch for other road users, these allegations could form the basis of the particulars of negligence. The paragraph pleading breach of duty might therefore be drafted as follows:

2. The said accident was caused by the negligence of the Defendant.

PARTICULARS OF NEGLIGENCE

(a) Driving too fast.

(b) Failing to keep any or any proper lookout.

(c) Driving into a major road from a minor road when it was unsafe to do so.

(d) Failing to stop before driving from a minor road into a major road.

(e) Failing to stop, slow down or so to steer or control the Defendant's car so as to avoid the accident.

You may have noticed that these particulars conform with the practice mentioned at Chapter 3 by beginning with precise allegations and ending with a general catch-all allegation.

Note that the facts of the collision, which must be pleaded as the occasion of the alleged breach of duty, have already been pleaded at para 1 on p 148 above. In the example given they are pleaded in neutral terms so as to facilitate admission by the defendant of the basic facts of the accident.

FACTS SHOWING A CAUSAL LINK BETWEEN DEFENDANT'S BREACH OF DUTY AND HARM SUFFERED BY PLAINTIFF

In the paragraphs pleading negligence set out above, one aspect of causation has already been pleaded in alleging that the accident was caused by the defendant's negligence.

However, as with any action, the statement/particulars of claim must also plead a causal link between the defendant's wrongful conduct and the harm suffered by the plaintiff. As we have noted,[18] the standard practice is to plead loss and damage together with causation in the same paragraph by using the following, or similar, words:

---

[18] See above, p 63.

By reason of the matters aforesaid, the Plaintiff has suffered loss and damage.

Here the 'matters aforesaid' refer, of course, to the defendant's negligence and its consequences as pleaded in the preceding paragraphs.

FACTS IDENTIFYING THE LOSS AND DAMAGE SUSTAINED

As we saw in Chapter 3, the rules and practice relating to pleading require that particulars be given of any special damage claimed. You will recall that special damage in this sense means monetary loss sustained to the date of trial. Other damage (general damage) need not be particularised.[19]

The structure of the entire paragraph pleading loss and damage, causation and particulars of special damage can be illustrated in the context of the road traffic accident referred to above. If, as a result of the accident, the plaintiff's motorcycle was damaged beyond repair, the relevant paragraph might read:

By reason of the matters aforesaid, the Plaintiff has suffered loss and damage.

PARTICULARS OF SPECIAL DAMAGE

Cost of replacing Suzuki TS 125 R (1994)

motorcycle damaged beyond repair   £3,500.00

In addition to the essential elements of negligence, two other matters must be pleaded in the statement/particulars of claim. These are the remedy claimed, namely damages, and the claim for interest.

THE CLAIM FOR DAMAGES

The plaintiff's claim for damages is pleaded in the prayer. The way in which the claim is drafted is shown in the sample pleading on p 155 below.

THE CLAIM FOR INTEREST

The claim for interest must be made in both the body of the statement/particulars of claim and the prayer. This is illustrated in the sample pleading on p 155 below.

---

19   See above, p 51.

We have now examined matters which must be pleaded in the statement/particulars of claim. However, as you will remember the rules provide that any matter which is material should be pleaded.[20] Three matters which may, in appropriate circumstances be material and are commonly pleaded are vicarious liability, convictions and the principle of *res ipsa loquitur*. The ways in which these may be pleaded are therefore considered below.

VICARIOUS LIABILITY

The vicarious liability of an employer is pleaded by setting out the facts which give rise to liability. The statement/particulars of claim must therefore allege that at the relevant time the relationship between the person who committed the tort complained of and the person said to be vicariously liable was one of employee and employer and that the employee was acting in the course of his employment.

Take, for example, the situation where the driver of an articulated lorry, acting in the course of his employment, has negligently collided with a car, causing substantial damage to that vehicle.

In that case, if both employee and employer are sued as, say, first and second defendants respectively, the opening paragraph of the statement/particulars of claim[21] might plead the relationship of employee and employer as follows:

1. At all material times the First Defendant was employed by the Second Defendant as the driver of an articulated lorry, registration number K210 BDP.

The paragraph setting out the facts of the accident might then include a phrase pleading that the first defendant was acting in the course of his employment at the time of the collision. In the example below the relevant phrase is italicised:

2. On 3 March 1995 the said lorry was being driven by the First Defendant northwards along the A5 *in the course of his said employment with the Second Defendant* when at about 2 miles south of Bicester the First Defendant lost control of the lorry which crossed onto the opposite side of the road and collided with a Ford Escort motor car registration number L567 ROL being driven towards Bicester by the Plaintiff.

---

20 See above, p 58.

21 It is often convenient, but not essential, to plead these matters in the opening (rather than a later) paragraph.

Alternatively, all the relevant facts could be pleaded in the paragraph stating the facts of the accident. In the example below, the relevant phrase is again italicised.

1. On 3 March 1995 the First Defendant *in the course of his employment with the Second Defendant* was driving an articulated lorry registration number K210 BDP northwards along the A5 when at about 2 miles south of Bicester he lost control of the lorry which crossed onto the opposite side of the road and collided with a Ford Escort motor car registration number L567 ROL being driven towards Bicester by the Plaintiff.

Where only the employer is sued the facts material to vicarious liability may be pleaded as in the paragraph above, substituting the name of the lorry driver for the description 'First Defendant'. The employer then becomes simply the 'Defendant'.

CONVICTIONS

As has been mentioned earlier,[22] a party who intends to adduce evidence at trial that another party to an action has been convicted by a court in the United Kingdom of an offence relevant to matters in issue must plead that conviction.

Suppose, for example, that the plaintiff motorcyclist in the road traffic case considered earlier in this chapter wished to rely at trial on the fact that the defendant driver had been convicted of driving without due care and attention as a result of the accident in which the plaintiff's motorcycle was damaged. The statement/particulars of claim should include a paragraph giving particulars of the conviction, the court which made it and the issue to which the conviction was relevant.

An appropriate paragraph could read as follows:

Further, on 10 August 1995 at the Bath Magistrates' Court, the Defendant was convicted of the offence of driving without due care and attention. The conviction arises out of the said accident and the Plaintiff will rely on the same as evidence of the Defendant's negligence herein.

For an alternative form of wording see below at p 160 at para 4.

---

[22] See above, p 48.

RES IPSA LOQUITUR

Where the cause of an accident is unknown, or there is insufficient evidence on causation, a plaintiff may seek to establish liability by alleging that negligence on the part of the defendant can be inferred from the fact that the accident happened. See below at p 156.

Drafting in practice I

A sample particulars of claim

Throughout this section of the chapter references have been made to a property claim in negligence in a straightforward road traffic accident case in order to illustrate pleading practice. To make clear how some of the various paragraphs used as illustrations would fit together in the particulars of claim, the pleading is set out in full on the following pages.

Sample particulars of claim

IN THE BATH COUNTY COURT [1]   **Case No** [2]

BETWEEN

JUSTIN TURNER   <u>Plaintiff</u>

and   [4]

FREDERICK MICHAEL BARRY   <u>Defendant</u> [3]

PARTICULARS OF CLAIM

1. On 1 May 1995 at about 9 pm the Plaintiff was riding his motorcycle registration number [   ] along the Bristol Road towards Wilsdown when as he passed the junction with Albert Road he was struck by a Lada motor car registration number [   ] driven out of Albert Road by the Defendant. [5]

2. The said accident was caused by the negligence of the Defendant.

PARTICULARS OF NEGLIGENCE

(a) Driving too fast.

(b) Failing to keep any or any proper lookout.

(c) Driving from a minor road into a major road when it was unsafe to do so.

(d) Failing to stop before driving from a minor road into a major road.

(e) Failing to stop, to slow down or so to steer or control the said motor car so as to avoid the accident. [6]

3. By reason of the matters aforesaid, the Plaintiff has suffered loss and damage.

PARTICULARS OF SPECIAL DAMAGE

Cost of replacing Suzuki TS 125 R (1994)
    motorcycle damaged beyond repair   £3,500.00 [7]

4. Further the Plaintiff claims interest pursuant to section 69 of the County Courts Act 1984 on the amount found to be due to him at such rate and for such period as the court thinks fit. [8]

AND the Plaintiff claims

(1) Damages.

(2) Interest pursuant to section 69 of the County Courts Act 1984. [9]

[signature] [10]

Dated etc [11]

Notes

1 *Court* in which the action is brought.

2 *Case number* is inserted by the court office.

3 *Heading* is the names of the parties.

4 *Description* of the pleadings.

5 *1st element; duty of care.* This paragraph pleads the facts from which the defendant's duty of care can be inferred and the facts of the collision. When breach of duty is pleaded separately from the facts of the collision, the latter should be pleaded in neutral terms to facilitate their admission by the defendant.

6 *2nd element; breach of duty (negligence).* This paragraph pleads the allegation that the defendant breached his duty of care, and gives the material facts alleged to constitute breach of duty under the heading 'Particulars of Negligence'. See also Hendy et al at pp 114–15

7 *3rd and 4th elements.* This paragraph pleads the allegation that the plaintiff has suffered loss and damage and gives particulars of special damage which is the monetary loss to the date of trial. The allegation that the loss and damage was caused by the defendant's negligence is also pleaded here.

8 *The claim for interest* pleaded as required in the body of the pleading.

9 *The prayer* pleading the remedy sought and re-pleading the claim for interest.

10 *The signature* of the barrister, solicitor or litigant in person who drafted the pleading.

11 *The date* the pleading is sent to the court for issue plus name and address of the plaintiff's solicitor or litigant in person.

Except in so far as para 3 pleads loss and damage and causation in the same paragraph,[23] following the usual practice, this pleading conforms with the rule that each allegation should be contained in a single paragraph.

However, you will certainly come across pleadings which to achieve conciseness plead duty of care, the facts of the accident, breach of duty and the resulting damage in one paragraph. If this can be done without loss of clarity, there can be no objection. Moreover, it is worth noting that pleading the facts of the accident in neutral terms and negligence in a separate paragraph may simplify the defendant's task by enabling him to admit the accident paragraph and deal separately with the issue of breach of duty.

In the present case, a single paragraph on the lines indicated above might read:

1. On 1st May 1995 at about 9 pm the Plaintiff was riding his motorcycle registration number [   ] along the Bristol Road towards Wilsdown when as he passed the junction with Albert Road the Defendant so negligently drove or controlled his Lada motor car registration number [   ] that he caused the same to collide with the Plaintiff's said motorcycle whereby the Plaintiff suffered loss and damage.

<u>PARTICULARS OF NEGLIGENCE</u>

(as in pleading)

The remainder of the pleading follows the sample pleading, with paras 3 and 4 becoming the 2nd and 3rd paragraphs respectively.

A sample paragraph pleading *res ipsa loquitur*

The doctrine need not be expressly pleaded (SCP 18/18/15) but it often is in practice. You may see the doctrine pleaded as one of several particulars of negligence, but, strictly speaking, it has no application

---

23 RSC Ord 18 r6(2).

where the cause of an accident is known. *Res ipsa loquitur* may, however, be pleaded in the alternative to particulars of negligence based on probable causes. See further, Curran, *op cit*, p 10.

When pleading *res ipsa loquitur*, it is better to avoid Latin words and to use plain English as in the following example:

> The Plaintiff will rely on the happening of the said accident as evidence in itself of the negligence and/or breach of statutory duty of the Defendants, their servants or agents.

Drafting on behalf of the defendant

Assuming that the defendant does not wish to admit the plaintiff's claim in its entirety, the arrival of the statement/particulars of claim imposes upon the defendant in person, or on his or her lawyer, the task of drafting a defence to the plaintiff's action.

As discussed earlier,[24] the most basic form of defence is putting the plaintiff to proof on some or all of the allegations made in the statement/particulars of claim. Thus in a negligence action, the defendant may traverse material facts pleaded by the plaintiff so as to put in issue any or all of the elements of negligence which the plaintiff must prove.

This approach can be considered in the context of the particulars of claim set out above.

Paragraph 1

This paragraph sets out the material facts from which duty of care can be inferred and pleads the facts of the collision. Unless the defendant says some or all of the facts pleaded in the paragraph are wrong, it is likely that it will be admitted. The practice of pleading the collision in neutral terms facilitates this response. The defendant could, of course, challenge the existence of a duty of care but, in the absence of special circumstances, a claim that a road user did not owe a duty of care to other road users would not succeed. Paragraph 1 is therefore admitted.

Paragraph 2

The material facts which the plaintiff alleges constitute breach of duty by the defendant are pleaded here together with causation. It is possible that a defendant might admit breach of duty and deny

---

24   See above, p 44.

causation, but such a response would be unusual. Most defendants will force the plaintiff to prove breach of duty and causation. This could be done by pleading as follows:

> It is denied that the Defendant was negligent as alleged in paragraph 2 of the Particulars of Claim or at all. It is further denied that the said accident was caused by the negligence of the Defendant.

The defendant is not required to plead to particulars of negligence, but may do so if he or she wishes to plead a positive case in response to one or more of the particulars.[25]

Paragraph 3

This paragraph pleads both loss and damage and causation. The standard response to allegations of loss and damage is non-admission, since it is unlikely to be within the defendant's knowledge whether or not the loss and damage alleged was incurred. No response need be made to the particulars of loss.

Causation is unlikely to be admitted, and may be traversed by non-admission or denial. A paragraph responding to para 3 of the particulars of claim might therefore read:

> No admissions are made as to the alleged or any loss or damage or as to the amount and causation thereof.

It is arguable, however, that it is unnecessary to deny causation in respect of both the accident and loss and damage flowing from the accident, and in some defences the latter is not traversed separately.

Paragraph 4

The defendant is not required to plead to the claim for interest.[26]

The prayer

The defendant should not plead to the prayer.[27]

In most cases, of course, the defendant will not merely traverse allegations made in the statement/particulars of claim, but will also

---

[25] See above, pp 43, 44.
[26] *Ibid.*
[27] *Ibid.*

plead the defendant's affirmative case on the matters put in issue by the defence.[28]

This can be illustrated by considering again para 2 of the particulars of claim set out above. Suppose that the defendant doesn't simply deny that he was negligent, but insists that the plaintiff was wholly, or at least partly, to blame for the accident and so for his own loss and damage. In this case the paragraph of the defence denying negligence and causation would be followed by a paragraph alleging and giving particulars of contributory negligence.

A simple example would be where the defendant claimed that the accident could have been avoided if the plaintiff had been keeping a proper lookout for other vehicles. The relevant paragraph would then read:

Further or alternatively the said accident was caused or contributed to by the negligence of the Plaintiff.

PARTICULARS OF NEGLIGENCE

(a) Failing to keep any or any proper lookout.

(b) Failing to observe the defendant's car.

(c) Failing to stop, to slow down or so to steer or manage the said motorcycle so as to avoid the accident.

The sub-heading used in this paragraph could simply have read 'Particulars'. The sub-heading 'Particulars of Contributory Negligence' is also commonly used. However, some lawyers feel that this is inappropriate where it is alleged that the plaintiff may have caused rather than merely contributed to the accident. This would seem to be technically correct unless one takes the view that it is possible to have 100% contributory negligence.

An example of a somewhat more complex response to para 2 of the particulars of claim above would be where the defendant claims that the reason the plaintiff was not keeping a proper lookout was because he had been drinking alcohol and that this had affected his ability to drive. Suppose in addition that, as a result of the accident, both parties were breathalysed by the police and that the plaintiff was, on the basis of the breath test, subsequently convicted of driving with excess alcohol.

---

[28] See above, p 44ff.

In these circumstances, the particulars of negligence on the part of the defendant could include an allegation that the plaintiff was unfit to drive due to the effect of drinking alcohol, and the conviction for excess alcohol could be pleaded. This is illustrated in the sample defence below.

In the example given, putting the defendant's case involved pleading the defence of contributory negligence. The pleading of other defences is discussed in Chapter 3.

Drafting in practice II

A sample defence

To illustrate how the paragraphs discussed above would appear when integrated into the full defence, the pleading is set out below.

Sample defence

IN THE BATH COUNTY COURT   **Case No**

BETWEEN

JUSTIN TURNER   Plaintiff

and

FREDERICK MICHAEL BARRY   Defendant [1]

DEFENCE [2]

1. Paragraph 1 of the Particulars of Claim is admitted. [3]
2. It is denied that the Defendant was negligent as alleged in paragraph 2 of the Particulars of Claim. It is further denied that the said accident was caused by the negligence of the Defendant. [4]
3. Further or alternatively [5] the said accident was caused or contributed to by the negligence of the Plaintiff.

PARTICULARS OF NEGLIGENCE

(a) Driving when he had been drinking alcohol in such quantities as to impair his judgment and render him unfit to drive safely.
(b) Failing to keep any or any proper lookout.
(c) Failing to stop, to slow down, or so to steer or manage the said motorcycle so as to avoid the accident. [6]

4. Further the Defendant will rely upon the conviction of the Plaintiff on 21 July 1995 at the Bath Magistrates' Court for the offence of

driving a motor vehicle with a breath/alcohol reading in excess of the permitted legal limit. The conviction arises out of the said accident and is relevant to the issue of negligence herein. [7]

5. No admissions are made as to the alleged or any loss or damage or as to the extent thereof. [8]

[signature] [9]

Dated etc [10]

Notes

1 *Heading* as in the particulars of claim. See above, p 154.
2 *Description* of pleading.
3 Admits the facts from which a *duty of care* owed by the defendant to the plaintiff (1st element) can be inferred, together with the facts of the collision.
4 Denies *breach of duty* (2nd element) and *causation* (3rd element).
5 Phrase indicating that the pleader relies on the matter(s) pleaded in this paragraph either in addition to, or as an alternative to, the defence(s) pleaded in preceding paragraphs.
6 This paragraph pleads and particularises by giving details of *contributory negligence* on the part of the plaintiff.
7 *Conviction.* The defendant intends to rely at trial on the fact of the plaintiff's conviction under the Road Traffic Act 1972, s 6(1)(a) and the Road Traffic Act 1988, s 5. He must therefore plead particulars of the conviction, the court which made it and the issue to which it is relevant as required by RSC Ord 18 r7A. The conviction could be pleaded under the particulars of negligence as particular (d) at para 3.
8 This paragraph traverses *loss and damage* (4th element) by non-admission. This is standard practice since it is not usually known to the defendant whether the plaintiff suffered the alleged loss and damage or not. *Causation* has already been traversed with respect to the accident and generally need not be separately traversed in respect of loss and damage.
9 *Signature* of the barrister, solicitor or litigant in person who drafted the defence.
10 *Date* on which the defence was issued, to be completed by the court office.

Adding a counterclaim

A defendant who alleges that the plaintiff's own negligence was wholly or partly to blame for an accident may counterclaim against the plaintiff for damages in respect of any injury, loss or damage which the defendant suffers as a result of the accident.[29]

If, for example, in the case pleaded above the defendant's car had been damaged in the collision with the plaintiff's motorcycle, he could counterclaim for the cost of repairs to his vehicle.

To plead a counterclaim successfully it is only necessary to understand how to draft a statement/particulars of claim, for the counterclaim is really the defendant's statement/particulars of claim attached, for convenience, to the defence.

In the present case these elements are, of course:

- duty of care (owed by the plaintiff to the defendant);
- breach of duty;
- causation;
- damage.

As with the statement/particulars of claim, particulars of negligence must be given in the pleading. Consequently the counterclaim must plead:

- the facts giving rise to a duty of care owed by the plaintiff to the defendant;
- the facts constituting breach of that duty;
- the facts which establish a causal link between the plaintiff's breach of duty and the harm suffered by the defendant;
- the facts identifying the injury and/or damage suffered.[30]

In addition the counterclaim must, of course, plead the facts of the collision which was the occasion of the plaintiff's alleged breach of duty.

However, since both the plaintiff's claim and the defendant's counterclaim arise out of the same accident, some of the material facts which must be pleaded by the defendant to establish the elements of a claim in negligence have already been pleaded by the plaintiff to establish his claim.

First, the particulars of claim pleaded facts establishing that the plaintiff and defendant were road users in such proximity as to impose a duty of care owed by the defendant to the plaintiff. The same facts are of course relied upon by the defendant to establish that the plaintiff owed him an identical duty of care.

---

[29] See above, p 23.
[30] See above, p 56.

Secondly, the plaintiff pleaded the facts of the collision which was the occasion of the defendant's alleged breach of duty and which must be pleaded by the defendant as the occasion of the plaintiff's alleged breach.

It would obviously be a waste of time and space to set these matters out in full again. However, since the defendant has already admitted them in para 1 of his defence, they can be incorporated into the counterclaim simply by re-pleading para 1 of the defence.

In addition, some of the matters pleaded by the defendant in order to establish his defence are relevant to the counterclaim. Thus the contributory negligence which is pleaded and particularised in para 3 constitutes the breach of duty which must be pleaded and particularised in the counterclaim. Similarly the allegation in that paragraph that the accident was caused by or contributed to by the negligence of the plaintiff constitutes the element of causation which must be pleaded as part of the defendant's counterclaim. These matters are also incorporated in the counterclaim by re-pleading the relevant paragraph of the defence.

Any matters which must be pleaded to establish the defendant's claim but have not been the subject of paragraphs in the defence must be set out in full in the counterclaim. In the present example, the matters which must be pleaded in full are the allegations that the defendant suffered loss and damage as a result of the plaintiff's negligence (the 3rd and 4th elements of negligence), the remedy sought, namely damages, and the claim for interest.

As with the statement/particulars of claim, the claim for damages is pleaded in the prayer and the claim for interest both in the body of the pleading and in the prayer.

By listing the elements of the cause of action relied upon and any other matters which must be pleaded by the defendant to establish his claim, it is easy to identify what matters can simply be re-pleaded from the defence and what must be set out in full in the counterclaim as the table below illustrates.

MATTERS WHICH MUST BE PLEADED	PARTICULARS OF CLAIM	DEFENCE	COUNTERCLAIM
Element 1 duty of care	Paragraph 1 pleads material facts from which duty of care is inferred	Paragraph 1 admits	Paragraph 1 of defence is repeated
Element 2 breach of duty (1) occasion of breach	Paragraph 1 pleads facts of collision	Paragraph 1 admits	Paragraph 1 of defence is repeated
(2) Breach and particulars		Paragraphs 3 and 4 plead and particularise the plaintiff's negligence and the plaintiff's conviction	Paragraphs 3 and 4 of defence are repeated
Element 3 causation		Paragraph 3 pleads that plaintiff's negligence caused or contributed to the accident	Paragraph 3 of defence is repeated
Element 4 damage			Pleaded in full in the counterclaim
Remedy sought			Pleaded in full in the prayer
Claim for interest			Pleaded in full in body of counterclaim and repeated in the prayer

To make clear the way in which a counterclaim is pleaded, the defendant's defence and counterclaim in the present case is set out below. Paragraphs 1 to 5 are as set out at p 160 and are not reproduced.

Sample defence and counterclaim

IN THE BATH COUNTY COURT **Case No**

BETWEEN

JUSTIN TURNER <u>Plaintiff</u>

and

FREDERICK MICHAEL BARRY <u>Defendant</u> [1]

DEFENCE AND COUNTERCLAIM [2]

DEFENCE [3]

1. ⎫
2. ⎪
3. ⎬ as in defence set out on p 160
4. ⎪
5. ⎭

COUNTERCLAIM [4]

6.[5] Paragraphs 1, 3 and 4 herein are repeated. [6]

7. By reason of the matters aforesaid the Defendant has suffered loss and damage.

Particulars of Special Damage

Cost of repairs to motor car £1,050.00 [7]

8. Further the Defendant claims interest pursuant to section 69 of the County Courts Act 1984 on the amount found to be due to him at such rate and for such period as the court thinks fit. [8]

AND the Defendant counterclaims: [9]

(1) Damages limited to £3,000,00. [10]

(2) The aforesaid interest pursuant to section 69 of the County Courts Act 1984. [11]

[Signature][12]

Dated etc[13]

Notes

1 *Heading* as in particulars of claim.

2 *The description* indicates that this is a composite document made up of two distinct pleadings. The counterclaim is an independent cross-claim capable of being heard separately from the main action and joined with it for convenience and to avoid re-litigation of matters common to the plaintiff's claim and that of the defendant.

3 *The sub-title* describing the first pleading.

4 *The sub-title* describing the second pleading.

5 The paragraph numbers follow on continuously.

6 Paragraph 6 repeats the paragraphs of the defence which deal with *duty of care*, *breach of duty* and *particulars of breach* including the *plaintiff's conviction* and *causation*.

7 This paragraph pleads the allegation that the plaintiff's negligence caused the defendant loss and damage and gives the required particulars of special damage which is the monetary loss to the date of trial.

8 The defendant's *claim for interest*.

9 *The prayer*. Do not forget to put 'counterclaims' instead of 'claims'.

10 The remedy sought. The fact that the damages claimed do not exceed £3,000 is pleaded so that costs are limited to Scale 1.

11 The claim for interest must be repeated in the prayer.

12 The *signature* of the barrister, solicitor or litigant in person who drafted the pleading.

13 *Date* of issue.

Drafting in practice III

Drafting on the basis of instructions from a client

Question for self-testing

We have now examined the way in which the statement/particulars of claim and the defence are constructed in a property claim in negligence. The next step is for you to put into practice what you have learned by drafting a pleading on the basis of instructions from a client.

BACKGROUND TO THE CASE

The client in this case, Mr Robert McDonald, wants compensation from a neighbour, Mr George Pritchard, for losses he incurred when a tree which Mr Pritchard was cutting down fell onto Mr McDonald's greenhouse. After interviewing Mr McDonald, his solicitor, Ms Frances Williams, was able to advise that he had a good claim for compensation from Mr Pritchard. On instructions from Mr McDonald she wrote to Mr Pritchard making a claim on behalf of her client and warning that legal proceedings might be taken if no reply was received. Mr Pritchard did not respond to the letter and a summons is to be issued on behalf of Mr McDonald in the Shrewsbury County Court.

This case provides an opportunity for you to draft the particulars of claim which will be served with the summons. A sample particulars of claim with which you can compare your draft is provided at the end of this chapter.

The information which you will need for this task is contained in the documents set out below. These are the client's proof of evidence, an initial letter from Ms Williams to Mr McDonald and a letter to Mr Pritchard. These are all documents of a kind that solicitors are frequently required to draft on behalf of clients, and while explaining their nature we shall take a preliminary look at how they should be drafted.

MR MCDONALD'S PROOF OF EVIDENCE

An early task for a solicitor whose client is, or is likely to become, a party to litigation is to take a proof of evidence from the client and from anyone who is a potential witness in support of the client's case. This document, which is drafted on the basis of an interview with the client, or potential witness, contains all the relevant evidence that person is able to give. The proof may therefore, and frequently does, contain inadmissible evidence, for example, hearsay or non-expert opinion evidence. It may also include matters which are potentially damaging to the client's case.

There is therefore a clear distinction between a proof of evidence and a witness statement. The latter, though drafted on the basis of the proof of evidence, is a written statement of the oral evidence which is to be adduced at trial. Consequently it must not contain inadmissible evidence and should not include matters damaging to the case of the party adducing the evidence. Drafting a witness statement therefore requires skill and care, particularly since witness statements are exchanged by the parties to an action before trial as part of the process of discovery.[31]

Although a proof of evidence is not disclosed to the other side in an action, the creation of an effective proof also requires skill, care and

---

[31]   RSC Ord 38 r2A; CCR Ord 20 r12A.

effort on the part of the solicitor who drafts it. He or she must be skilled in interviewing techniques in order to ensure that all relevant matters are dealt with by the person giving evidence. Drafting skills are also required for the proof which, though full, must be clear, concise and well-structured. It must also be accurate and this can be ensured by dictating the proof in the presence of the maker of the statement so that errors can be corrected immediately. Alternatively the solicitor can draft it on the computer and forward a copy for the client to correct and sign.

The checklist below sets out the key matters to be covered by a proof of evidence.

- maker's name and address;
- maker's date of birth and National Insurance number if relevant for a personal injury claim;
- maker's occupation and position if relevant;
- all relevant evidence which the maker can give in relation to the matters in dispute;
- maker's signature and date proof signed;
- date proof taken by solicitor;
- solicitor's name and address.

Be careful to ensure that the proof is signed by the maker and includes the date of signing together with the date the proof was taken by the solicitor. This will facilitate its admission in evidence under the Civil Evidence Act 1968 should this become necessary.

The proof of evidence taken by Ms Williams from Mr McDonald is set out below.

Proof of George McDonald of 4 Wingate Lane, Old Fordham, Shropshire SH5 3JT [1]

I am a retired lecturer [2] and have lived at the above address for 43 years. The cottage belongs to me as I inherited it from my great aunt, Miss Eve McDonald.

The cottage is one of a pair situated about half way down Wingate Lane, about one quarter of a mile from the centre of Old Fordham. Both cottages have large gardens which are separated from each other by a low wooden fence. This belongs to number 6. The neighbouring cottage, number 6, is owned by Mr John Edward Pritchard who has lived there about 10 years. He is very keen on do-it-yourself and has done a lot of work on his cottage. Most of it has been done in a very shoddy manner – I don't think he knows what he is doing. [3]

I have always been a very keen gardener, and since I retired five years ago, gardening has been my main occupation. I have always enjoyed growing flowers, but some years ago I bought my wife an orchid and since then growing orchids has been my great passion. My collection of orchids was my pride and joy.

The orchids were kept in a large greenhouse at the far end of my garden. The greenhouse was brand new. I bought it a year ago with some of the lump sum I received on retirement, as my collection had become too large for my previous greenhouse. The new greenhouse was a very expensive model, and I installed a sophisticated sprinkler system to regulate the temperature and humidity. The greenhouse cost £3,800 including the cost of erecting it. The sprinkler system cost £1,500 and I paid £250 to have the system installed.

My problem arose two weeks ago on 10th October 1995 when Mr Pritchard decided to cut down a very large old apple tree at the bottom of his garden. Instead of hiring an expert, Mr Pritchard obviously decided to do the job himself. I have never been on very good terms with Mr Pritchard, who is a very difficult person to get on with, but I did decide to have a word with him when I saw him going at the old tree with a electric saw. In fact I was pretty certain that he had no idea how to tackle the job, but he would not take any advice so I could only warn him to be careful because the tree was so close to my greenhouse.

Unfortunately, the tree collapsed onto the greenhouse, demolishing a large part of it, and destroying much of my orchid collection. I spoke to Mr Pritchard immediately, but he was totally uncooperative. He just said it was an unfortunate accident for which no-one was to blame and that I should claim on my insurance. Since then he has refused to discuss the matter further.

I don't know how much my orchid collection was worth. It would take some time to value the plants lost.

George McDonald [4]   22 October 1995 [5]
(Proof taken on 22 October 1995 by Frances Williams) [6]
Ref FW/McDonald/30451
Pembury, Wilson & Porter, Solicitors [7]
5 High Street
Old Fordham
Shropshire
SH5 2RL

Notes

1 Name and address of maker.
2 Occupation of maker.
3 Inadmissible non-expert evidence. This would have to be excluded from a witness statement based on the proof.
4 The proof should be signed by the maker.
5 The date on which the proof was signed should be indicated.
6 The date on which the proof was taken should be indicated.
7 The proof should indicate the name and the address of the solicitor taking the proof.

Legal advice to Mr McDonald

Mr McDonald presented his solicitor with a clear-cut case, and the solicitor was therefore able to advise immediately that there was a legal remedy for Mr McDonald's problem.

Mr McDonald was told at the interview that he appears to have a strong claim in negligence against Mr Pritchard. What this meant was explained and Mr McDonald was advised to instruct his solicitor to write to Mr Pritchard setting out Mr McDonald's claim against him and requesting compensation for the loss suffered by Mr McDonald. The solicitor explained that this letter would warn Mr Pritchard that if he did not reply within 14 days, legal proceedings might be issued against him. She also explained that if no reply was received from Mr Pritchard the next step would be for Mr McDonald to commence proceedings against Mr Pritchard. This would be done by the solicitor requesting the Shrewsbury county court to issue a summons against Mr Pritchard.

Mr McDonald's solicitor then wrote two letters.

INITIAL LETTER

The first was an initial letter to the client following a first interview. Such a letter will usually confirm the instructions given by the client, the advice given to him and the action to be taken. It must also give the client certain information in accordance with the Solicitors' Practice Rules. The checklist below sets out the key matters covered by the letter.

* reference to interview;
* confirmation of instructions;
* outline of advice given;
* information on client care;
* costs.

The initial letter to Mr McDonald reads as follows:

Mr George McDonald
4 Wingate Lane
Old Fordham
Shropshire SH5 3JT

22 October 1995

Dear Mr McDonald

Thank you for calling at my office yesterday. [1] As promised I am writing to confirm your instructions and my advice.

As I explained to you yesterday, it appears that you have a good claim at law to be compensated by your neighbour Mr Pritchard for the loss you incurred when a tree he was cutting down fell on your greenhouse damaging the greenhouse and the collection of orchids you kept in it.

As instructed I have written to Mr Pritchard requesting him to solve this matter by paying an appropriate sum in compensation. A copy of that letter is enclosed. I will contact you by letter as soon as Mr Pritchard replies to this letter.

If Mr Pritchard fails to respond to this letter I shall, as instructed, commence proceedings on your behalf in the county court. At court you will need to prove that Mr Pritchard was negligent in that he failed to take adequate precautions to avoid damage to your property while felling the tree. I believe that you have a good prospect of establishing this. [2]

I shall personally be responsible for the conduct of your case and may from time to time be assisted by other members of this firm. If at any time you are not satisfied with the service you receive, you can raise the matter with Mrs Jane Fox who is one of the firm's senior partners and who will investigate your complaint.

The firm's offices are open from 9 am to 5.30 pm Monday to Friday. If at any time it is difficult for you to visit during these hours, it may be possible for a meeting to be arranged out of office hours. If you have any queries concerning your case, please write to me or telephone if the matter is urgent. If you need to discuss any matter with me personally, please contact my secretary who will arrange a meeting. [3]

I shall write to you separately on the question of costs. [4]

If you require any further information, please do not hesitate to contact me.

Yours sincerely,

Frances Williams
Pembury, Wilson & Porter

Notes

The notes to this letter show how the matters in the checklist above are dealt with in the letter. A more detailed example of an initial letter to a client is illustrated and discussed at p 182 below.

1   The opening sentence links the letter to the interview with the client.

2   *2nd, 3rd* and *4th paragraphs.* These paragraphs confirm the client's instructions, the advice given to him by the solicitor, and the steps which are being or may be taken to deal with his problem.

3   *5th* and *6th paragraphs.* These paragraphs provide information on the solicitor handling the client's case, the firm's complaints procedure, its hours of business and how the client can contact his legal advisor. This is information which the solicitor is required to give the client under r15 Solicitors' Practice Rules 1990. It is common practice for this information to be in a separate letter which is automatically sent by the firm to every new client when instructions are given.

4   This paragraph indicates that information on costs likely to be incurred in pursuing the case will be provided separately. The Written Professional Standards issued by the Law Society require that at the outset of a case the client should be given such information.

Where the client will be funding proceedings himself, he should be informed in writing of the following matters:

• the hourly rate charged by the solicitor for his or her services and how this is calculated;

• the disbursements likely to be made by the solicitor on the client's behalf which must be repaid to the solicitor by the client;

• the way in which the client will be required to make payments to the solicitor;

• an estimate of the costs of the case.

It is usual to give this information to the client in a separate information sheet.

Alternatively, a legally-aided client must be advised on behalf of the Legal Aid Fund about the statutory charge. This is a first charge for the benefit of the Legal Aid Board which will attach to any money or property recovered or preserved in the case. This charge is redeemed to reimburse the Legal Aid Fund for the cost to the Fund of conducting the case.

LETTER BEFORE ACTION

The second letter drafted by Mr McDonald's solicitor was a letter sent to Mr Pritchard setting out Mr McDonald's claim and requesting him to compensate Mr McDonald for his losses. The letter warned that if no reply was received by the solicitor, legal proceedings might be commenced against Mr Pritchard. This is the letter referred to by Ms Williams in her letter to Mr McDonald. It is known as a letter before action. Failure to send such a letter before commencing proceedings may result in a successful plaintiff losing some of his costs.

The checklist below sets out the key matters to be covered in a letter before action:

- identity of client;
- a brief account of what happened;
- the resulting damage suffered by the client;
- a concise statement of why the recipient of the letter is alleged to be liable for the client's loss;
- what the recipient is being asked to do;
- what steps will be taken if the recipient fails to comply.

The letter before action sent to Mr Pritchard reads as follows.

Mr John F Pritchard
6 Wingate Lane
Old Fordham
Shropshire SH5 3JT

                                                        22 October 1995

Dear Mr Pritchard

re: George McDonald of 4 Wingate Lane, Old Fordham

I am instructed by the above-named [1] in respect of damage to his property which resulted from an incident on 10 October 1995. [2]

I understand that on that date you were attempting to cut down an apple tree located on your property when the tree fell onto adjacent land owned by my client, and damaged a greenhouse and a collection of orchids kept in the greenhouse, which belonged to my client. [3]

From my instructions it would appear that the incident was caused by your negligence in failing to take the precautions necessary to prevent my client's property from being damaged when the tree was felled. [4] I therefore claim, on behalf of my client, compensation for the damage caused to his property as a result of this incident. [5]

My client is currently obtaining estimates of the expenditure necessary to rectify the damage and I expect to be in a position to quantify his claim when these are forthcoming. [6]

I must point out that if I do not hear from you within 14 days of the date of this letter, proceedings may be issued against you without further notice. [7]

In view of the contents of this letter, you may wish to take independent legal advice in which case I suggest that you consult a solicitor. [8]

Yours sincerely,

Frances Williams
Pembury, Wilson & Porter

Notes

1   Identifies the client.
2   Identifies the incident.
3   Gives a concise account of the incident and the resulting damage to the client's property.
4   States precisely why the recipient of the letter is alleged to be liable for the client's loss.
5   Makes clear what the recipient of the letter is being asked to do, namely, to compensate the client for the damage suffered.
6   The claim should be quantified if possible.
7   Warns the recipient of the letter of the consequences if he fails to respond to it.
8   Indicates to the recipient of the letter that it may be advisable to seek legal advice on its contents.

Preparing to draft the particulars of claim

You are now in a position to be able to draft the particulars of claim in this case. It is of course a claim in negligence for damage to property.

Even if you had only the above documents before you, the cause of action would be clear from Mr McDonald's proof and is confirmed in the third paragraph of Ms Williams' letter to Mr Pritchard. See note 4 to this letter.

Remember, it is the elements of the cause of action that provide the basic framework for the particulars of claim. To remind you, these are:

- duty of care (owed by the defendant to the plaintiff);
- breach of duty (negligence);
- causation;
- damage.

Remember, too, that negligence must be particularised so you must plead the facts which are necessary to establish the elements of negligence. Below is a checklist of matters that must be pleaded:

- *duty of care*:
  plead the facts from which the duty owed can be inferred;
- *breach of duty*:
  plead the occasion of the breach and the facts constituting breach;
- *causation*:
  plead the causal link between the breach of duty alleged and the harm suffered by the plaintiff;
- *damage*:
  plead loss and damage and particularise special damage, ie monetary loss to trial;
- *interest*:
  this must be claimed in the body of the pleading and in the prayer;
- *remedy sought*:
  plead the claim for damages in the prayer.

If, after reading the documents with the checklist in mind, you are still uncertain as to what facts to plead, the points below may assist you.

DUTY OF CARE

Mr Pritchard owes Mr McDonald a duty of care because their relationship as occupiers of adjoining properties means that it is reasonably foreseeable that work undertaken negligently by Mr Pritchard on his land might cause harm to Mr McDonald's property.

How should this be pleaded?

Remember that in the road traffic accident case considered earlier the court would be able to infer a duty of care owed by the defendant to the plaintiff, and *vice versa* from the fact that the plaintiff and the defendant were fellow road users in such proximity that it was reasonably foreseeable that negligence by one of them might cause harm to the other. Refer back to the particulars of claim to see how this was pleaded by the plaintiff.

BREACH OF DUTY

The occasion of Mr Pritchard's negligence was the felling of the apple tree. What facts need to be pleaded to give the defendant and the judge a clear picture of the alleged context in which the wrongful conduct complained of by the plaintiff occurred? Breach of duty must be particularised. In what ways was Mr Pritchard careless? What did he do that he should not have done? What did he fail to do that should have been done to prevent damage to Mr McDonald's property? The answers to these questions will give you the particulars of negligence.

DAMAGE

Particulars must be given of special damage. What is the monetary loss that Mr McDonald will have incurred as at the date of trial? Can you plead figures for this? A claim must be made for compensation for the orchids destroyed, but no figure can be given for this as yet. You must, therefore, leave a blank space at the relevant place in the pleadings.

Sample particulars of claim in *McDonald v Pritchard*

IN THE SHREWSBURY COUNTY COURT [1]   **Case No** [2]
BETWEEN

GEORGE McDONALD [3]   Plaintiff
and
JOHN EDWARD PRITCHARD [3]   Defendant

PARTICULARS OF CLAIM [4]

1. The Plaintiff is the freehold owner of the land and premises at 4 Wingate Lane, Old Fordham, Shropshire. The Defendant is the occupier of the neighbouring land and premises at 6 Wingate Lane. The land to the rear of the premises at 4 is separated from the land to the rear of the premises at 6 by a wooden boundary fence ('the fence'). [5]

2. On the Plaintiff's land and adjacent to the fence is located a greenhouse ('the greenhouse') in which the Plaintiff keeps a collection of orchids. [6]

3. On 10 October 1995 the Defendant felled a tree ('the tree') which was growing on his land and adjacent to the fence causing the tree to fall onto the Plaintiff's land, and to demolish the greenhouse and destroy the Plaintiff's collection of orchids. [7]

4. The matters aforesaid were caused by the negligence of the Defendant. [8]

PARTICULARS OF NEGLIGENCE

(a) Felling the tree when he was neither qualified nor competent to do so.

(b) Felling the tree without using the appropriate equipment.

(c) Failing to control the tree as it fell so as to ensure that it did not fall onto the Plaintiff's land.

(d) Failing to take any or any adequate precautions to prevent the tree from falling onto the Plaintiff's land. [9]

5. In the premises the Plaintiff has suffered loss and damage. [10]

PARTICULARS OF LOSS AND DAMAGE

(a) cost of replacing greenhouse	£	3,800.00
(b) cost of replacing heating/humidifier system	£	1,500.00
(c) cost of installing replacement heating/ humidifier system	£	250.00
(d) value of plants destroyed	£	
TOTAL		[11]

6. Further the Plaintiff claims interest pursuant to section 69 of the County Courts Act 1984 on the amount found to be due to the Plaintiff at such rate and for such period as the court thinks fit. [12]

AND the Plaintiff claims: [13]

(a) Damages exceeding £5,000.00. [14]

(b) Interest pursuant to section 69 of the County Courts Act 1984 to be assessed. [15]

[signature] [16]

Dated, etc [17]

Notes

1   The name of the appropriate county court was given at p 167 above.

2   Leave the case number blank. This is inserted by the court office.

3   Don't forget to put the parties' full names. See above at p 26.

4   The description of the pleading.

5   This paragraph pleads the facts which show that the plaintiff and defendant are the occupiers of adjacent land. It is from these facts that a duty of care owed by the defendant to the plaintiff (1st element) can be inferred.

6   The existence and location of the greenhouse is pleaded separately for clarity. Inclusion of this information in para 3 would result in a longer, more complicated paragraph.

7   This paragraph pleads the facts identifying the occasion of the alleged breach (2nd element).

8   The opening sentence of this paragraph pleads breach of duty (2nd element) and causation (3rd element).

9   The breach of duty is particularised in para 4, sub-paras (a) to (d). You may have variations on these particulars. Don't forget to begin with specific allegations and end with a general 'catch-all' particular.

10 This paragraph pleads damage (4th element) and causation (3rd element). The phrase 'in the premises' means by reason of the matters which have been pleaded in the preceding paragraphs. In this pleading, it therefore means by reason of the defendant's breach of the duty of care owed to the plaintiff.

11 The particulars of special damage. Item (d) has been left blank because the client cannot yet put a figure on this element of his loss.

12 The claim for interest.

13 The prayer.

14 Where damages are likely to exceed £5,000 this must be pleaded. Failure to do so may result in the case being listed before the district judge whose jurisdiction is limited to £5,000. See above, at p 50.

15 Don't forget to plead the claim for interest in the prayer as well as in the body of the pleading.

16 Don't forget to sign the draft pleading.

17 The date of the pleading. See above, at p 28.

Chapter 8

Drafting in a Personal Injury Case in the County Court

Scope of chapter

This chapter explains how to construct the drafting of pleadings and a letter of advice to the client who wishes to seek compensation for her personal injuries.

At any time accidents occur and not unnaturally the person who is injured will look for someone to blame for the accident. The first job the lawyer must do, when approached for advice, is to examine the facts surrounding the accident and come to a conclusion as to whether the responsibility for the accident can be placed on someone else. It is important to remember that some accidents are just that – accidents, and there may be no possibility of recovering compensation because there was no negligence. However, the doctrine of *res ipsa loquitur* may help to prove negligence if your client can remember nothing and finding proof of negligence is difficult or impossible.

Responsibility for an accident can be laid on another person under the tort of negligence if the person injured and the party who it is alleged caused or contributed to the injury are in a certain relationship.

The relationship may be defined by statute, as under the Occupiers' Liability Act 1957, or may be a common law duty of care owed to neighbours under the rule in *Donaghue v Stevenson* (1932).

The case considered in this chapter is a simple accident that happened in a public place where the only relationship that is consistent with the facts is that of the common duty of care. Below is a synopsis of the information given by the injured person.

The plaintiff's view of the facts of the accident

Mrs Janet Simpson was walking on the pavement of High Street, Westchester on her way to work on Wednesday, 24 May 1995. At about 8.30 in the morning she stopped to look in the window of Electric City, a shop at 23 High Street.

Michael Andrews, a shop assistant at Electric City, was helping unload a delivery of new products. Carrying a large and heavy box from the van towards the shop, he bumped into Mrs Simpson and knocked her down. Mrs Simpson suffered a fractured ulna and made a full recovery six months later. She now wishes to sue and obtain compensation because of her injury.

The law

From these facts it is now possible to work out if Mrs Simpson can establish the basic elements of a claim in negligence. These elements which must be proved by Mrs Simpson are:

- a duty of care owed to Mrs Simpson;
- breach of the duty;
- causing;
- loss and damages.

The action before issuing proceedings

From the facts set out above, the legal advisor is now in a position to work out if Mrs Simpson has a claim in negligence which she can bring before the court. The next step will be to establish who Mrs Simpson will sue, whether they are able to pay Mrs Simpson, should she win her case, and whether Mrs Simpson has sufficient evidence to prove her case should the matter go to trial.

A final consideration is how Mrs Simpson is going to pay for her legal costs up to the trial.

The legal advisor will have discussed some of these matters at the initial interview with Mrs Simpson. But it is good practice, after the interview, to write to Mrs Simpson confirming her instructions, setting out the legal advice, asking for further information if needed, and stating what action he or she will next take on Mrs Simpson's behalf.

The legal advisor is also given an extra professional duty under r15 Solicitors' Practice Rules 1990. This duty is to keep the client informed about all issues which are relevant to the matter. This includes in this particular case:

- the name and status of the person responsible for the case on a day to day basis and the name of the principal solicitor supervising the case;
- the person the client should approach if they feel they have a problem with the service given by the firm;
- detailed information as to the likely costs of the case.

The subject of costs is often a contentious issue between solicitor and client. The Law Society has issued detailed Written Professional Standards which give guidance as to the information that solicitors should properly give to their clients. These include:

- a discussion of the availability of legal aid, or insurance cover;
- information as to how the solicitor's fee will be calculated (eg the hourly charging rate);

- confirmation in writing of an agreed fee, if relevant, and whether it includes VAT and disbursements;
- informing private clients that they are at all times responsible for their own solicitor's bill even if they win their case, and that if they lose their case they will probably have to pay, in addition, their opponent's costs.

It is important that r15 and the written professional standards are followed in practice. This is not the place for a full discussion of the professional rules. The postgraduate professional course covers the detailed rules which must be borne in mind when conducting a client's case and writing a letter of advice.

Construction of letter of advice

The structure of the letter will be similar to that of an opinion. But it will differ in two important ways.
- It must give Mrs Simpson the information described under r15 above.
- It is usual also to confirm Mrs Simpson's instructions so that there can be no later misunderstanding.

The letter should therefore also, like an opinion, contain:
- the names of the parties;
- establish the duty of care;
- confirm that there appear to be breaches of the duty of care;
- assess the nature, cause and extent of the loss and damage;
- advice on the relief claimed.

These elements are set out in brackets in italics at the end of each paragraph in the advice letter.

Procedural matters

The following matters should be dealt with by instructing solicitor before issuing proceedings:
(1) A signed and dated statement should be taken from Mrs Simpson to be used as admissible evidence should she die or become unavailable before trial.
(2) An initial letter of claim must be sent to the tortfeasor inviting him to refer the matter to his insurer.
(3) A medical report must be obtained.
(4) A schedule of special damages must be prepared.

The advice letter, which follows, deals with the contents of (3) and (4). There is no prescribed form for (1) and (2) above.

Sample letter of advice

> Messrs Stones
> Solicitors
> 21 Low Road
> Westchester
> Devon

5 December 1995

Mrs J Simpson
Three Ways
Ross Lane
Westchester
Devon

Dear Mrs Simpson

I was pleased to meet you at our offices last week and discuss with you the action you wish to take to claim damages for the injury to your arm, compensation for your loss of wages, and reimbursement for the money you spent on drugs and travel because of the injury. *(Introduction confirming instructions.)*

Should you instruct us to commence proceedings, I will be the solicitor in charge of the conduct of your case, and Mrs Green, our litigation partner, will be responsible for overall supervision. Either of us will make ourselves available should you feel you have any problems. *(Information for client required under r15 Solicitors' Practice Rules 1990.)*

Summary of advice

As I explained, I think you are in a good position to prove that the shop assistant at Electric City was responsible for your accident and therefore will be ordered to compensate you for your subsequent suffering, the wages you lost and the money you spent as a direct result of the accident. As Mr Andrews was working at the time, his employer will also be liable to meet the claim, so I would advise suing him as well as Mr Andrews. There is, of course, no double recovery. *(Summary of advice and information about vicarious liability of employer.)*

You will claim in court that Mr Andrews was negligent, in that he failed to take adequate precautions to avoid an accident while transferring goods into the shop and this failure led directly to your injury. As I understand it, he was carrying a large box which was bulky, unwieldy and appeared to be heavy. *(Cause of action in negligence and proof of causation.)*

Evidence

It is possible that Mr Andrews, if he defends the case, will say that you did not try to avoid him. For this reason, I asked you where you were standing when Mr Andrews knocked you over. You told me that you had your back to the road and were standing still, looking at the window display. You said you couldn't avoid him, because you couldn't see him. You also told me that as far as you know you and Mr Andrews were the only witnesses. You have no recollection of seeing the driver of the delivery van and heard no warning shouts before you were knocked over. *(This is a vital paragraph which assesses the facts and asks for confirmation of the evidence. It is included to enable the solicitor to: (i) confirm the client's instructions about the absence of witnesses and (ii) explore the possibility of the defendant pleading contributory negligence.)*

In the paragraph above, I have tried to set out the key facts of the accident. It is important that I have stated them correctly. Please could you let me know if there is anything with which you cannot agree.

Compensation

As I explained to you, if you prove that Mr Andrews was negligent, and I see no reason to doubt this, you are entitled to be compensated for the loss you have suffered. *(Assessment of damages.)* This will be made up in the following way.

(1) You will be awarded a sum for your pain, suffering and the loss of opportunity to do things while your arm was mending. This will be assessed by the district judge who will look at previous judgments concerned with similar injuries. I have looked at recent cases, and estimate you should receive between £1,500 and £1,750 for this. *(This figure is an estimate arrived at after the solicitor has looked in Kemp and Kemp, The Quantum of Damages, and found an award in a similar recently decided case.)*

(2) You will also be compensated for your direct losses that have arisen because of your injury. Please therefore send me details of the following:

(a) wage slips both before and after the accident;

(b) details and cost of drugs;

(c) cost of travel to hospital, doctor's surgery, physiotherapy;

(d) value of clothing damaged or destroyed by the accident.

From this figure will be deducted half of any benefits you have received from the DSS. Could you let me have details of these?

I need all this information before I can start your court proceedings.

I also need a report from your hospital consultant which must be filed at court when you start proceedings. Please could you arrange to be examined by him or her and ask for the report to be prepared as soon as possible. You will have to cover the cost of the report.

Costs of your case

You kindly paid on account £300, for which we acknowledge receipt. Our charges for handling this case are £80 per hour for my time and £100 per hour for my partner's time. This figure is exclusive of VAT. In addition, you will be required to pay disbursements such as court fees, counsel's fees and the cost of a medical report.

I would point out that at all times you are personally responsible for the payment of our costs. Should you win your case it is likely that the defendants will be ordered to pay these costs. However, should the defendants have no resources, you personally will be responsible for our bill of costs. Should you lose your case, you are likely to be responsible for both our bill of costs and the defendants' costs.

I am not at this time able to estimate the costs of your action, since we have no idea how the defendants will respond when you start court proceedings. At the time they serve their defence I will look to you for a further advance, and will then be in a better position to give you an estimate of the whole fee. (*This information is required to be given to the client in writing under the Written Professional Standards issued by the Law Society. The standards are not mandatory, but represent a safe and preferred method of practice.*)

Your help in dealing with detailing your losses and obtaining a medical report is appreciated, and on receipt of that information I look forward to taking your instructions to start proceedings.

Yours sincerely,

A Solicitor
Messrs Stones

Drafting the claim

Having summarised the basis of the claim in the advice letter, the next step, if instructed by the client, is to draft the particulars of claim. The aim of this is to tell the client's side of the story to the district judge and the defendants.

It is important to recall that only matters referred to in the pleadings can be brought to the attention of the court and therefore the entire compass of the case must be included in the pleadings. This is because to win a case the plaintiff must prove, on the balance of probabilities, that the facts alleged in the particulars of claim are true. These facts must be included in the pleadings so evidence can be brought at trial to prove these alleged facts. If they are not in the pleadings, the plaintiff cannot, except with leave of the court, bring evidence to prove the claim. Leave is granted only very exceptionally.

Below is a brief checklist to reinforce the rules on drafting particulars of claim which are discussed in Chapter 2 of this book at greater length. Please look back at the chapter if you can't remember the meaning of the rules in the checklist.

Checklist for pleading a claim

- Plead all material facts and do not plead immaterial facts.
- Do not anticipate the defence.
- Do not plead evidence and do not plead law.
- Identify and sue under the correct cause of action.

Material facts

The structural problem, before starting to draft, is to identify the material facts to be included. These must be pleaded: CCR Ord 6 r1(1). This rule gives no definition of a material fact, but RSC Ord 18 r7 is more helpful. This is discussed more fully in Chapter 3 of this book.

Here, the material facts relevant to this claim are:

(a) the names of the parties;

(b) the date of the accident;

(c) the place of the accident;

(d) the plaintiff was hit from behind by the first defendant;

(e) no warning was given;

(f) the plaintiff was injured because of the accident;

(g) the first defendant was working for the second defendant at the time of the accident, and the accident occurred during the course of his employment;

(h) the plaintiff suffered loss because of her injury.

Immaterial facts which should not be included are indicated in the notes following the pleading.

Sample particulars of claim

IN WESTCHESTER COUNTY COURT [1]   **Case No** [2]

BETWEEN

JANET SIMPSON   <u>Plaintiff</u>

and

(1) MICHAEL ANDREWS

(2) ELECTRIC CITY (a firm) [4]   <u>Defendants</u> [3]

PARTICULARS OF CLAIM

---

1. On Wednesday 24 May 1995 the Plaintiff was standing on the pavement facing 23 High Street, Westchester which is a ground floor shop owned and managed by the Second Defendant when she was knocked to the ground by the First Defendant. [5]

2. At all material times the First Defendant was the servant or agent of the Second Defendant Company and was acting in the course of his employment. [6]

3. The said accident was caused by the negligence of the First Defendant. [7]

<u>PARTICULARS OF NEGLIGENCE</u> [8]

The First Defendant was negligent in that he:

(a) Carried goods which obscured his vision.

(b) Carried goods that were too heavy to control.

(c) Failed to control the goods he was carrying.

(d) Failed to keep any or any proper lookout.

(e) Failed to observe or heed the presence of the Plaintiff.

(f) Failed to take any or any sufficient steps to warn the Plaintiff.

(g) Knocked down the Plaintiff.

(h) In all the circumstances failed to take any or any adequate regard for the Plaintiff's safety and exposed her to an unnecessary risk.

4. By reason of the Defendants' said negligence, the Plaintiff suffered personal injury, loss and damage. [9]

PARTICULARS OF INJURY [10]

The Plaintiff was born on 16 March 1950 and was 43 years old at the date of the accident. She was conveyed by ambulance to St Charles Hospital, Westchester where she was found to have suffered a fracture to her right ulna; she was taken to theatre, a plate was applied to her under general anaesthetic and her arm put into plaster. She attended a course of physiotherapy for three weeks and suffered a decreasing amount of pain in her right arm for a period of around six months. The Plaintiff is right-handed and was unable to work as a secretary for four months after the date of the accident. She was unable to pursue her hobbies of gardening and calligraphy and had difficulty in dealing with household tasks and playing with her two children.

The Plaintiff will rely on the report of Mr Tibber FRCS which gives a full account of her injuries which is served herewith.

PARTICULARS OF SPECIAL DAMAGE [11]

(a) Loss of earnings [12]

Plaintiff absent from work for 24 weeks

@ £120 net per week	£2,880.00
Less sick pay advanced	£480.00
TOTAL LOSS OF EARNINGS	£2,400.00
(b) Cost of painkillers	£5.00
(c) Cost of travel to doctor, hospital and for physiotherapy	£20.00
(d) Cost of home help to assist the Plaintiff in the care of her home and her family for six weeks commencing 27.5.1995 @ £20 per week	£120.00
TOTAL	£2,542.00

5. Further the Plaintiff claims interest pursuant to section 69 of the County Courts Act 1984 on such damages as may be awarded to her at such a rate and for such a period as the Court thinks fit. [13]

AND the Plaintiff claims against the First and/or the Second Defendants: [14]

(1) Damages. [15]

(2) Interest as pleaded. [16]

> Messrs Stones [17]
> Solicitors
> 21 Low Road
> Westchester
> Devon

Dated etc [18]

Notes

1 The overall total of damages will be less than £50,000 and so must be brought in the county court: s 15 County Courts Act 1984. The plaintiff can start proceedings in any county court: CCR Ord 4 r2(1)(c). In this case, the plaintiff's costs will be less if the case is heard in the local court, so proceedings will be issued by instructed solicitor in Westchester.

2 This will be allotted by a court official when proceedings are issued. The first letters refer to the name of the local court.

3 The actions against both defendants are separate but because they arise from the same incident, the actions should be heard together: CCR Ord 5 r2. The second defendant faces liability because the company is vicariously liable for the torts of its servants or agents committed in the course of their employment.

4 The second defendant is sued in this style if it is the trading name of a partnership: CCR Ord 9 r9. If Electric City is in fact the trading name of an individual carrying on business in a name other than his own, then the plaintiff can sue either the individual as 'James Long (trading as Electric City)' or 'Electric City (a trade name)': CCR Ord 5 r10. The individual, however, can only sue in his own name. Accurate information should be available because s 4 Business Names Act 1985 requires the identity of each partner to be stated on all business letters, invoices, receipts etc.

It is perfectly acceptable to list the defendants as:

MICHAEL ANDREWS   First Defendant
and
ELECTRIC CITY (a firm)   Second Defendant

Material fact (a) here included.

5 The general rule is to set the scene and in this paragraph plead the identity of the parties and non-contentious matters that can be agreed by the defendants. In this case the address of the plaintiff is not in contention and is not a material fact and is therefore not included. Her employment, which is a material fact, relates to her damages and is therefore included in the particulars of injuries and not in this paragraph.

The time of the accident has not been included in the pleading because it is not relevant in evidential terms, is unlikely to be in contention and is not a material fact. If the accident had happened in the evening in poor light, it might have been a material fact.

Material facts included here are: (b),(c),(d).

6 'At all material times' is used as shorthand to avoid repeating the date and (if a material fact) the time of the accident. Here it is included to explain why the second defendant, the employer, is vicariously liable for the acts and omissions of the first defendant, the employee.

Company is referred to in the singular throughout this book. There is no rule to reflect this position we have taken, but it is important to be consistent throughout the pleading.

Referring to the second defendant company rather than just second defendant in this paragraph emphasises why it is being brought into the action.

Material fact (g) here included.

7 This pleads the cause of action, here the tort of negligence, which is the vehicle that enables the plaintiff to bring the matter to court. This is required by CCR Ord 6 r1(1). It is not necessary to include the liability of the second defendant which has been stated in para 2 of the pleadings. It would not be wrong however here to refer again to their liability.

8 Set out the breaches of the cause of action. To cover all possible negligent acts by the defendant it is necessary to analyse the accident in detail. Here the first two pleaded acts in the particulars of claim were positive acts of negligence. The next five were acts of omission and the final act is a sweeping-up clause.

All these allegations must be proved by the plaintiff so they must relate directly to the letter of advice which confirms the client's instructions. If there is any area of doubt it is vital that further instructions are obtained from the client.

Material fact (e) included in particular (f).

9   This is to establish causation; that the breach of the duty of care alleged in para 3 actually caused injury and loss. There are a number of ways of pleading causation, the important elements to include are: that the plaintiff suffered the loss, injury and damage pleaded and the loss was caused by the negligent acts pleaded.

Material fact (f) included here.

10   This is the pleading which sets out for the district judge and the defendants the matters to consider when deciding the figure to award for general damages.

Under CCR Ord 6 r1(5)(a) a medical report must be served with the particulars of claim. This is defined under CCR Ord 6 r1(7) as 'a report substantiating all the personal injuries alleged in the particulars of claim which the plaintiff proposes to adduce in evidence as part of his case at trial'. It can be annexed to the pleading by using words like:

The Plaintiff's injuries are set out in the medical report served herewith in compliance with Order 6 rule 1(5)(a) of the County Court Rules.

This will be sufficient if the medical report is completely comprehensive. However it may be necessary to add information which is not addressed by the consultant or GP in the medical report. For example, the doctor may not have stated the plaintiff could not follow a hobby while ill. To bring evidence to show this loss, this information must be included in the pleading and it is usual to do this under the particulars of injury.

The object of the particulars of injury is to give a general idea of the seriousness of the case and to include the information required under the rules. These include the plaintiff's age, and features that are special to each particular plaintiff. Here the special features are how the loss of the use of her right arm at work and at home has affected the plaintiff. The fact that the plaintiff made a good recovery will be shown in the medical report and need not be pleaded in this particular case.

11   These are the plaintiff's quantifiable losses that directly relate to the accident. All special damages that are pleaded need to have figures attached to them. It is acceptable that, if these figures are not available when the summons has to be issued, they can be supplied at a later date.

A schedule of special damages is required under CCR Ord 6 r1(5)(b) and is defined under CCR Ord 6 r1(7) as, 'a statement giving full particulars of the special damages claimed for expenses and losses already incurred and an estimate of any future expenses and losses (including loss of earnings and of pension rights)'. There is no set form for the schedule which must be served with the particulars of claim.

The schedule can be annexed to the pleading with words such as:

The Plaintiff's losses are set out in the Statement of Special Damages served herewith in compliance with Order 6 rule 1(5)(b) of the County Court Rules.

If the list of losses is not very long, it is accepted practice to list them directly in the particulars of claim as shown here. It is important that the plaintiff keeps receipts to prove the special damages claimed.

12 Since the introduction of the Social Security Administration Act 1992 it is no longer necessary to put into the pleading the amount of money that the plaintiff has received from DSS. Section 81(5) of the Act makes it a general rule that the court should leave benefits out of account when assessing damages. If the plaintiff succeeds in her action and receives over £2,500 a deduction will be made by the Compensation Recovery Unit and a certificate must be issued before she is entitled to receive her damages.

However if she recovers £2,500 or less, the DSS does not under reg 3 Social Security (Recoupment) Regulations 1990 have the power to recover the social security payments made to her. The defendant however is at liberty to deduct the amount she has received from the DSS from the damages it is ordered to pay.

Material Fact (h) included here.

13 *Interest* must be specifically pleaded: CCR Ord 6 r1A. There are a number of views on how to plead interest and variations can be found throughout this book. But in an unliquidated claim, as here when general damages are claimed for injury etc, the court does not require a calculation of the interest. If successful the plaintiff will be entitled to interest on both special and general damages.

Under s 69 County Courts Act 1984 the judge has wide discretion to award interest for such period and at such a rate as he thinks fit. The usual rule is that 2% is awarded on general damages from the date of issue of the summons. Interest on special damages is usually calculated at half the 'special account rate', currently 8% from the date of the accident. If, however, as here, the special damages have ceased to accrue, there are strong reasons to argue for the full special account rate.

14 The *prayer* sums up the remedies the plaintiff wishes the court to grant against any or all of the defendants. It has be included in the pleading: CCR Ord 6 r1(1). It is possible to take the view that the case against both defendants is properly pleaded and there is no point in reiterating that both the First and/or the Second Defendant are both held to be liable (as is pleaded here). This is a personal decision. An alternative pleading would name only 'the Defendants'.

15 In the county court it is sometimes desirable to limit the amount of damages claimed to avoid increasing the costs of the case should the plaintiff lose the action. If the claim will not exceed £3,000, and if the pleading is so limited in the prayer with such words as 'Damages limited to £3,000.00' it will mean that if the plaintiff loses she will only have to pay costs on Scale 1, not the more expensive Scale 2. The scale of the costs, ie the amount a solicitor is entitled to charge for each procedure, is listed in the *Green Book*.

It is not advisable to limit the claim in this pleading since the special damages claim is for £2,545, and this takes no account of the general damages that the plaintiff hopes to be awarded for her pain and suffering.

16 Claiming costs is not strictly necessary, RSC Ord 18 r6, but it is sometimes included to warn the defendant that contesting cases in court is expensive. If you consider this tactically desirable, it should be claimed after interest in the prayer.

17 *Signature* of particulars and the address for service is mandatory and the rules are in CCR Ord 6 r8. Some courts accept a rubber stamp and under CCR Ord 50 r6A an acceptable signature is one printed by computer or other mechanical means.

18 The date of the pleading is inserted by the court if it is issuing and serving proceedings by post, or by instructed solicitor if the firm is effecting service. It is an important part of the pleading, because the plaintiff can obtain judgment in default if the defendant does not respond to the summons within 14 days after the service of the summons: CCR Ord 9 r6(1).

Defending the action

The defendants' story

Mr Andrews will say that he was aware that Mrs Simpson was standing outside the shop looking at the goods for sale in the shop window. He was told by his employer, the boss of Electric City, to go and start unloading the van while the van driver was talking to his employer inside the shop.

He had done this before on a number of occasions, and felt that there was no particular problem. He was not carrying boxes that he could not manage, and the reason that he fell and knocked Mrs Simpson down was that he tripped on a protruding paving stone. When he fell on Mrs Simpson, he did not hurt himself, but the new television set he was carrying was broken beyond repair.

He told all this to his employer after the accident and his employer took a photograph which clearly showed that the flagstone was protruding three inches. They both thought that the local authority, who were responsible for the upkeep of the pavement, caused the accident. After the accident his employer telephoned the town hall to complain and asked for the pavement to be repaired.

His employer had talked to his insurance company about Mrs Simpson's court action when he received a letter from Mrs Simpson's solicitors setting out her claim. The insurance company had given his employer the name and address of their solicitors and told him to forward any court documents to them. If Mrs Simpson took the claim to court, they would file a defence.

Checklist for drafting the defence

The most important rule in drafting a defence is to: **ensure every material allegation in the statement of claim has been pleaded to**. This is because unless an allegation of fact is specifically denied or not admitted it is deemed by the court to be admitted: RSC Ord 18 r13(1).

The county court does not have rules that contain an equivalent provision, but by s 76 County Courts Act 1984 these provisions apply in both the High Court and the county court.

The three basic ways of dealing with an allegation are:

- admit it – but limit its scope to matters not in contention.
- deny it – if it is disputed and there is evidence to show the defendant's side of the story.
- not admit it – if the defendant has no evidence to rebut the allegation and wishes the plaintiff to prove it.

There is a full explanation of the rules governing drafting defences in Chapter 3 and these should be looked at again before attempting to draft a defence.

Finally, it is important to remember that a defence must both tell the defendant's story and deny, admit or not admit the alleged facts set out in the plaintiff's particulars of claim.

Structure for drafting the defence

Having received these instructions from Mr Andrews, the solicitor must now draft a document that tells both defendants' side of the story to the judge and to the plaintiff.

The kernel of the defendants' story is:

1   the first defendant saw the plaintiff standing outside the shop before the accident;
2   he was employed by the shop at the time of the accident and was unloading the van on the instructions of his employer;
3   he fell and knocked Mrs Simpson down;
4   when he fell he broke the new television set he was carrying but he did not hurt himself because he landed on Mrs Simpson;
5   he fell because he tripped on a protruding paving stone;
6   the local authority, which has responsibility for the upkeep of the pavements, was responsible for his accident and therefore for the injury to Mrs Simpson.

Bearing these factors in mind, the defence lawyer in this case has to draft a defence that will:

- admit that Mr Andrews saw Mrs Simpson standing outside the shop;
- admit he was working as an employee at the time of the accident;
- admit he fell and knocked down Mrs Simpson;
- claim he fell because of the negligence of a third party, the local authority;
- claim Mrs Simpson's injury was therefore not caused by Mr Andrews' fault but the fault of the local authority.

The defence lawyer will also have to draft a third party notice to join the third party in the proceedings. In that third party notice will be a claim for the costs of the television set broken when Mr Andrews fell onto Mrs Simpson. This draft and an explanation will follow after the draft defence.

Sample defence

IN THE WESTCHESTER COUNTY COURT [1]   Case No WC631234 [2]

BETWEEN

<table>
<tr><td></td><td>JANET SIMPSON</td><td>Plaintiff</td></tr>
<tr><td></td><td>and</td><td></td></tr>
<tr><td></td><td>(1) MICHAEL ANDREWS</td><td></td></tr>
<tr><td></td><td>(2) ELECTRIC CITY (a firm)</td><td>Defendants</td></tr>
<tr><td></td><td>and</td><td></td></tr>
<tr><td></td><td>WESTCHESTER DISTRICT COUNCIL</td><td>Third Party [3]</td></tr>
</table>

DEFENCE

1. Paragraphs 1 and 2 of the Particulars of Claim are admitted. [4]

2. It is denied that the First Defendant was negligent as alleged in paragraph 3 of the Particulars of Claim or at all. It is further denied that the said accident was caused by any negligence on the part of the First Defendant. [5]

3. The alleged accident was caused or contributed to by the uneven surface of the pavement which caused the First Defendant to trip, fall onto the Plaintiff, and so damage the new television set he was carrying. [6]

4. The uneven surface of the pavement, and accordingly the accident, was caused by or contributed to by the negligence of the Third Party, their servants or agents who were, at all material times, responsible for the upkeep of the pavements in the borough [7] including the pavement outside 23 High Street, Westchester ('the pavement'). [8]

PARTICULARS OF NEGLIGENCE [9]

(a) Causing or permitting the pavement to be and/or remain in disrepair so that it was not reasonably safe for use by the First Defendant.

(b) Allowing at all material times a paving slab to protrude three inches above the surface of the pavement.

(c) Failing to give any or any adequate warning to the First Defendant of the unsafe condition of the pavement.

5. No admission is made as to the alleged or any pain, injury, loss or damage suffered by the Plaintiff or as to the amount thereof. [10]

Raspberry & Apple [11]
10 Station Road
Westchester

Dated etc [12]

Notes

1   When the defendant files a defence, the court will automatically transfer the case to the county court serving the district where the defendant lives: CCR Ord 9 r2(8).

2   Case number will remain for the duration of the case. It consists of a two-letter court identifier, a single number identifying the year and five further numbers. This number will stay with the case even if the case is transferred to a new court.

3   The defendants' instructions are that another party is responsible for part, if not all, of the damages and loss caused by the accident. The third party must therefore be brought into the case. Details of how and why this is done is explained on p 198 following these notes on this draft defence.

4   The possibilities are to admit or not admit the facts alleged in paras 1 and 2 of the particulars of claim. There is nothing in the instructions which indicates there is evidence to deny the facts alleged. Further there is nothing which the defendant disagrees with in these paragraphs. The bold action is to admit them, so the plaintiff is not put to the expense of proving it. The costs of that might have to be met by the defendants should the defence fail. If there is any doubt seek further instructions. In this case there may be problems because there are no instructions from the first defendant's employers.

It makes for a clear and simple pleading to join the admissions of para 1 and 2 of the particulars of claim into one paragraph in the defence.

5   The first sentence is a straightforward denial of the plaintiff's allegation of negligence. The second sentence denies the causation; the defendants state they did not cause the accident by their alleged negligence.

6   The defendants' side of the story is now introduced. The drafting should follow the structure of a particulars of claim and must

include the defendants' material facts that will be supported by their evidence.

If the case goes to trial, the judge will apportion blame and damages between the defendants if he finds in favour of the plaintiff. From the facts so far disclosed, it seems likely that the local authority would only be liable for some of the losses claimed by Mrs Simpson since Mr Andrews couldn't see where he was going. Therefore the correct method of pleading is to claim that the accident was caused by, as well as 'contributed to' by the local authority. The right to a contribution is a statutory right under s 1 Civil Liability (Contribution) Act 1978.

7   This establishes the defendants' claim in negligence against the third party and alleges both the duty of care of the third party, the breach of the duty and the fact that the breach caused the accident. This statement contains all the elements of the claim in tort that the defendants propose to advance against the local authority. Further details of these elements are found in the third party notice on p 200 which is served together with the particulars of claim and the defence on the third party, the Westchester County Court and the Plaintiffs.

This claim is included in the defence to give notice to the plaintiff of the way in which the defendants wish their claim and defence to proceed. It is in theory possible for the defendants to start a new action against the local authority, but it saves money and court time to combine cases where the claim is based on the same incident. The defence therefore, as well as defending the plaintiff's action, gives notice to the third party of their involvement, and the case they have to meet.

8   Since the allegation of negligence by the defendants against the third party refers to a specific paving stone in a specific pavement it is useful here to use the device of ('the pavement'). This is defined when first referred to in the pleadings and the short form is added at the end of the definition in quotation marks and brackets. Thereafter, throughout the pleadings, the word can be used without quotation marks or brackets and will be regarded as referring to the originally defined term.

9   Particulars of negligence are structured in the same way as particulars in a statement of claim and set out the alleged breaches of the duty of care, in this case owed by the local authority to the defendant. Here the allegations concern one omission (particular (b)) and two negligent acts (particular (a) and particular (c)) by the third party which resulted in the breach. These are again

particularised in full in the third party notice on p 200. The third
party notice contains all the allegations that the third party has to
meet and defend.

10 Because the defendant has no knowledge of the allegations of loss
and damage in para 4 of the particulars of claim, he does not admit
them and leaves the plaintiff to prove them at trial. However, it is
important to remember that the amount of the damages and loss is
deemed to be admitted unless specifically denied or not admitted
as in the defence.

It is not necessary to admit or deny or not admit para 5 of the
particulars of claim. This is because the plaintiff has a statutory
right to interest if she is awarded damages. The award of interest is
in the discretion of the judge and is therefore not relevant to
pleading a defence.

11 Signature and service address of the defendants' solicitor.

12 The date must be set out as in the particulars of claim.

Third party proceedings

Because the defendants' instructions are that someone else was
responsible for the accident, the solicitor must ensure that the clients, if
found liable to pay damages and costs to the plaintiff, will be able to
claim them from the person they consider caused the accident.

They must therefore, as well as drafting and filing a defence, issue a
third party notice which in this case is addressed to the local authority.
Under this third party notice, the defendants can claim a contribution
or an indemnity from the third party.

An indemnity is a claim for the recovery of all the damages and
costs which may be awarded against the defendants. A contribution is
for the proportion of the damages that the court considers is the
responsibility of the third party.

Because the defendants claim that they, as well as the plaintiff,
suffered loss because of the third party's negligence, they will include
in their third party notice a claim for damages for the cost of replacing
the broken television.

Once a third party notice is issued, the third party is in the position
of being the defendant to the defendant in the main action. To defend
his position, he must therefore serve a defence to the third party notice.

This diagram shows the relationships between the parties at the time of the issue of third party proceedings.

A. Main action: JANET SIMPSON   <u>Plaintiff</u>
                                    and
                  (1) MICHAEL ANDREWS
                  (2) ELECTRIC CITY (a firm)   <u>Defendants</u>

B. Third party action:
                  (1) MICHAEL ANDREWS
                  (2) ELECTRIC CITY (a firm)   <u>Defendants</u>
                                    and
         WESTCHESTER DISTRICT COUNCIL   <u>Third Party</u>

The rules governing third party proceedings are under CCR Ord 12. This gives the correct procedure to be followed before a third party notice can be issued and served on the third party.

In this particular case a third party notice can be issued and served without the leave or permission of the court. This is because automatic directions are now followed in personal injury cases, and so leave of the court will not be required under CCR Ord 12 r1(2)(c) in this case before a third party notice is issued. The reason for this is that the defence will issue and serve the third party notice with the defence, and therefore pleadings will not have closed. Under automatic directions, pleadings close 14 days after the delivery of a defence: CCR Ord 17 r11(11)(a).

Leave is however required under CCR Ord 12 r2 in a fixed date action (as a possession case) or in a default action when a pre-trial review date has been set and, of course, when pleadings are closed.

The defendants must serve the third party notice together with the defence on the plaintiff, and on the court. They must also serve these two documents, together with a copy of the summons and a copy of the particulars of claim, on the third party. This ensures that the third party is fully informed of all the previous pleadings and knows the case that he has to meet and defend.

Printed is an example of a third party notice and an explanation of its content.

Sample third party notice

IN THE WESTCHESTER COUNTY COURT   **Case No: WC631234**

BETWEEN

JANET SIMPSON   <u>Plaintiff</u>

and

(1) MICHAEL ANDREWS

(2) ELECTRIC CITY (a firm)   <u>Defendants</u>

and

WESTCHESTER DISTRICT COUNCIL   <u>Third Party</u> [1]

THIRD PARTY NOTICE [2]

TO THE THIRD PARTY, WESTCHESTER DISTRICT COUNCIL of Crown House, 331–335 High Street, Westchester WPC 2DG

TAKE NOTICE that this action has been brought by the Plaintiff against the Defendants. In it the Plaintiff claims against the Defendants damages arising out of an accident on 24 May 1995 as appears from the Particulars of Claim a copy of which is served herewith.

The Defendants deny that they are liable to the Plaintiff as appears from their Defence, a copy whereof is served herewith, but if contrary to that contention the Defendants are found liable to the Plaintiff, the Defendants claim against you to be indemnified against the Plaintiff's claim and the costs of this action, alternatively they claim a contribution to such extent as is deemed just. [3]

AND the Defendants' claim against you is made on the following grounds: [4]

1. At the time of the said accident you were responsible for the safe condition of the pavement. [5]

2. The surface of the pavement was uneven at all material times. [6]

3. The First Defendant tripped on a paving slab that was three inches above the surface of the surrounding pavement and fell onto the Plaintiff. [7] The condition of the pavement therefore caused or contributed to the Plaintiff's accident. [8]

4. At the time of the accident the First Defendant was carrying a new boxed television set. When the First Defendant tripped on the pavement, knocking down the Plaintiff, he fell and damaged the said television set beyond repair. [9]

5. The matters complained of by the Plaintiff were caused wholly or in part or contributed to by the negligence of yourself, your servants or agents in not carrying out repairs to the said pavement. [10]

6. By reason of the matters aforesaid, the Defendants have suffered loss and damage. [11]

PARTICULARS OF SPECIAL DAMAGE

Cost of replacement for Sommi CDE Super
Television set damaged beyond repair   £500.00

7. Further the Defendants will claim interest pursuant to section 69 of the County Courts Act 1984 on all sums awarded at such rate or rates for such period or periods as the Court may think fit.

AND the Defendants claim: [12]

(1) An indemnity or contribution in respect of the Plaintiff's claim, any costs which the Defendants may be ordered to pay to the Plaintiff, and any costs incurred by the Defendants in defending the Plaintiff's claim. [13]

(2) Damages.

(3) The aforesaid interest.

If you dispute the Plaintiff's claim against the Defendants or the Defendants' claim against you, you must within 14 days after the service of this notice upon you take or send to the Court two copies of your defence.

AND TAKE NOTICE that you should attend at

on   at   o'clock when directions will be given for the further conduct of these proceedings. [14]

If you fail to attend you may be deemed to admit:

(1) The Plaintiff's claim against the Defendants; and

(2) The Defendants' claim against you; and

(3) Your liability to contribute to the extent claimed or indemnify the Defendants; and

(4) The Defendants' right to relief or remedy claimed in paragraph (3) hereabove; and

(5) The validity of any judgment in the action:

And you will be bound by the judgment in the action.

Raspberry & Apple
10 Station Road
Westchester

Dated etc

Notes

1 *Heading*: parties, case number and court name are the same as in the particulars of claim and the defence.

2 *Third party notice* is the notice that informs the third party and the plaintiff of the allegations of the defendants that they have to meet. In the *Green Book*, Form N 15 gives guidance as what this notice should contain. It is however acceptable to the court to adapt it to suit the defendant's particular case as has been done here.

3 *Indemnity or contribution* are both claimed because at the point of drafting the third party notice, the defendants do not know which they will be awarded. They will not be penalised for claiming both, but if they claim only one remedy, and the judge, after deciding on liability, feels another remedy is more suitable, he will not be in a position to award it at the trial if it is not within the pleadings.

4 *Defendants' claim* is similar in structure to a plaintiff's particulars of claim.

5 The defendants state that the third party owes them a duty of care. The standard of care is that the pavements must be safe. It is not desirable to detail why a local authority owes pedestrians a duty of care. There are a number of cases that could be brought to the court's attention, should this be the form of defence taken by the local authority. This is an example of the basic rule – do not plead law.

Breach of statutory duty is not pleaded because the writers did not want to confuse readers by pleading two causes of action.

6 This is pleading the material fact that the pavement was uneven that is relied on by Mr Andrews and his employer to found their claim. This goes to the breach of the standard of care. Note the use of the shorthand words 'at all material times' which saves

repetition of the date and time of the accident. This claim is further referred to in paras 2 and 3 of the defence.

7   The first sentence refers to point 5 on p 194 which gives the kernel of the Mr Andrews' case. This is the material fact that must be pleaded to show the breach of duty of care.

8   The second sentence pleads causation; that the negligence of the local authority caused both the accident to the plaintiff as well as to the defendant, Mr Andrews.

9   This is split from para 3 because it refers to the background of the loss caused to the defendants by the incident. Details of the loss are particularised in para 6.

10 This is a fairly standard paragraph which pleads breach of the duty of care by the local authority. Because a local authority cannot itself perform any actions, except through its employees, members or councillors, it is necessary to use the words 'servants or agents' in this pleading.

11 This claims that as a result of the breach, the defendants have suffered loss, and details under the particulars of special damage the actual item and value of the damaged item. There is no claim for general damages because Mr Andrews was not hurt in the accident. See note 4 of Mr Andrews' instructions on p194.

12 *The prayer* is similar to the prayer in a plaintiff's particulars of claim in that the defendants are claiming damages and interest on the damages. It is not strictly necessary to include a prayer in a county court third party notice. It has been included here to reflect the defendants' claim for interest on the cost of the damaged television.

13 But here the defendants also claim for a contribution or an indemnity from the third party, because if they are found liable to the plaintiff at the trial, they want total or partial financial relief from the third party.

14 *Notice of hearing* is completed by the court staff when the third party notice is served on the court. They will seal the third party notice and fix a time and a date for a pre-trial review and will serve the dated notices by first class post on the plaintiff, the defendants and the third party.

15 *Failure to attend pre-trial review hearing* can be treated as an admission. Therefore the third party notice must indicate what can happen if the third party does not attend the pre-trial review.

The position of the plaintiff

Joining the local authority as another defendant

Once the defendants have served the third party notice on the plaintiff, Mrs Simpson should consider her position. The serving of the third party notice on the local authority does not make the local authority a party to the proceedings between herself and the defendants. But it does mean that at the trial, the issue of liability as between the defendants and the third party will be dealt with by the judge. Mrs Simpson on the advice of her solicitors must decide if she feels she needs to bring the third party directly into her action by joining them as another defendant.

The risk of not doing so is that if the third party is found wholly to blame for the accident, the defendants would not be held liable at the trial. The plaintiff would have no direct claim on the third party and would therefore lose her case and have to start a new action against the original third party.

This would not only be costly, but might bring additional problems if the limitation period had passed by the time of the trial.

The plaintiff will also have to bear in mind, in making her decision, that joining the third party into her action could mean that if she loses her case, she will be liable for the costs of the defendants as well as that of the third party.

Because of the risk of completely losing her case if the third party is found solely liable, it is likely that in this case Mrs Simpson will instruct her solicitor to join the local authority as a third defendant at the time of the pre-trial review.

Continuing the claim

At this point it should be obvious that what appeared to be a simple claim for damages which would probably not exceed £5,000 looks like becoming complicated. As a result it could be an expensive case for the plaintiff should she want to continue the action.

This point must be brought to her attention by the solicitors instructed by Mrs Simpson, and she will probably be asked to provide more money if she wishes to continue her claim. That decision is of course for her to make, but those advising her must bear in mind the Written Professional Standards issued by the Law Society referred to on p 184.

Question for self-testing

One of the most frequent tort claims in the county court is for damages for personal injury arising from a car accident. It is therefore a claim that you will be expected to draft early in your career or training. Below are simple details of a straightforward accident where there is no problem about liability. The only question for the court to decide will be as to the amount of damages that the plaintiff will be awarded.

You may wonder why these cases go to court. The answer is that defendants do not pay damages willingly, and insurance companies, the most frequent defendant, will not settle a case until proceedings are issued.

You will issue proceedings on Form N2, a copy of which is on p 14. You are unlikely to be able to fit the particulars of claim on the form in the box provided. It is therefore quite in order to complete the box which is headed 'Particulars of the plaintiff's claim against you' with the words 'See particulars of claim attached'.

An example of a particulars of claim that could be used to start proceedings in this case will be found on p 207.

The facts

James Johnson was driving his girlfriend, Belinda Blue, home after a night out. James's car was a Ford Sierra, registration number H708 ABD. It was a company car. The time of the accident was about 11.30 pm and it happened on the wet and windy night of 25 September 1995.

James had stopped at the traffic lights at the junction of Maze Road and North End Road in Westchester. He was stationary on Maze Road and was facing in an easterly direction. A lorry which bore on its side and front the name of 'Robert Taggart & Sons' drove into the back of his car causing considerable damage to the car. The driver gave his name as Ian Williams.

As a result of the accident, James was badly bruised and took two weeks off work for which he was paid by his company. He has had no further medical problems. His company gave him another car while the Sierra was repaired.

Belinda was not so fortunate. She was in considerable pain the day after the accident and went to her GP who referred her to physiotherapy, after telling her that she was probably suffering from whiplash. She went to hospital on 10 occasions for physiotherapy and wore a neck brace for three weeks.

She went back to work after three weeks and her firm paid her in full in her absence. She continued to have shooting pains in her neck and the upper part of her back for about six months after the accident. She found the neck brace uncomfortable to wear and found it difficult to sleep and relax because of the pain. She now wishes to sue for compensation.

The police did not go to the scene of the accident, and no criminal action was taken against Ian Williams following this accident.

Draft the particulars of claim on the basis that the driver was not convicted of any offence as a result of the accident.

Sample particulars of claim for whiplash injury

IN THE WESTCHESTER COUNTY COURT   **Case No**

BETWEEN

BELINDA BLUE   <u>Plaintiff</u>

and

IAN WILLIAMS   <u>First Defendant</u>

and

ROBERT TAGGART & SONS LIMITED [1]   <u>Second Defendant</u>

PARTICULARS OF CLAIM

1. On 25 September 1995 the Plaintiff was the passenger in a Ford Sierra motor car, registration number H708 ABD which was stationary at the traffic lights at Maze Road, Westchester when the First Defendant drove his motor lorry registration number K123 LMN into the rear of the said Ford Sierra.

2. At all material times the First Defendant was the servant of the Second Defendant Company, and was driving the said motor lorry in the course of his employment. [2]

3. The said collision was caused by the negligence of the First Defendant.

PARTICULARS OF NEGLIGENCE

The First Defendant was negligent in that he:

(a) Drove into the back of the stationary Ford Sierra.

(b) Failed to keep any or any proper lookout.

(c) Drove too fast.

(d) Drove too close to the vehicle in front of him.

(e) Failed to brake in time or at all.

(f) Failed to stop, slow down, swerve, or in any other way so to manage or control the motor lorry as to prevent the collision. [3]

4. By reason of the First Defendant's negligence, the Plaintiff, who was 26 years of age at the time of the accident, suffered personal injury, loss and damage.

PARTICULARS OF PERSONAL INJURY

The Plaintiff suffered whiplash injury together with bruising and shock. She was treated by her GP and referred for a physiotherapy programme to Westchester Hospital. She attended hospital on 10 occasions and wore a neck collar for the first 3 weeks which she found uncomfortable. She continued to suffer pains in her neck and back for 6 months after the collision. The Plaintiff will rely, *inter alia*, on the report of Dr Smith dated 11th March 1996, a copy of which is annexed hereto. 4

PARTICULARS OF LOSS AND DAMAGE

(a)	Cost of painkillers		£5.00
(b)	Cost of travel to hospital, doctor and physiotherapy		£15.00
		TOTAL	£20.00

5. The Plaintiff further claims interest on such damages as may be awarded to her, at such a rate and for such a period as the Court may deem fit, pursuant to section 69 of the County Courts Act 1984.

AND the Plaintiff claims against the First and/or the Second Defendants:

(1) Damages;

(2) Interest as aforesaid;

(3) Costs.

James Joyce & Co
15 High Street
Westchester
Solicitors for
the Plaintiff

Dated etc

Notes

1 Before you issue a summons, it is sensible to do a company search to find the correct name of the defendant company, the registered office (for service of the summons) and the financial status of the company (for payment of damages).

2 From instructions from the client, you cannot assume that Ian Williams was an employee of the firm. If the assumption in the

pleading, at para 2, proves incorrect it can be later amended. It is more difficult to add a new party to a pleading (because leave is required) than to amend the contents of the pleading.

3   It is important to put in particulars of all the negligence that you can visualise. This is because it may be that the defendant can prove at trial that he did not fail to keep any or any proper lookout (particular (b)). This could have been because the weather was so awful that his visibility might have been obscured.

    If you fail to put in all the details of the negligence at the time of the issue of the summons, it is expensive to rectify these mistakes at a later date.

4   In a claim such as this, a medical report of the GP will be of sufficient status to annex to this summons. In more serious cases, a report from a consultant would be required. This is because the defendant will insist that the plaintiff is examined by his expert, and both experts will probably be called as witnesses.

Time spent drafting a summons or a writ is always time well spent, because this is the document that must state the plaintiff's total case and the issues to be resolved by the court.

Chapter 9

A Fatal Accident Claim

A fatal accident claim could be one of the most difficult cases that you have to plead. This is not because of the difficulty of drafting the statement of claim but because you will need to do extensive legal research and may have difficulty in estimating the damages that the surviving dependants are likely to recover.

The rules on pleading are largely based on two Acts: the Fatal Accidents Act 1976 (as amended) and the Law Reform (Miscellaneous Provisions) Act 1934. The most useful book for legal research on the damages recoverable for personal injuries and death is *The Quantum of Damages* by Kemp and Kemp.

The law

Under s 1 Fatal Accidents Act 1976, the dependants of the deceased have a right of action for damages. By s 1 Law Reform (Miscellaneous Provisions) Act 1934, the estate of the deceased also has a right to an action for damages. These two actions are combined in pleadings under RSC Ord 15 r1 (relief against the same defendant in respect of more than one cause of action).

Claims for loss and damage by the estate between injury and death pose particular research problems. This is because many of the cases cited in the law reports relate to deaths which occurred before 1 January 1983. Before that date, damages for expectation of life, as well as for continuing loss of earnings before and after the death of the deceased, were recoverable under the Law Reform (Miscellaneous Provisions) Act 1934. Cited cases therefore do not distinguish between the claims for damages and loss before and after death.

But when deaths have occurred after 1 January 1983, claims for loss and damage after death have to be brought under the Fatal Accidents Act 1976. But claims for loss and damage before death continue to be brought under the Law Reform (Miscellaneous Provisions) Act 1934.

Method of calculation

Before any calculations as to losses can be made, it will be up to the legal advisor to assess two vital figures. These are the *multiplicand* and the *multiplier*.

The multiplicand

This is the annual sum of money that the dependant survivors will lose because of the death. The most important constituent will be the earnings of the deceased. However, not all the earnings would have gone to the survivors and the judges have used a number of different ways to calculate this figure. This is called the multiplicand.

One method of arriving at this figure is by calculating the money spent yearly by the deceased on the dependant survivors before his death. This involves considerable work in looking up details of old bills, many of which are often not available.

But the most popular calculation now appears to be expressing the dependency of the survivors as a percentage of the deceased's income. It is fairly common, for example, to hold that the surviving spouse and children, who were supported by the deceased, were 75% dependant. This assumes that the deceased spent 25% of his income on himself. The multiplicand would therefore be 75% of the deceased's net annual income.

There have been attempts to persuade the courts to adjust the figures to reflect inflation. This has been consistently resisted by the superior courts and the Court of Appeal again rejected this in *Auty v National Coal Board* (1985).

The multiplier

The multiplicand, a yearly figure, must be multiplied by another figure to produce a global figure that reflects the dependants' total loss of support on the death of the deceased.

The starting point in the calculation of the multiplier is the number of years that it is contemplated that the plaintiff dependant will incur this loss.

The court seeks, in calculating the multiplier, to arrive at a capital sum (the multiplicand x (times) the multiplier) which would purchase an annuity to provide the lost income for the survivors. The figure reached therefore will take into account the fact that the survivors receive the sum immediately, not over a long period of time.

This figure is assessed at the date of death of the deceased, not the date of trial. The most important factors in assessing the multiplier are the age and expectation of working life of the deceased. The future prospects of the deceased, if he had not been killed, will also affect the multiplier. If he had good prospects of achieving promotion and salary increases the court will apply a higher multiplier.

The modern practice of judges is to state in any particular case the value of the dependency and the multiplier adopted. Thus it is possible, with legal research, to analyse cases and advise clients of the likely multiplier and a multiplicand. Before finally arriving at the estimated figure for damages recoverable, the researcher must use the inflation tables in *Kemp and Kemp* to estimate the current value of the award.

Any advice given to clients should be heavily qualified because each case is decided on its own particular facts and in any event different judges may arrive at different figures.

Evidence of the client

This is the information taken by the instructing solicitor that counsel will be given to enable him or her to draft the pleadings, or advise on quantum or liability as requested by the solicitor.

Statement by Mr Ramsey

Taken: 6 December 1995

My name is Alfred George Ramsey, I was born on 12 November 1955 and live at 3, The Drive, Northam. I work for the Sun Provident Assurance Company as a claims assessor and earn £25,000 a year (gross), £22,000 a year (net). I have worked there for 15 years.

My deceased wife Rebecca Jane was born on 13 August 1962. We have two children:

Richard Alfred Ramsey, dob 11.8.82

Sarah Rebecca Ramsey, dob 1.3.86

Both the children attend local schools, and Richard hopes to go to university to study transportation.

My wife was a clerk at the Sun Provident before our marriage, but has not worked since the children were born. She felt her job was to be at home and look after us. She was a very good and careful housewife and managed the family income. She did most of the redecorating, all the cooking, all the washing, cleaning and gardening. She took the children to and from school each day and to and from their after-school activities. She also supervised their homework. It is impossible for me to say how much the children and I miss her.

She had planned to go back to work when Sarah was 14. Sun Provident wanted to offer her a job and hoped to retrain her in IT.

She was knocked down on a pedestrian crossing on 1 September 1994 and as a result of her injuries died just over three months later on 5 December 1994. From the time of the accident until her death she was in St George's Hospital, Northam and there underwent a number of operations to try to save her life. She had not made a will before the accident, and afterwards she was too ill for me to talk to her about it. My solicitor arranged for me to take out letters of administration.

The driver of the Vauxhall Astra who knocked her down was Mr Joseph Agnew who lives at 22 Main Road, Northam. He was convicted of careless driving at Northam Magistrates' Court on 14 July 1995. I went to the court hearing and heard evidence from Mr Agnew and his passenger that my wife had rushed out in front of them and not given them time to stop. My wife was a very careful woman and I don't think that is at all likely.

I have had great difficulty managing to keep my home together without my wife. There are no members of either my own family or Rebecca's, who can help me look after the children. My employers have been very good to me, but I have had to employ Janet Roe for 25 hours a week since 30 September 1994 to cook for us, clean the house, do the ironing and look after the children after school and in the holidays. I pay her £3 an hour which comes to £75 a week.

I have also paid £1,250 for the cost of Rebecca's funeral.

I now wish to start proceedings to help me with this financial burden and I would like advice as to how much the court is likely to award me and the children.

The draft advice

It is usual for the solicitor to instruct counsel to advise the client in fatal accident cases. This is because counsel will provide continuity by drafting the pleadings and also representing the client at the hearing. The advice that Mr Ramsey requests in this case is called 'Advice on quantum' or 'Advice'.

There are a number of ways that counsel will draft the advice and there are no rules of the court to look to, since the advice is a privileged document and does not have to be disclosed on discovery. However, when drafting an advice on quantum, the most important thing to remember is to whom the advice is addressed. In this case, it is to Mr Ramsey, who wants actual real figures, and instructing solicitor who needs to be up-dated on the legal issues and possibly also needs to know if counsel needs any additional evidence.

A draft statement of claim and an explanation of the pleadings in the statement of claim follows the advice. It is usual for a barrister to draft the statement of claim as well as the advice.

The advice may be needed by the Legal Aid Board in order for them to decide on the grant or refusal of a legal aid certificate. It also serves as an opinion for the client and the solicitor as to the likely success of the claim and an estimate of the damages that will be awarded.

The date of the advice on quantum is also important. The figures given will reflect the decisions reported by that date, and will not reflect later decisions, or later inflation. This advice is dated as at the middle of January 1996.

RE: REBECCA RAMSEY

ADVICE ON QUANTUM

1. I am asked to advise Mr Ramsey as to the quantum of damages that he can expect to be awarded by the court in respect of the very sad death of his wife. I understand that liability is in dispute only to the extent of a possible discount for contributory negligence which I have discussed in paragraph 29 below.

2. This tragic accident occurred when a car driven by Mr Joseph Agnew knocked down Mrs Ramsey on a pedestrian crossing on 1 September 1994. I am obliged to instructing solicitors for enclosing the medical report of Mr T Evans FRCS dated 18 August 1995, which sets out the injuries suffered by Mrs Ramsey, her treatment in the hospital, and information as to the cause of her death.

3. This report shows that Mrs Ramsey suffered a fracture to her skull causing severe concussion, and also fractures to several of her ribs and left arm and leg. She suffered severe loss of blood and substantial internal bleeding. Two operations were undertaken to relieve the pressure resulting from the fracture of her skull, but because of the nature of her original injuries they were unfortunately not successful and Mrs Ramsey died in St George's Hospital, Northam, on 5 December 1994.

Claim by the estate of Mrs Ramsey

4. My instructing solicitor is aware that there are two claims to be made in this case. The first claim, on behalf of the estate, will be under the Law Reform (Miscellaneous Provisions) Act 1934. This claim will be for special and general damages.

Special damages

5. The special damages will be:

(a)	funeral expenses	£1,250
(b)	damage to clothing	£200
(c)	cost of employment of help in the home from 30.9.94 to 5.12.94 @ £75 pw	£300
(d)	any other expenses which arose directly as a result of the accident (please advise)	[ ]

With regard to (d) above, I would ask you to let me know if payments have been made for any other expenses. I have in mind paid help from friends or extra travel if the children were cared for elsewhere before Janet Roe was employed.

General damages

6. The general damages are to compensate for the pain, suffering and loss of amenity suffered by Mrs Ramsey who was in great pain for 14 weeks before her death.

7. In *Stratford v BREL* (1990) the estate of a 74 year old man was awarded £18,000 for the pain and suffering from work-related cancer of the lungs. The length of time this reflected is difficult to estimate from the report, but it appears he had been under hospital treatment for three months before his death, and had consulted his doctor before he went to hospital.

8. In a similar case, *Mills v BREL* (1992), an award of £20,000 for 13 months' pain and suffering for a 61 year old man was reduced on appeal by the Court of Appeal to £15,000.

9. However, I would refer instructing solicitor to the helpful case of *Jefferson v Cape Insulation* (1981) where Farquharson J awarded £18,000 general damages. In this case the judge said that a major factor to be taken into account in assessing the general damages for pain and suffering were the prospects in the plaintiff's mind of being parted from her family. In particular he noted her great distress of leaving behind her young daughter.

10. The other end of the scale is an award of £750 general damages to the estate of a man who lived for 12 days after an accident though he was unconscious throughout this period. This is the case of *Davies v Hawes* (1990).

Level of general damages for the estate

11. In my opinion the likely award of general damages is between £15,000 and £20,000, but I am sure that instructing solicitor will draw to Mr Ramsey's attention the fact that these cases give guidelines only

and the judge may arrive at a different figure at trial. The special damages will be £1,750 plus any other specific items that Mr Ramsey recalls.

Claim by the dependants of Mrs Ramsey

12. The second claim will be on behalf of the dependants of Mrs Ramsey. These are her husband and her two children. This is a calculation of the financial loss that her husband and children will continue to suffer as a result of her death.

13. Before I consider in detail how this sum is arrived at, I would like to point out that Fatal Accidents Act claims depend so much upon their particular facts for assessment, and the figures I have arrived at are at best estimates and only to be used as guidance.

Assessment of claim

14. The technique used to arrive at an ultimate figure for loss under this heading is to assess a yearly total loss, and multiply that figure by the number of years during which that loss will be sustained. The figure for the number of years, the multiplier, is reduced to take into account that the dependants have the benefit of receiving a lump sum to cover present as well as future expenditure.

15. The only substantiated figure for the total loss that I have note of is the weekly figure of £75 that Mr Ramsey has paid to Janet Roe since the end of September 1994. This comes to £3,900 a year and is paid to help him look after his home and his children.

Decided cases

16. I have looked at past cases to take me further. Since as long ago as *Regan v Williamson* (1976) Watkins J expressed the view that the services to be brought into account should not be considered too narrowly and that it should be acknowledged that a housewife and mother was in virtually constant attendance upon her husband and children. He was prepared therefore in that case to put a value on services that could not be provided by another.

17. A recent example of an award under this head is *Re Wilson* (1992) where the two children of the deceased, who were aged seven and eight, were awarded £12,000 each for the loss of a mother's services. After her death they went to live with their father, who had been divorced from their mother prior to her death.

18. The most useful recently decided case is *Khan v Duncan* (1989). There, Mr Justice Popplewell arrived at a compensation figure of £5,000 a year for a mother's and wife's services with a reduction of £1,500 a year as the child got older. There was further, a final figure of

£500 a year, awarded for three years, for the dependency of Mr Khan alone, which was assessed to arise after the child was 18.

19. In *Khan v Duncan* (1989) the youngest and only dependant child was eight at the time of the accident. The judge agreed with the plaintiff that she would be a dependant for 10 years and therefore assessed the multiplier as seven. This seems a figure likely to be followed in this case.

Preliminary assessed figures

20. Basing my advice on these figures, I would assess that the dependency for the family until Sarah Ramsey is 18 would be at least £22,000. I would assess a further £1,500 would be awarded to Mr Ramsey, giving a total award of £23,500.

Further considerations

21. I would however like to bring to your attention the fact that my assessment based on Mr Khan's award may be on the low side. I have a number of reasons for coming to this conclusion.

Remarriage

Firstly, under s 3(3) of the Fatal Accidents Act 1976 (as amended) the courts were no longer to consider the widow's prospects of remarriage when arriving at a figure, but the statute did not consider the position of widowers such as Mr Ramsey.

23. However in *Stanley v Saddique* (1992) the Court of Appeal followed the statutory line and disregarded prospects of remarriage for a widower, though Popplewell J in *Khan v Duncan* (1989) indicated remarriage was a factor he took into account. Much will depend, I suspect, on the evidence as to how much of the household tasks Mrs Ramsey took over, the value to Mr Ramsey's career of his status as a married man, and his evidence as to whether he is contemplating remarriage.

Return to work

24. Secondly, there is also the probability of Mrs Ramsey returning to work at a later date. In *Regan v Williamson* (1975) the judge increased the dependency figure to take account of the deceased wife's future contributions and this sum should be included in an assessment of damages in this case.

Adjustment for inflation

25. The figure given in paragraph 20 above must be multiplied by 1.34 to allow for inflation since March 1989, the date of the decision in *Khan v Duncan*.

Level of general damages for dependants

26. I would therefore assess the total claim for general damages under this Act to between £30,000 and £35,000.

27. There is also in addition a claim for £7,500 which is the bereavement allowance granted under the Act. This has to apportioned by the court between Mr Ramsey and his children.

Will the two claims be granted in full?

28. I would like to point out that if Mrs Ramsey's estate is awarded damages for her pain and suffering, these will be taken into account when assessing damages under the Fatal Accidents Act claim. In the cases referred to in paragraphs 7 to 10 no deduction was made by the judges. They do, however, of course have the right to make such adjustments should the circumstances of the case dictate.

Contributory negligence

29. I see from Mr Ramsey's statement that there is some indication that the defendant will claim that Mrs Ramsey was in part responsible for the accident. At this point I am not in a position to judge the weight of this evidence. I would however like to point out to Mr Ramsey the procedure taken by the court when such an allegation is made.

It will firstly decide whether Mrs Ramsey was in any way responsible for the accident. Secondly, it will fix the contribution as a number, expressed as a percentage, and finally the damages awarded will be reduced by that figure. Should Mr Ramsey need further advice on this, I would need to see the police accident report and any other witness material that instructing solicitor possesses.

Conclusion

31. In conclusion, in my opinion the likely award of damages will be between £55,000 and £65,000. There could be a deduction in respect of contributory negligence, but upon this I am not yet in a position to advise. I can see no difficulty with proving liability. I would therefore advise commencing proceedings in the High Court without delay and would be happy to draft the statement of claim if so instructed.

32. Please do not hesitate to contact me if there is any further help I can give to yourself or to Mr Ramsey.

A Counsel

(signature)

10 Timber Court
Old Building
Temple EC4
14.1.96

Sample statement of claim

IN THE HIGH COURT OF JUSTICE [1]   **1996 R No** [3]
QUEEN'S BENCH DIVISION [2]

BETWEEN

ALFRED RAMSEY
(Widower and Administrator
of the Estate of Rebecca
Jane Ramsey deceased) [4]   Plaintiff
and
JOSEPH AGNEW   Defendant [5]

STATEMENT OF CLAIM [6]

1. The Plaintiff is the widower and administrator of the estate of Rebecca Jane Ramsey deceased ('the deceased'), letters of administration having been granted to him from the Northam District Registry on 6 October 1995, and he brings this action on behalf of the deceased's estate under the Law Reform (Miscellaneous Provisions) Act 1934 and for the benefit of her dependants under the Fatal Accidents Act 1976. [7]

2. On 1 September 1994 the deceased was crossing Lime Road, Northam on a pedestrian crossing when the Defendant drove his Vauxhall Astra car registration number H123 LMN in such a negligent manner that he ran into the deceased causing her a fatal injury. [8]

PARTICULARS OF NEGLIGENCE [9]

The Defendant was negligent in that he:

(a) Drove at a speed that was excessive in the circumstances.

(b) Failed to keep any or any proper look out for pedestrians.

(c) Failed to observe or heed the presence of the deceased on the road.

(d) Failed to give way to the deceased.

(e) Knocked down the deceased.

(f) Failed to stop, slow down, brake, swerve, or otherwise steer or control the motor car so as to avoid colliding with the deceased.

3. Further the Plaintiff intends in reliance on section 11 of the Civil Evidence Act 1968 to adduce evidence at trial that the Defendant was, on 14 July 1995 at Northam Magistrates' Court, convicted of careless driving contrary to section 3 of the Road Traffic Act 1988 as evidence of the negligence alleged in paragraph 2. [10]

4.[11] By reason of the matters aforesaid the deceased suffered pain and injury[12] in consequence of which she later died on 5 December 1994.[13] As a result of her death the deceased's estate and dependants have suffered loss and damage and the Plaintiff has suffered bereavement. [14]

PARTICULARS OF INJURY

[Sufficient particulars of the injuries would be inserted here.][15]

PARTICULARS PURSUANT TO STATUTE [16]

The claim herein under the Fatal Accidents Act 1976 is brought on behalf of the following dependants:

(a) The names of the persons for whose benefit the action is brought are:

The Plaintiff, who was born on 16 June 1955, widower of the deceased;

Richard Alfred Ramsey, born 11 August 1982, son of the deceased;

Sarah Rebecca Ramsey, born 1 March 1986, daughter of the deceased.

(b) the nature of the claim in respect of which damages are sought is:

At the time of her death the deceased was 34 years old. She enjoyed good health and lived a full and busy life. She was not employed and devoted her time to the care and welfare of her family. She did all the housework, cooking, cleaning, washing and other household chores for the family. She did most of the decorating in and outside the house and transported the children to and from school and to and from their after-school activities. In 2000 she intended to return to work as an insurance clerk working for her previous employers. Therefore from about the age of 40 the Plaintiff would have been financially dependant on the deceased for a portion of her anticipated earnings.

The Plaintiff has lost the value of his wife's services and the children have lost the benefit of her maternal care for which claims are made.

Since 30 September 1994 the plaintiff has had to pay £3,900 a year to obtain domestic help and £200 a year for redecoration of parts of the family home.

There is a lost financial dependency of £1,560 per annum from the deceased's anticipated earnings when she returned to work.

The Plaintiff and the children of the deceased were wholly dependent on her for support as a wife and mother and by her death they have lost this means of support and have suffered loss and damage.[17]

PARTICULARS OF SPECIAL DAMAGE [18]

Damage to clothing	£200.00
Funeral expenses [19]	£1,250.00
	£1,450.00 [20]

5. Further the Plaintiff claims interest pursuant to section 35A of the Supreme Court Act 1981 on the amount found to be due to the Plaintiff at such rate and for such period as the court thinks fit. [21]

AND the Plaintiff claims: [22]

(1) Damages on behalf of the deceased's estate under the Law Reform (Miscellaneous Provisions) Act 1934

(2) Damages on behalf of the deceased's dependants under the Fatal Accidents Act 1976

(3) Damages for bereavement under section 1A of the Fatal Accidents Act 1976 [23]

(4) The aforesaid interest pursuant to section 35A of the Supreme Court Act 1981 to be assessed.

J Bull

(signature of Counsel)[24]

Served etc [25]

Notes

Precedents of pleadings for fatal accidents are to be found in books such as *The Encyclopaedia of Forms and Precedents*. They are fairly simple to follow. These notes are to indicate which elements are important to include in your draft and to give the reason for their inclusion.

1   Because the value of the claim is £50,000 or more, the action should start in the High Court: Art 5(1) High Court and County Courts Jurisdiction Order 1991. Value, by Art 9 of the same Act, does not include interest.

2 The choice of the division of the High Court in which to commence proceedings is left to the barrister or solicitor. Schedule 1 Supreme Court Act 1981, which lists the distribution of business in the High Court, does not refer to claims for personal injury and death. But s 64(1) of the same Act confers on the plaintiff the initiative to choose the division he thinks fit to commence proceedings. The Queen's Bench Division is the division most often selected for these cases.

The writ must be endorsed with the words 'This writ includes a claim for personal injury but may be commenced in the High Court because the value of the action for the purposes of Article 5 of the High Court and County Courts Jurisdiction Order 1991 exceeds £50,000'. This endorsement must be signed by the plaintiff's solicitor.

When the statement of claim is served after the writ has been issued, then 'Writ issued (relevant date)' should be added to the pleading below the words 'QUEEN'S BENCH DIVISION'.

3 The numbering system in the High Court consists of firstly the year of issue, followed by the first letter of the surname of the plaintiff, followed by the writ number which is given by the court when the writ is issued. Do not make one up when drafting pleadings.

4 It is perfectly acceptable to put the name of the deceased in capital letters rather than the script type face that has been used in this example. If the deceased had left a will, the status of the plaintiff would have been widower and executor rather than widower and administrator.

5 Even if the defendant is insured, the insurance company has the right of subrogation, and will continue the action in the name of the insured defendant. The plaintiff does not, therefore, sue the insurance company as defendant since they owe no duty to the plaintiff. It is usual for a solicitor for an insurance company to indicate he or she will accept service on behalf of the defendant. There is therefore no necessity to join them as a third party once they acknowledge proceedings.

6 The description of the pleading must be stated: RSC Ord 18 r6(1)(d). Statement of claim is used in the High Court, and in the county court the term is particulars of claim.

7 This is a fairly standard paragraph. Facts to be included are:
   • The plaintiff has the capacity to sue as administrator on behalf of the estate. This is granted under s 2(1) Fatal Accidents Act 1976.

- Since the deceased died intestate, the plaintiff's capacity to sue runs from the date of the grant of letters of administration. The date of the grant of the letters as well as the name of the court granting the letters must be included in the pleading.
- The action must be for the benefit of the dependants of the deceased. Dependant is defined in s 1(3)(a) to include the husband of the deceased and (e) any child or other descendant of the deceased.
- By s 1 Law Reform (Miscellaneous Provisions) Act 1934, causes of action after the death of any person shall survive against, or for the benefit of the estate. Section 5 of the Act states that these rights do not derogate from the rights under the Fatal Accidents Act. It is usual for both causes of action to be brought by the same plaintiff in one proceedings.
- The names and dates of the two statutes that give the right of the dependants to sue must be stated, but further particulars are not required.
- The lay-out that pleadings must follow is described by RSC Ord 18 r6(2). This states that every pleading must, if necessary, be divided into paragraphs numbered consecutively, and each allegation should so far as convenient, be contained in a separate paragraph.
- It is a useful tool of pleading to put a word in quotation marks and brackets and then use that word as shorthand in the pleadings to represent several words. The most obvious use is 'the property' which refers to a particular address, or as in this case 'the deceased'. Please, however, make sure that this shorthand word is used later in the pleadings. If it is not, it looks amateur.

8 This is a simple and clear explanation of the fatal accident. The material facts are:

- the date of the accident;
- the place of the accident;
- the location of the deceased at the time of the accident. This pleading states that the plaintiff was on a pedestrian crossing which thus infers the negligent act of the defendant;
- the details of the defendant's car;
- the loss, damage and injury resulting from the negligent act.

The source of the rule to plead only material facts is RSC Ord 18 r7(1). An explanation of this is to be found on p 55. When the duty of care is owed not to one particular plaintiff but is common to everyone, it is unnecessary to plead the existence of this right, for it is implied by law. These rights include the right to security of life, limb, liberty and reputation. In such cases the pleading should merely state the violation of the right. This is why this pleading does not refer to the duty of care owed by the defendant to the plaintiff.

9   The particulars of negligence are arrived at by a detailed analysis of the accident. The particulars need to cover every negligent act since these are the allegations that the defendant must meet and defend and the plaintiff must prove.

10 Section 11 Civil Evidence Act 1968 permits evidence of a criminal conviction by a court in the United Kingdom to be admissible as evidence in civil proceedings. This is an exception to the rule against pleading evidence, see p 50. The object of pleading the conviction is to give the opposite party fair notice that such criminal conviction is intended to be relied on.

The party wishing to rely on this evidence must include in his pleading a statement of his intention to do so, particulars of the conviction, including the date and the court, and the issue to which the conviction relates: RSC Ord 18 r7A.

The effect of pleading and proving a criminal conviction is to shift the legal burden of proof to the convicted party who has to disprove the offence. In cases of negligent conduct it is particularly important, since instead of the plaintiff having to prove the defendant was negligent, the defendant, as a result, will have to prove he or she was not negligent. In many such cases, therefore, the only matter before the court will be deciding the level of damages.

There is no set pattern for pleading convictions. Provided the details set out in RSC Ord 18 r7A are included, the draft may follow any form.

11 This is the paragraph which alleges causation and the loss and damage flowing from the breach of the duty of care.

12 Because Mrs Ramsey did not die immediately after the accident, she had a claim against the driver of the car for pain, suffering and loss of amenity. These are called general damages. These are damages that the law will assume to be the natural and probable consequence of the defendant's act. They do not have to be pleaded as specific sums, because the judge will decide at trial on the level of general damages to be awarded.

13 It is important to give the subsequent date of death of the deceased to indicate that the plaintiff is claiming general damages on behalf of the estate before her death.

The claim for pain and suffering will only be allowed if it is based on a medical report that indicates the deceased suffered pain before her death. In the Hillsborough Stadium case, *Hicks & Others v Chief Constable of the South Yorkshire Police* (1992), Parker LJ rejected the claim for damages for pain and suffering, because the claim was based on 30 minutes of mental anguish. This, he stated, did not come within the remit of pain and suffering.

14 The claim for bereavement is a claim granted under s 1A Fatal Accidents Act 1976. It is a claim that can only be made by a spouse of the deceased or the parents of an unmarried minor. The sum awarded is currently £7,500. This was last raised on 1 April 1991. This claim does not extinguish the right to damages at common law for bereavement where seeing the fatality causes nervous shock: *Watson v Willmott* (1990).

15 There is now considerable pressure under the rules to persuade litigants to show their evidence to each other at an early stage. It is hoped that this will enable the parties to have more information, and so possibly reach a settlement. RSC Ord 18 r12(1A) states that a plaintiff in an action for personal injuries shall serve with his statement of claim a medical report and a statement of the special damages claimed.

A medical report means 'a report substantiating all the personal injuries alleged in the statement of claim which the plaintiff proposes to adduce in evidence as part of his case at the trial': RSC Ord 18 r12(1C).

The effect of this rule is that the medical evidence will take on the character of a pleading and the plaintiff will not be able to change it without asking the court for permission to amend it. It is therefore important that it should be approved by the plaintiff's solicitor before it is filed at court.

16 This is the information required by s 2(4) Fatal Accidents Act 1976 to be delivered to the defendant or his solicitor. It is usual to include these in the statement of claim since the statement of claim must be served on the defendant and his solicitor, and this ensures that s 2(4) is complied with. These particulars include:

- the identity of the dependants;
- their ages and/or date of birth;
- their relationship to the deceased;

- the age and/or date of birth of the deceased;
- details of the value of the dependency.

17 Section 3(1) defines the damages as '... proportional to the injury resulting from the death to the dependant respectively'. The value of the dependency will include accurate details of the deceased's job, salary, future salary and prospects, the extent to which his or her work supported the dependants and the value of any other work that he or she undertook for the benefit of the family or the family home. It is necessary to put a figure to this valuation, and bring evidence to support it at trial.

18 Whenever the plaintiff has suffered any special damage, this must be alleged in the statement of claim with all necessary particulars. Special damage is loss that will not be presumed by the court to be a consequence of the defendant's act, but will arise due to the circumstances of a particular case. The defendant therefore must have notice of such damages that are claimed before the trial.

The plaintiff is not likely to be allowed at the trial to give evidence of any special damage which is not claimed explicitly in his statement of claim: *Ilkiw v Samuels* (1963).

19 The cost of funeral expenses is recoverable under both acts. In this case, the funeral expenses were paid by the plaintiff and are recoverable under s 3(5) Fatal Accidents Act 1976. Case law indicates that they must be reasonable, taking into account the deceased's station in life, creed and racial origin, *Gammell v Wilson* (1982), and may include travel expenses: *Schneider v Eisovitch* (1960).

In this pleading the cost of employing help in the home at £3,900 per annum is stated in the particulars pursuant to statute. When the judge makes the award of damages he will apportion the cost of this employment between a claim on behalf of the estate before the death of Mrs Ramsey and a claim by the dependants for loss after her death.

In addition, the judge has to make a further apportionment. By s 3(1) Fatal Accidents Act 1976, the judge must apportion all the damages awarded under the act between the dependants. The only exception is the award for bereavement referred to in note 14 above.

20 In every pleading, dates, sums and other numbers must be expressed in figures and not in words: RSC Ord 18 r6(3). This rule is designed to ensure that dates, sums and other numbers in the pleadings can be speedily assimilated.

21 Interest can be awarded in the High Court at the discretion of the judge under s 35A Supreme Court Act 1981 in proceedings for recovery of a debt or damages. The rules of recovery of interest and the amount recoverable are set out in case law and the Rules of the Supreme Court. The *White Book* has an excellent explanation after RSC Ord 6 r2 at SCP 6/2/10–18.

Interest must be specifically pleaded; RSC Ord 18 r8(4). It is pleaded in the body of the pleading as well as in the prayer. The overriding principle as stated by Lord Herschell LC in *London, Chatham & Dover Ry Co v South Eastern Ry Co* (1893) is that interest should be awarded to the plaintiff not as compensation for the damage done, but for being kept out of money which ought to have been paid to him.

In an action seeking damages for personal injury or death, the court should normally award interest unless there are special reasons to the contrary, but interest will be calculated differently on the awards that are made under the different heads of damages. The Court of Appeal in *Jefford v Gee* (1970) stated the principles to be applied when awarding interest on damages for personal injury or death.

- For special damages, interest is awarded at half the appropriate rate from the date of the accident to the date of trial. The appropriate rate is the rate for the special investment account for the relevant period. This figure frequently changes; from 1 February 1993 it was 8%.

- On damages for pain and suffering, general damages, interest is normally awarded at 2% from the date of issue of the writ to the date of trial: *Wright v British Railways Board* (1983).

- There is no interest on damages for loss of future earnings or future earning capacity, as these damages do not relate to money that has been withheld from the plaintiff.

- Interest normally ends at the date of judgment, but may end on the date the type of damage ceases if earlier. The judgment should state the rate of interest and the amount on which interest is awarded and the period for which awarded.

- The judgment debt, which will include the interest awarded, itself carries interest. This is set at the prescribed rate under the Judgment Act 1838. The rate since 1 April 1993 is 8% per annum and was changed to this by the Judgment Debts (Rate of Interest) Order 1993.

- The lost dependency during the pre-trial period attracts interest: *Cookson v Knowles* (1977).
- Interest should be computed and awarded as a gross sum without any deduction of tax.
- Interest on the statutory award for bereavement (currently £7,500) should be awarded from the date of death at the full special investment account rate: *Khan v Duncan* (1989).

Because of the delay in cases going for trial, the sum awarded for interest is therefore often very significant. It is vital therefore that interest is pleaded.

22 At its conclusion the statement of claim must state specifically the relief or remedy which the plaintiff claims, but costs need not be specifically claimed: RSC Ord 18 r15(1). Costs are however at the discretion of the court under s 51(1) Supreme Court Act 1981.

23 A plaintiff may claim his relief or remedy in the alternative since, as in this pleading, he is entitled to rely upon several different rights alternatively.

If the plaintiff omits to ask for any relief or remedy claimed in the writ, he will be deemed to have abandoned the claim: *Lewis & Lewis v Durnford* (1907). However the court has discretion to grant relief appropriate to the facts as proved, so the absence of a claim for a particular remedy in the prayer may result in an adjournment being granted if the relief has not been claimed: *Belmont Finance Corpn Ltd v Williams Furniture Ltd* (1979).

24 Every pleading must be signed by counsel if it has been settled by him or her: RSC Ord 18 r6(5). The signature of counsel reflects the responsibility for the formulation of the case on behalf of a party, and this requires the exercise of great care, skill and art to present this case with clarity, precision and effectiveness: *Associated Leisure Ltd v Associated Newspapers Ltd* (1970).

25 Every pleading must bear on its face the date on which it is served: RSC Ord 18 r6(1)(e). If it is amended, it must be re-served and the date and authority of such amendment and re-service must be shown on its face.

Defending the action

The defendant's story

Joseph Agnew will say:

He was the driver of the Vauxhall Astra motor car registration number H123 LMN on 1 September 1994. The car is owned by his girlfriend, Mandy Miller, who was the front seat passenger in the car on that date. He was 35 at the time of the accident and in good health.

Lime Road is in a built-up area and he was driving at about 30 mph which is the speed limit for that area. The time of the accident was about 7.30 pm. Before 1 September there had been a long dry period but on that evening the drought had ended and there was a complete downpour. The driving conditions were therefore atrocious.

The streets were very empty and the traffic was light and he and Mandy were going home after work.

Neither of them had seen Mrs Ramsey until she was on the road. He thought she must have darted out in front of them without looking for oncoming traffic. He wasn't aware that she had been crossing the road on the pedestrian crossing.

He had slammed on the brakes as soon as he saw her, but the car had skidded because the surface of the road was oily after the long dry period before the rain.

He felt very bad when he heard that she had died, but he had done everything he could to avoid hitting her. He could only think that she had rushed out into the road without looking because she wanted to avoid the downpour.

He has no previous convictions for road traffic offences, though he had been in a minor crash five years ago. After the accident he took the car to his regular garage to ask them to check the brakes, but they were found to be completely in order. He can only assume that the accident occurred because of the appalling weather, combined with the fact that Mrs Ramsey dashed out onto the crossing without looking.

He was breathalysed by the police after the accident, and they found, as he expected, that he had no alcohol in his system. He pleaded guilty to the offence of careless driving at Northam Magistrates' Court in July 1995.

Other than his girlfriend, he was not aware of any other witnesses to the accident.

Mandy Miller's story

Mandy Miller will say that she was being driven home by Joseph Agnew after work on the evening of 1 September 1994. The car was owned by her, but Joseph often met her after work and drove her home in it.

She remembered that it had been pouring with rain that evening. She didn't recall much before the accident, but she remembered seeing someone dash in front of the car, and the scream of brakes as Joseph tried to avoid hitting that person. She wasn't aware that the pedestrian she now knew as Mrs Ramsey was on the pedestrian crossing at the the time of the accident.

Joseph and she were no longer together. She thought that the accident had probably led to the breakdown of their relationship.

She was comprehensively insured by the First Law Insurance Company and Joseph Agnew was an approved driver.

Structure for drafting the defence

These instructions, combined with the criminal conviction of careless driving, leave little room for the defence lawyer to draft anything other than a plea of contributory negligence and hope that this will reduce the damages that are inevitably going to be awarded to the plaintiff.

The function of the defence is to state the grounds and the material facts on which the defendant relies for his defence.

In addition, he must deal specifically with every material allegation contained in the statement of claim.

The kernel of the defendant's story is:

- The car was not owned by him, but by his girlfriend, but it is questionable that this is a material fact.
- He pleaded guilty to the offence of careless driving.
- The deceased was partly to blame for the accident.
- His girlfriend witnessed the accident and saw that the deceased was partly to blame.
- The other contributory factor was the appalling weather.

Bearing these factors in mind, all the defence lawyer can do is:

- Establish the correct ownership of the car, if he or she considers this is a material fact.
- Admit the criminal conviction.
- Not admit the negligence, thus leaving the plaintiff to prove it, but claim contributory negligence.

- Call Mandy Miller as a witness.
- Realise that the bad weather was unfortunate, and no doubt explains the accident. It is not however a defence because a driver is expected to drive at a standard that takes into account the prevailing weather conditions. Therefore driving within the speed limit in extremely bad driving conditions is no defence to a claim for negligence.
- Consider whether calling an expert witness to attest to the weather conditions, or rely on a meterological report and hope that this can be agreed with the plaintiff.

The only other consideration at this stage for the defence lawyer is whether the claim should be transferred to the county court under s 40 County Courts Act 1984. In fact this should not at present be pursued, though the defence will have to come to a decision at some time as to their preferred venue for trial. If the case goes to a hearing, it is likely that the High Court Master assigned to the case may on his or her own motion decide to send the case to the county court.

A draft defence on the following lines will serve to reflect the above considerations.

Sample defence

IN THE HIGH COURT OF JUSTICE   **1996 R No 1234**
QUEEN'S BENCH DIVISION

BETWEEN

ALFRED RAMSEY
(Widower and Administrator
of the Estate of Rebecca
Jane Ramsey deceased)   <u>Plaintiff</u>
and
JOSEPH AGNEW   <u>Defendant</u>

DEFENCE [1]

1. No admission is made as to paragraph 1 of the Statement of Claim. [2]
2. Save that it is admitted that the deceased was crossing Lime Road, Northam on 1 September 1994, paragraph 2 of the Statement of Claim is denied. [3]

3. In particular it is denied that the Defendant is the owner of the Vauxhall Astra car registration number H123 LMN. The said car is the property of one Mandy Miller. [4]

4. It is further expressly denied that the Defendant was negligent as alleged in the Statement of Claim or at all. [5]

5. Further or in the alternative the alleged accident was caused wholly or in part by the negligence of the deceased. [6]

PARTICULARS OF CONTRIBUTORY NEGLIGENCE

(a) Failing to look to see if it was safe to step on to Lime Road before doing so.

(b) Failing to observe the car driven by the Defendant.

(c) Failing to stop, step aside or take any other action to avoid being struck by the car driven by the Defendant.

(d) Failing to take account of the poor visibility due to the weather conditions. [7]

6. Paragraph 3 of the Statement of Claim is admitted. [8]

7. No admission is made as to the alleged or any pain or injury or loss or damage suffered by the Plaintiff or the deceased, or as to the causation thereof, or to the amount thereof. [9]

[10]

Eric Wilwood
(signature of Counsel)

Served this   day of   199
by Messrs Jones & Wood,
Solicitors for the Defendant
who will accept service of
proceedings on behalf of
the Defendant at ....

Notes

1 *Heading* is as in the statement of claim. Remember to call the pleading a defence; RSC Ord 18 r6(1)(d). It is suprising how often this is missed.

2 Mr Agnew has no knowledge of the material facts alleged in this paragraph. It is right therefore that he should not admit them and let the plaintiff prove them.

3   There are a number of material facts that have to be pleaded to in para 2 of the statement of claim. The evidence of Mr Agnew is vital when it comes to deciding how to deal with these facts.

Mr Agnew agrees with the alleged date of the accident and the place of the accident. He also agrees that Mrs Ramsey was on the road at the time of the accident. It is therefore sensible to admit to these elements of the statement of claim.

He will wish to deny all the other material facts in para 2 of the statement of claim, and this he does by a general denial. In particular, Mr Agnew was not aware that Mrs Ramsey was on a pedestrian crossing, but he has no evidence to show that she was not on the crossing. He therefore should not admit to that fact, and this is covered by this general denial.

4   Mr Agnew says in his statement that he is not the owner of the car. The ownership of the car does not appear to be a material fact, but for the sake of truth it is better that the matter is now dealt with and denied. The name of the true owner should be included to place the matter before the plaintiff.

It is likely that this slip was made when the particulars of claim were drafted. The plaintiff's solicitors would have had copies of the police accident reports that would have shown the ownership of the car. It is common in practice to find defective pleadings, and correcting them may help to convince the other side that when you litigate you mean business.

5   Mr Ramsey denies that he was negligent. The fact that he has a criminal conviction for careless driving will be the plaintiff's evidence for negligence, but the defendant will not admit negligence because his defence is that the deceased brought about the accident by running onto the road without first looking for oncoming traffic.

It is therefore not inconsistent for the defence to agree that the defendant has been convicted of careless driving, but that, of itself, this does not mean that the defendant was negligent.

Another defence, which is common in road accident cases, is that the accident was caused by defective workmanship by the garage, or the manufacturer. If the defendant can prove this, for example by expert reports, the third party, the garage or the manufacturer, may well be found negligent rather than the defendant who had the criminal conviction. This is not applicable here.

6 It is perfectly possible in pleading to appear to do the impossible and appear inconsistent. This arises because the defendant will often rely on more than one defence and these must all be pleaded however inconsistent they appear.

In this case, the defendant is trying to make this statement. Firstly, he was not negligent; secondly, even if he was negligent it wasn't his fault, it was the fault of the deceased; and thirdly, if it wasn't entirely the fault of the deceased, it was partly the fault of the deceased. One method of achieving this is shown in the drafting of this paragraph.

Contributory negligence must be specifically pleaded as a defence to a plaintiff's claim for negligence. RSC Ord 18 r8(1) states, 'a party must in any pleading subsequent to a statement of claim plead specifically any matter, for example, performance ... which raises issues of fact not arising out of the preceding pleading'. The statement of claim does not raise the fact that Mrs Ramsey, by her action in rushing out in front of the car, could have caused the accident. It must therefore be raised in the defence. In the absence of such a plea, the trial judge is not entitled to find that the plaintiff's negligence contributed to the accident: *Fookes v Slaytor* (1978).

The defence therefore must state what facts the defendant will rely on at trial. If it does not do so, the plaintiff may legitimately claim that he had no knowledge of these alleged facts and had no opportunity to meet them.

7 The fresh facts raised by the defence must be pleaded in a summary form, giving enough information for the plaintiff to appreciate the case he has to respond to. The evidence of Joseph Agnew and his girlfriend, Mandy Miller, will not be given in the defence pleading since RSC Ord 18 r7(1) specifically states 'every pleading must contain, and contain only, a statement in summary form of the material facts on which the party pleading relies for his claim or defence ... but not the evidence by which those facts are to be proved'.

If the defence of contributory negligence is raised, then the defence lawyer has to face a two-stage hurdle. He or she must firstly prove by evidence that there was contributory negligence. That this evidence is available is shown in the statements of both Joseph Agnew and Mandy Miller. Secondly, the defence lawyer has to argue what effect this should have on damages. This will mean proving to what extent the deceased was responsible and arguing in what proportion the damages should be reduced.

When a finding of contributory negligence is made, the judge will express it as a percentage of the general damages. Damages, which are payable by the defendant, can therefore be considerably reduced by the difference between an award of 10% and 25%.

8 The defence should admit any allegations made by the other side which the client agrees are true. If the plaintiff has to go to the cost of proving such an allegation, the defendant may find himself being penalised by bearing the plaintiff's costs that arose from having to prove the agreed allegation.

An express admission in the pleading ought to be clear and should specify exactly what is being admitted. Here the defence are admitting the whole of para 3 of the statement of claim.

Should the defendant deny to this paragraph, the burden of proof will be on him to prove that the allegation was wrong, and the defendant has no evidence to prove this.

9 It is a general rule of pleading that each material fact must be pleaded to, and if for any reason they are not denied, or dealt with by a non-admission, they will be deemed by the court to be admitted: RSC Ord 18 r13(1). This is engraved in stone on all draftsman's hearts, because it will mean that there is no issue between the parties on that part of the case, and therefore no evidence is admissable with regard to those facts.

It is necessary therefore in these circumstances not to admit to the damage suffered by the plaintiff and not to admit to the amount claimed by the plaintiff. It is for the plaintiff, through evidence, to prove the amount of general and special damages he alleges he suffered.

It is important also to not admit the fact that the injury caused the deceased's pain and death. In proceedings in negligence, the plaintiff has to prove causation as an element of the tort of negligence and, in this particular case, the defendant has no evidence to disprove the causation. He will, therefore, by this pleading ensure that the plaintiff has to prove that the road accident caused the deceased's death.

It should be remembered that in this case the plaintiff is pleading on his own behalf under the Fatal Accidents Act 1976 and on behalf of the deceased's estate. The claims by both the plaintiff and the deceased should therefore be addressed in the defence, and in this case be not admitted.

10 It is not necessary to plead to the claim for interest. Interest is awarded at the discretion of the judge and is announced when the judge makes the assessment of damages.

It is also not necessary to plead to the prayer of the statement of claim which lists the remedies sought by the plaintiff. It is for the judge to make the orders at the trial, and it is open to both parties to argue what remedies should be awarded.

The position of the plaintiff

Once the solicitors for the plaintiff receive this defence, they will be in a position to decide on the strength of the opponent's case in claiming contributory negligence. It is likely that they will take the view that the only matters of issue will be the percentage of discount for contributory negligence, and the quantum. With proper management it is likely that an agreement can be reached before the matter gets to trial.

However, before agreement is reached, there are two procedural matters that need to be considered.

Firstly, any settlement on behalf of a minor has to be approved by a court. Secondly, any sum adjudged or ordered or agreed to be paid in satisfaction of a claim under the Fatal Accidents Act 1976 must be apportioned between the various dependants. The apportionment is effected by the court.

There is very little authority on the principles that the court follows when apportioning the damages. But the usual rule is to award the greater sum to the widower or widow on the assumption that he or she will maintain the children so long as they are dependant. The sums awarded to the children therefore are comparatively small, with the younger child being awarded more than the elder child on the basis that the period of dependency is greater.

In this particular case, the plaintiff has no need to serve a reply. When and how a reply is drafted is discussed in more detail on p 49.

Question for self-testing

As you would expect, most of the claims for damages for fatal accidents are brought by widows and children of men who have been killed at work. Part of the difficulty of researching a case like the one included in this chapter of the book arises because there are significantly fewer cases in *Kemp and Kemp* vol 3 under Section M3 'Death of wife' than under Section M2 'Death of husband'.

The question set for self-testing therefore involves the death of a husband. You will find, when you research the quantum, that there are more cases to choose from when advising on quantum.

When drafting an advice and a statement of claim in such a case, you are likely to be presented with statements from a number of people. It is part of the job of the draftsman to go through these statements and extract the information needed to draft the proceedings and the advice.

In this case, you are not asked to draft an advice on quantum. The answer on p 242 will give in note form the information that should be included and indicate the structure of the advice.

Below are the statements needed to draft the claim and the skeleton advice.

1   Statement of Jane Seymour of 212 West Road, Westchester

Jane Seymour will say:

I was born on 22 February 1960. I married Keith Seymour on 22 December 1980. We have two children: Kate who was born on 12 November 1986 and James who was born on 22 July 1990. I worked as a secretary before the birth of Kate but did not return to work after her birth and since that date Keith has solely supported us.

Keith, who was born on 20 November 1958, was a civil engineer and worked for James Jones & Sons plc on their road building programme. I understand that he was very well regarded by the company. He had to travel a lot to take charge of the road building contracts that they won. This meant that he was away from home a lot, particularly in the summer, when he and the men worked throughout the daylight. I think that he was due to be promoted to a job that would mean less travel, but I don't know the details.

Keith's salary was paid into a joint account and I paid all the bills from this. We were trying to save for a larger house and any money left over at the end of the month was transferred automatically into a high income savings account. We also had the advantage of Keith having a company car which made it possible for me to use it during the weekend for household shopping.

Keith was a very practical man and had done all the decorating and maintenance at our house. He had also improved the value of our house by putting in a shower, re-wiring the upstairs and putting in a new kitchen. I can't do any maintenance work, and since his death I have spent £600 on small jobs that have had to be done. I know that sounds a lot, but these are jobs that were vital.

I do not intend to go back to work. I need to be with the children as they are so young, and they and I miss their father so much.

I have a widow's pension of £100 a week which comes from Keith's company. This continues until I die. I was also given a lump sum of £25,000 from the company's life policy on Keith. We had a life policy on the mortgage and this has paid off the mortgage on 212 West Road, Westchester, our home.

I have had to pay for Keith's funeral and headstone and the bill came to about £2,000. I paid this out of our joint bank account.

Keith had made a will a few months before he died. Perhaps he had a feeling about something awful happening. Anyway, he left everything to me. My solicitor has been dealing with that.

The boy who killed Keith was called Jo Snap. He was convicted of causing death by careless driving at Kingstone Crown Court on 12 February 1995 and sentenced to prison. He was, I understand, very drunk at the time. It is wholly wrong that he who killed my husband is walking around today while my husband is dead. Jo Snap didn't even get hurt in the accident. The police told me that Mr Snap had car insurance and had paid his road tax.

2   Statement by Stephen King, construction manager, James Jones & Sons plc

Stephen King will say:

My name is Stephen King and my address is Jones House, Well Road, Crofton, Leeds. I am construction manager of James Jones & Sons and in charge of their road building programme which is an important part of the company. We currently have work in hand to the value of £10m. Keith was recruited in 1989 when the board decided that our company should tender for more road construction work when other building work started to decline.

We have been very successful in winning large contracts, and Keith was particularly good in managing them on site. Good site management makes all the difference between a project making money and losing it, and Keith's management was very good. All the projects he had undertaken with the company had been profitable.

He was earning £35,000 pa net when he died. But his salary would have increased when he finished the project he was working on when he died. The managing director and the board had decided that they needed him in head office as a development manager and trouble shooter to oversee the entire road construction programme. When that happened I was to move on to develop other projects which are emerging as the recession recedes. This move would have happened at the end of 1994. I don't think that all the details of his new job had been worked out, but I would expect that his salary would have been about £40,000 pa net, which is what I earn.

I am happy that this statement should be disclosed to the defendants in any action, and confirm that I will give evidence, if so required, at trial.

3   Statement by Joseph MacCuish, site agent of 14 North Road, Cumnor, Norfolk

Joseph MacCuish will say:

I am a site agent employed by James Jones & Sons on their construction site for the Cumnor bypass. I know Keith Seymour very well and saw him about twice a week when he came to the site.

This particular project was the contruction of a bypass round the town of Cumnor. The road had to be built over fields, and a bridge had to be constructed to take the road over the railway line.

On the day of the accident, 23 August 1994, I was in Keith's car with him.

We had left the site at about 8.30 in the evening and Keith was taking me back to my digs in Cumnor. I got a lift from Keith because I wasn't able to start my car that morning.

I still can't believe that it is Keith who died, and I am still around. I suppose you would call it fate.

Anyway, Keith was driving towards the town centre of Cumnor on the London Road. It was an open road and he was driving quite fast, about 50 mph I think. The next thing I remember was an enormous noise and tremendous movement as the car veered off the road. I later realised that another car had dashed out from a side road and slammed into the driver's side of Keith's car.

I suffered shock but, except for bruises and scratches, I was not badly injured.

Keith however was very bad. As soon as I got myself clear of the car and while we waited for the ambulance, I knew that he was very very sick.

The ambulances took us both to the local hospital, the Princess Mary. He died later that night and never regained consciousness.

I had to give a statement to the police, and they later prosecuted a boy called Jo Snap. He pleaded guilty to causing death by careless driving when under the influence of drink, and was sentenced to 6 months in prison. He was only young, about 20 I think, and had been drinking because his girlfriend had given him the push.

The whole thing was a tragic accident. Keith was a smashing chap and a very good engineer. He had a wife and young family as well.

I agree that this statement can be used in evidence and I am prepared to give oral evidence to the court if that is needed. If that happens, could you give me a witness summons, otherwise my employer will not give me time off work.

4 Statement by Philip Smith, partner of Nelson & Co, Estate Agents, 32 High Street, Westchester

Philip Smith will say:

I am a partner in Nelson & Co, an estate agency and property management company. My firm specialises in managing property on behalf of non-resident landlords. An important part of my job is to ensure that the properties are kept in good repair and to arrange for repairs to be undertaken when they are necessary. Many of our client landlords wish for advice on what proportion of their rental income they should put aside for repairs and redecoration, and this estimate is part of the work I undertake on their behalf.

On behalf of Mrs Seymour I visited her house at 212 West Road, Westchester. The property is a fairly standard three-bedroomed semi-detached house built in 1938 I would estimate. I advised her that the money she will have to spend will not be the same every year. Some years she will be required to make quite a large investment, as for instance when she needs the exterior to be repainted. I have therefore decided, for convenience, to express my estimate for total labour costs on an average yearly basis.

As the house has been well maintained I would estimate that she would need to spend on average about £750 a year on labour costs to keep it in a good state of repair and redecoration.

I agree that this statement can be used in evidence and I am prepared to give oral evidence to this effect at trial.

5   Medical Report by Mr Philip Houstead FRCS

On 23 August 1994 Mr Keith Seymour was admitted to the Accident and Emergency Unit of the Princess Mary Hospital, Cumnor. I was then the consultant orthopaedic surgeon on call and I was called to see him.

On my arrival I found Mr Seymour conscious and in great pain. He had been given nitrous oxide by the paramedical staff on duty in the ambulance but the effects were starting to wear off.

I found he had sustained the following injuries: crush injury to the chest, gross bruising and swelling of the abdomen, broken and contused right arm, a severe head wound over the right side of the skull.

He was taken to theatre where a laparotomy was carried out. It was immediately obvious that he had ruptured his spleen and lost a great deal of blood internally. Despite being given five pints of blood, his condition deteriorated and he died whilst on the operating table at approximately 1.30 am on 24 August 1994.

Dated 10.3.1995

Draft structure for the advice

All this information is difficult to handle. One of the key skills of a successful drafter is the ability to sift out the irrelevant and useless information and swiftly incorporate the material facts into the advice and the pleadings.

Here the information needed for this advice is expressed in note form in numbered paragraphs.

1   Statement about nature of advice wanted and details of the accident. These will include date, time, name of defendant and witness.

2   Possible short summary of injuries and date and time of death.

3   Details of claim by the estate of Mr Seymour; special and general damages and assessment of general damages (if any).

4   Details of the claim by the dependants of Mr Seymour; special and general damages and assessment of general damages. This will involve assessing the dependency as a percentage of Mr Seymour's income. Here probably 75%. Also an assessment of the multiplier.

5   Proof of liability of the defendant.

6   Any other considerations such as bereavement allowance, time limitation, Mrs Seymour's return to work and apportionment of the damages.

7   Conclusions. These may also be placed after para 2 above.

Sample statement of claim for a fatal accident claim

IN THE HIGH COURT OF JUSTICE   1995 S No
QUEEN'S BENCH DIVISION

BETWEEN

JANE SEYMOUR
(Widow and Executrix
of the Estate of Keith
Seymour deceased)   <u>Plaintiff</u>
and
JO SNAP   <u>Defendant</u>

STATEMENT OF CLAIM

1. The Plaintiff is the widow and executrix of the estate of Keith Seymour deceased ('the deceased'), probate having been granted to her from the Westchester Probate Registry on 20 November 1994 and she brings this action on behalf of the deceased's estate under the Law Reform (Miscellaneous Provisions) Act 1934 and for the benefit of his dependants under the Fatal Accidents Act 1976.

2. On 23 August 1994, at approximately 8.45 pm the deceased was driving a Vauxhall Cavalier motor car, registration number L231 XYZ along the London Road towards Cumnor. The Defendant, driving a Volvo 240l motor car, registration number F456 OPR, negligently drove out of Holly Road hitting the deceased's car and fatally injuring him.

<u>PARTICULARS OF NEGLIGENCE</u>

The Defendant was negligent in that he:

(1) Drove his vehicle along the said road:

    (a) at an excessive speed;

    (b) in an aggressive manner;

    (c) when it was not safe to do so;

    (d) while under the influence of alcohol.

(2) Failed to observe the deceased's motor car.

(3) Failed to keep any or any proper lookout.

(4) Failed to take any or any sufficient steps to brake, steer or otherwise manoeuvre his vehicle to avoid the deceased's car.

(5) Failed to heed or observe the 'Give Way' sign.

(6) In all circumstances failed to drive with regard for other road users and in particular the deceased.

3. The Plaintiff will seek to rely on the fact that on 12 February 1995 at Kingstone Crown Court the Defendant pleaded guilty to an offence of causing death by careless driving when under the influence of alcohol contrary to section 3A of the Road Traffic Act 1988 as evidence of his negligence.

4. As a result of the said collision, the deceased suffered pain and injury in consequence whereof he died on 24 August 1994. As a result of his death his estate and dependants have suffered loss and damage and the Plaintiff has suffered bereavement.

PARTICULARS OF INJURY

Crushed chest, gross bruising of the abdomen, broken and contused right arm, severe head wound and considerable loss of blood.

A full report of the Plaintiff's injuries appears in the medical report of Mr Philip Houstead FRCS dated 10 March 1995 served herewith.

PARTICULARS PURSUANT TO STATUTE

The claim herein under the Fatal Accidents Act 1976 is brought on behalf of the following dependants:

(1) The Plaintiff who was born on 22 February 1960 and is the widow of the deceased.

(2) Kate Seymour who was born on 12 November 1986 and is the daughter of the deceased.

(3) James Seymour who was born on 22 July 1990 and is the son of the deceased.

The deceased, who was born on 20th November 1958, was a civil engineer employed at a salary of £35,000 pa net at the date of his death. This would have increased to £40,000 pa net at the end of 1993 when he would have been promoted to Construction Manager. The deceased was the sole support of his dependants and in addition carried out repairs, maintenance and decorations to the family home to an annual value of £750.

PARTICULARS OF SPECIAL DAMAGE

Funeral expenses   £2,000.00

5. Further the Plaintiff claims interest pursuant to section 35A of the Supreme Court Act 1981 on the amount found to be due to the Plaintiff at such rate and for such period as the court thinks fit.

AND the Plaintiff claims:

(1) Damages on behalf of the deceased's estate under the Law Reform (Miscellaneous Provisions) Act 1934
(2) Damages on behalf of the deceased's dependants under the Fatal Accidents Act 1976
(3) Damages for bereavement under section 1A of the Fatal Accidents Act 1976
(4) The aforesaid interest pursuant to section 35A of the Supreme Court Act 1981 to be assessed.

A Counsel
(signed)

Served etc

Chapter 10

A Claim Under the Occupiers' Liability Act

This Act of 1957 gives a visitor a statutory right to claim damages for personal injury from the occupier of premises. Because this is a negligence claim based on statute, there is likely to be less legal argument about the duty owed to the visitor, and, in this Act, the duty of care and the defences to this duty are set out in the Act.

For these reasons it is less difficult to draw up the pleadings for claims for personal injury due to breach of this or any statutory duty.

The facts of the accident – the plaintiff's view

Edith Jones was employed by Westchester local authority. It was her duty to inspect the facilities at the private nursing homes within the borough to ensure that the specified equipment was installed and the levels of cleanliness and health care offered were of a satisfactory standard.

Mrs Jones is a qualified state registered nurse and she had worked for the local authority for a number of years.

There had been publicity about a number of cases where old people had been scalded when they had been put in baths. For this reason Mrs Jones decided to look particularly at the water systems on her regular inspection visits to nursing homes.

On 21 April 1995 she had arranged to visit Wisteria House Nursing Home in Saleworth. This was a private nursing home run by Mr and Mrs Turner. Mr Turner was responsible for the maintenance of the property and Mrs Turner, who was a nurse, managed the business. The business had been in existence for about seven years, but at the time of the accident had recently been taken over by Golden Homes plc.

Wisteria House had been inspected a number of times and every recommendation that was made had in the past been implemented. Since Golden Homes owned no other homes in the borough, Mrs Jones was also looking for an indication as to whether the takeover would make a difference to the good working relationship that had previously existed between the borough and the Turners.

She also knew that the Turners, who were concerned about the quality of some of their internal pipework, had put in for a local authority grant. This had been approved by the council and Mrs Jones on her visit also wanted to check up on how the work was progressing.

Unfortunately, her visit was a total disaster. She found that Mr Turner was not interested in discussing pipework and Mrs Turner was not even at the home.

What Mr Turner was interested in discussing was the way he was being treated by Golden Homes. He told her that he had agreed at the time of the takeover to stay on for a further three months, until the end of June 1995, to look after the buildings and maintenance. He was being paid by them and was called a consultant.

This had seemed a good idea at the time, but it had turned out to be a disaster. He found he was expected to take instructions from the administrator Stella Little and she was only interested in not spending Golden Homes' money. He received all the complaints from problems with the hot water, but he wasn't allowed to spend money to put it right.

The reason Mrs Turner was not there was that the medical side of Wisteria House was being run by a series of agency nurses who had been sent on the instructions of Golden Homes administration manager.

Somewhat dismayed, Edith Jones toured the home escorted by Stella Little and Mr Turner who were obviously no longer on speaking terms.

Worse was to follow. When Mrs Jones asked Stella Little about the hot water, she said that there had been a number of problems and the nurses and carers were not at present bathing the patients. A plumber had been sent for and come and gone and promised to return and they were still waiting.

Mrs Jones, while this was being explained to her, turned on the hot tap in one of the bathrooms. A huge stream of boiling water shot out directly at her face, and severely burnt her face and her bare arms. As she fell back she landed on her right wrist which as a result was seriously damaged.

After some months of treatment, Mrs Jones still had severe scar tissue and scar marks on her face and arms. This scarring is now unlikely to improve and her consultant has warned her that she will continue to bear these marks for the rest of her life. She has also been told that she could need a further operation to stop her wrist deteriorating further.

She knows that there was an investigation into the causes of the accident soon after it occurred. She has not however received any information or a copy of this report.

The law

Mrs Jones has no contractual relationship with the Turners or the owners of Wisteria House Nursing Home. There is therefore no possibility of suing in contract.

She is however owed a duty of care in negligence even though the accident happened on private property.

However, usual practice is to consider first whether the pleadings can be based on the statutory duty under the Occupiers' Liability Act 1957 because of the advantages of making a claim under statutory authority.

The questions to ask before drafting, in order to decide if Mrs Jones is within the protection of the Act, are as follows:

Is Mrs Jones entitled to sue under the Act?

The answer is that visitors or invitees are, for the purposes of this Act, the same as in common law: s 1(2). Mrs Jones is at common law an invitee or visitor. Therefore she has a right to sue under the Act.

Further, s 2(6) gives the right of being an invitee or visitor to:

... persons who enter premises for any purpose in the exercise of a right conferred by law ...

Mrs Jones is therefore entitled to sue under the Act either under the common law definition of visitor, or the statutory definition of a visitor.

What is the duty of care?

This is called the 'common duty of care' in s 2(1) of the Act and defined in s 2(2) as:

... a duty to take such care as in all the circumstances of the case is reasonable to see that the visitor will be reasonably safe in using the premises for the purposes for which he is invited or permitted by the occupier to be there.

From the facts it would appear that there is a case to answer because she self-evidently was not reasonably safe in using the premises. The case of *Ferguson v Welsh* (1987) is authority for the proposition that there is liability arising from an unsafe system of work rather than 'use' of premises.

How does the occupier discharge the duty?

The statutory defences are a warning in s 2(4)(a) and that damage is due to the faulty work of an independent contractor in s 2(4)(b).

It is therefore important to plead that a warning was not given to Mrs Jones. A warning, on the authority of case law, must be placed in a suitably visible place and if it is an oral warning, it must be given seriously: *Bishop v J S Starnes & Sons Ltd* (1971).

To protect the position of Mrs Jones against the possible defence under s 2(4)(b), it is important to sue all the people who might be responsible for the faulty work. This is considered below.

The defendants

There are a number of possible defendants in this case. It is important to consider and determine who to sue before issuing the summons.

These possible defendants are:

(1) Golden Homes plc and/or

(2) The administration manager and/or

(3) Mr Turner and/or

(4) The plumber.

Taking each of the above in order, their possible liability is:

(a) Golden Homes plc is under a statutory duty under the Occupiers' Liability Act 1957. This duty of care is owed to a visitor by the owner of the property. They are primarily liable and they will therefore be pleaded as the first defendant.

(b) The administrator is also under the common law duty of care which is owed to any person who it is foreseeable could be injured. Since she is also employed by Golden Homes plc they will be vicariously liable for her acts or omissions. Even if she is found liable, her liabilities will be met by the first defendant

She is also an occupier by reason of *Wheat v Lacon & Co Ltd* (1966), which established that the test of whether a person is an occupier within the Act is whether that person has some degree of control associated with and arising from her presence in and use of or activity in the premises. The administrator therefore fulfils this definition.

(c) The position of Mr Turner is more complex. From the facts it is not entirely clear whether he is the occupier. He will however stand as a defendant under the common law duty of care in negligence. He might also be cited by the first defendant in their defence as an independent contractor under s 2(4)(b); for which see above.

(d) The plumber occupies a special position in this Act. As stated above, the first defendant may defend his position by passing liability to the independent contractor he employs: s 2(4)(b).

There is however a restriction on this defence in the same section of the Act. This is that the occupier had:

> ... acted reasonably in entrusting the work to an independent contractor and had taken such steps (if any) as he reasonably ought in order to satisfy himself that the contractor was competent and that the work was properly done.

This then is the possible liability of the potential defendants. It is now important to balance the advantages and disadvantages before deciding who to sue.

The first consideration is the financial status of the defendants. A company search might help, but here the primary defendant is a plc which indicates it is financially secure. Other defendants may or may not be so financially strong, but their liability is likely to be less than that of the first defendant. There is therefore no particular reason not to join them.

The second consideration is the Limitation Act 1980. Under s 2 of this Act there is a basic three year period from the time of the accident during which proceedings have to start. There have been a number of cases lost because the plaintiff has run out of time to start proceedings.

It is a legal fact of life that actions take a long time to get to court. If the three year time limit has passed before all the possible defendants have been joined into the case, there is little hope of adding a new defendant. Recovery may then only be possible by suing the legal advisor, and this will not endear the negligent litigator to his or her employer. It is therefore generally good advice to join all possible defendants at an early date.

There is no problem about causation since from the facts it appears likely that the accident caused the damage.

The structure

Even though the issues of law are here more complicated, the structure of the draft particulars of claim is still the same as for any tort pleading. This is:

- The parties
- The accident
- The cause of action

- The damage
- The claim for interest
- The prayer

The draft

For the purposes of this pleading we have assumed that the medical report filed with the summons contained all the information required under CCR Ord 6 r1(5)(a). We further assumed that it gives details of the client's prognosis and the pain and loss of amenity she has suffered because of the accident.

We have also assumed that the plaintiff filed a schedule detailing her special damages when her summons was filed at the county court.

> **Sample particulars of claim for breach of Occupiers' Liability Act**

IN THE EAST LONDON COUNTY COURT [1]   **Case No** [2]

BETWEEN

EDITH JONES   Plaintiff [3]

and

(1) GOLDEN HOMES PLC [5]

(2) STELLA LITTLE

(3) ALLAN TURNER

(4) FRED JACKSON (Trading as Pipeworks) [6] Defendants [4]

PARTICULARS OF CLAIM

1. On 21 April 1995 the Plaintiff during the course of her employment visited the Wisteria Nursing Home, Saleworth ('the home'), which at all material times was owned and occupied by the First Defendant and managed by the Second Defendant. The visit was to inspect, inter alia, the plumbing at the home. The Plaintiff was accordingly a visitor of the First and Second Defendant. [7]

2. The Third Defendant at all material times is believed to have been employed by the First Defendant as a consultant maintenance manager. Until 31 March 1995 he had been the maintenance manager and joint owner of the home. The Fourth Defendant had

been instructed to repair the hot water system ('the system') at the home and had visited the home on 14 April 1995. [8]

3. As the Plaintiff turned on a hot water tap in the bathroom in the home on the said day, a burst of steam and boiling water escaped from the tap and scalded the Plaintiff on her face and arms. The Plaintiff attempted to avoid the steam and boiling water and in doing so she fell and injured her wrist. [9]

4. The said accident was caused by the negligence and/or breach of statutory duty under section 2 of the Occupiers' Liability Act 1957 [10] on the part of the Defendants their servants or agents. [11]

PARTICULARS OF NEGLIGENCE AND/OR BREACH OF STATUTORY DUTY [12]

The First [13] and Second [14] Defendants their servants or agents were negligent and/or breached section 2 of the Occupiers' Liability Act in that they: [15]

(a) Allowed the Plaintiff to turn on the tap when the system was unsafe to use.

(b) Failed to give any or any adequate warning to the Plaintiff that the system was unsafe to use.

(c) Failed to supervise the Third and/or the Fourth Defendants, their servants or agents, adequately or at all.

(d) Failed to order the disconnection of the unsafe system.

(e) Failed to make any or any adequate arrangements for the repair of the system.

(f) Failed to instruct the Third and/or Fourth Defendants or any other expert to repair the system.

(g) Failed in all the circumstances to take any or any reasonable care for the Plaintiff's safety. [16]

Further or alternatively [17] the said accident was caused by the negligence [18] of the Third Defendant [19] in that he:

(h) Allowed the Plaintiff to turn on the hot water tap when the system was unsafe to use.

(i) Knowingly allowed the system to remain unsafe and in disrepair.

(j) Failed to give any or any adequate warning to the Plaintiff that the system was unsafe to use.

(k) Failed to make any or any adequate arrangements for the repair of the system.

(l) Failed to instruct the Fourth Defendant or any other expert to repair the system. [20]

Further or alternatively the said accident was caused by the negligence of the Fourth Defendant [21] in that he:

(m) Failed to repair the system adequately or at all.

(n) Failed to give any or any adequate warning to the First, Second or Third Defendant that the system was unsafe to use.

(o) Failed to turn off the system.

(p) Failed to attach a warning notice to any or any visible part of the system to alert the users of the system as to the dangerous condition of the system. [22]

5. By reason of the aforesaid, the Plaintiff suffered pain and injury, loss and damage and has been put to expense. [23]

PARTICULARS OF INJURY

The Plaintiff's injuries are set out in the medical report served herewith in compliance with Order 6 rule 1(5)(a) of the County Court Rules. [24]

PARTICULARS OF SPECIAL DAMAGE [25]

The Plaintiff's losses are set out in the Statement of Special Damages served herewith in compliance with Order 6 rule 1(5)(b) of the County Court Rules. [26]

6. By reason of the matters aforesaid, and in particular the fact that the Plaintiff's condition is likely to deteriorate seriously within the next 5–10 years, [27] necessitating an operation either to excise the ulnar styloid or to fuse her injured wrist, the Plaintiff is entitled to and claims an award of provisional damages pursuant to section 51 of the County Courts Act 1984. [28]

7. Further the Plaintiff is entitled to and claims interest pursuant to section 69 of the County Courts Act 1984 on the amount found to be due to the Plaintiff at such rate and for such period as the court thinks fit. [29]

8. The value of the Plaintiff's claim exceeds £5,000 but does not exceed £50,000. [30]

AND the Plaintiff claims:

(1) Damages.

(2) Provisional damages pursuant to section 51 of the County Courts Act 1984.

(3) Interest under paragraph 7 hereof. [31]

signature
(Counsel or Solicitor)

Dated etc

Notes

Precedent pleadings are to be found in a number of volumes. These can be referred to for the basic structure of a claim under the Occupiers' Liability Act. The facts that are essential to include in these pleadings are indicated below. Round them the draftsman must fit the other information that needs to be included in the pleading to tell the story behind the claim.

1 This case will commence in the county court because the value of the claim is less than £50,000: Art 5 High Court and County Courts Jurisdiction Order 1991. The assessment of potential damages is made either by a barrister or by the solicitor instructed by Mrs Jones. For an explanation as to how to value damages in personal injury cases, see p 183 in the paragraph headed 'Compensation'.

   By CCR Ord 4 r2 the case can commence in the court of the district in which the cause of action arose or in the court for the district in which the defendant resides or carries on business or any county court. Here the choice must be the court that covers the address of the home.

2 The case number and letters that identify the court are allotted by the court official when proceedings are issued.

3 The plaintiff is the name given by the court to the person who starts these court proceedings. At the trial, it is for the plaintiff to prove to the satisfaction of the court that she is entitled to damages for breach of duty under the Occupiers' Liability Act and for negligence. The standard of proof that she will have to meet is on the balance of probabilities.

   The full names of the parties are used in the heading to a pleading. Thereafter in the body of the pleading they are referred to as 'the Plaintiff' and 'the Defendant'.

4 A full discussion of the possible liability of all four defendants is on p 250. This also shows how a decision can be reached as to who should be sued.

   The defendants are joined in one action under CCR Ord 5 r2(a). This is because the rights of relief that are claimed by Mrs Jones arise out of a single incident. It is clearly desirable that these otherwise separate actions should be heard together.

5 The first defendant is a public limited company. It is a legal entity and therefore it must be sued in its company name with service at the registered office.

6   The fourth defendant is sued in his own name followed by his trading name: CCR Ord 5 r10(1)(a). This order sets out the correct form of the pleading. The alternative way of pleading as set out under CCR Ord 5 r10(1)(b) would be PIPEWORKS (a trading name). The choice is the plaintiff's, but will depend on the state of knowledge of the plaintiff at the time the proceedings have to be issued.

7   This is the non-contentious paragraph which traditionally pleads the time, the date and the geographical area where the incident took place. It is *essential* in all pleadings and not confined to pleadings in tort.

- For the purposes of pleading under the Occupiers' Liability Act it is *essential* that one or more of the defendants should be identified as an occupier under the Act and the plaintiff as a visitor.

- It is clearly good pleading to shorten the name and address of the property by introducing the short form 'the home'.

- The status of all the defendants is *essential* in this pleading because their liability will depend on their status.

- Because the second defendant's liability depends on that of the first defendant, this paragraph is a convenient place to include her.

- The reason for the visit of the plaintiff is given so there can be no doubt that she was a visitor under s 2(6) of the Act. See p 249.

- The words *inter alia* are Latin and mean 'amongst other things'. It is one of the few Latin tags now still used in pleadings. It has probably survived because it is a useful phrase.

8   It is often possible to put all the non-contentious information into one paragraph. Here, though there are four defendants, it makes for clarity to introduce them in one paragraph.

Mrs Jones' information about the current status of Mr Turner is not very clear. It is however better to plead what she believes than to give no information at all. This makes sense of her story. The previous status of Mr Turner is known to Mrs Jones and must be included because the cause of the defective system may have arisen during the time he was the owner of the home.

Even less is known about the plumber and the extent of his liability for the defects of the hot water system. For the reasons given on p 250 it is wise however to include him as a defendant. His liability will become clearer as the defences are filed.

9   Though the general rule is that only material facts must be pleaded it is often a useful device to use an adjective in a pleading to give an indication of the gravity of the accident. Here it is unlikely that the plaintiff can prove the water was boiling. But the effect on her skin, which can be proved, is enough to infer this fact.

A paragraph like this, detailing the breach of the duty of care, is essential in all negligence pleadings.

10 This pleads the cause of action. This is *essential* to any pleading. Here the plaintiff is claiming under the tort of negligence and breach of statutory duty, namely s 2 Occupiers' Liability Act. When, as here, the plaintiff is claiming damages for personal injury under the Act and/or in negligence both causes of action must be pleaded. It also also pleads causation which it is *essential* to establish in any pleading in tort.

11 It is not necessary to list all the defendants, but because one the defendants is a company, it is sensible to include the words 'their servants or agents' since the company can only operate through its employees or agents.

12 This is more complicated than other particulars discussed in this book. Four defendants are being sued and their individual liability must be assessed, so they can each answer the claims made against them.

The easiest way to construct such particulars is to work out the potential liability of each defendant, starting with the first defendant. When, as is often the case, the liability co-exists between several or all of the defendants, the device of pleading their liability together or in the alternative with the words 'and/or' is useful to cut down the number of words in the pleading.

13 The company bears the primary liability because the accident happened when it was both the occupier for the purposes of the Occupiers' Liability Act and the employer of staff who may have been responsible for the accident. If the staff are found to be liable, the company will be held to be vicariously liable for the actions of its staff.

Vicarious liability is a principle that states that in certain circumstances a person will be liable for the negligence of his servants or agents as if he were in their stead. The same principle is not applied to independent contractors. Therefore the employer will only be held liable in tort for employees and agents. The company will in these proceedings be liable for the actions of the second defendant, but not the third or fourth unless they can prove they are employees and not independent contractors.

14 Because the second defendant was also an occupier following the decision in *Wheat v Lacon & Co Ltd* (1966) she will be joined in the pleadings with the first defendant.

15 Liability for breach of s 2 of the Act and for negligence must therefore be pleaded against both the first and the second defendants.

16 One negligent act and six negligent omissions are particularised. It is certainly possible to think up further particulars. Probably six, however, are sufficient in most straightforward pleadings.

Particular (b) is important because one of the defences under s 2(4)(a) of the Act is that a warning was given. The plaintiff can give evidence to the fact that she was not given a warning and the defence will have to meet that claim if it is to defend itself on that ground.

Particular (g) is a general sweeping-up provision. The words 'reasonable care' are chosen because they reflect both the common law duty of care and the statutory duty under s 2(2) of taking '... such care as in all the circumstances of the case is reasonable ...'.

17 Because at the time of issue of proceedings it is not known which defendant will be found liable, the correct procedure is to plead all the defendants liable in the alternative. The mechanism for doing this is the words 'Further or alternatively'.

18 This defendant could liable in negligence, but not under a statutory duty. The pleading reflects this.

19 The legal advisors instructed by Mrs Jones have to take a view as to the status of Mr Turner at the time of the accident since the evidence of Mrs Jones is sketchy. It is likely that he is either an employee or an agent of the company and therefore if he is found to be liable or partly liable for the accident, the company will be vicariously liable for his acts or omissions. The pleading therefore refers to his liability at the time of the accident and before the accident as far as is known.

20 Mrs Jones knows of a report commissioned by the defendant company into the accident. This will not be disclosed to her until the process known as 'discovery'. That takes place 28 days after close of pleadings, CCR Ord 17 r11(3)(a). Her advisors must therefore bear in mind that on disclosure of this document their pleadings may have to be amended. It is therefore wise at the start of these proceedings to draft the particulars widely to encompass all areas of potential liability.

21 Even less is known about this defendant and his potential liability. For the reasons given on p 251 it is necessary to join him as a defendant and not wait for the third party notice that the first defendant is likely to issue.

22 The breaches have all been drafted as omissions. It may be necessary to amend the pleading of the particulars when the report is disclosed on discovery (see note 20 above). The negligence may be acts of commission, not omission, and may require amendment.

23 This is the *essential* paragraph which pleads in a general form causation and the particulars of the loss and damage flowing from the breach of statutory duty and breach of the duty of care. This loss includes general and special damages and claims for these are particularised after the general claim.

General damages are the type of damages that a court will assume have resulted from the wrong alleged by the plaintiff. The exact figure need not be expressly pleaded by the plaintiff. It is for the court to decide, after finding for the plaintiff, a suitable award for damages in all the circumstances. They include compensation for pain, suffering, loss of amenity, loss of future work prospects etc.

Special damages claims have to be expressly set out in the plaintiff's pleadings. The defendant can then have the opportunity to argue as to the merits or extent of any particular sum.

24 Because the medical report in this particular case is comprehensive, it is not necessary to repeat in the pleadings the extent of the plaintiff's injuries, her prognosis or the effect the injuries have had and will continue to have on her leisure activities, her work and her future.

A claim for personal injuries will include under general damages a claim for loss of amenity. Amenity in the legal sense means enjoyment of life and will include losses suffered because the plaintiff is no longer able to continue with previous hobbies and other leisure activities. If the plaintiff, because of the injury, is no longer able to enjoy these activities, a claim may be made to compensate her financially for this loss. But, in order to obtain these damages, evidence must be brought to the court. This can be included in the medical report, because the loss relates to a medical condition, as hearing or sight, or may be pleaded separately in the particulars of injury.

A claim may also be made for compensation for pain. This has been pleaded in these particulars. If the claim is to succeed, evidence must be brought that the plaintiff did suffer pain. If there is evidence in the medical report this need not be repeated in the particulars of injury.

If the medical report is not comprehensive and does not give evidence of the pain, the loss of amenity, or the medical prognosis for the plaintiff, these must be pleaded in addition to the medical report. See 'Particulars of Injury' pleaded on p 187 in Chapter 8 for an example.

A medical report must be filed with the particulars of claim under CCR Ord 6 r1(5)(a). The words used in this pleading annex the medical report to the pleading, and it thus becomes part of the pleading.

25 Under CCR Ord 6 r1(5)(b) the plaintiff in an action for personal injury must file with the court, with the particulars of claim, a statement of the special damages claimed. This can be done either by listing the details of the special damages on a schedule and annexing this to the pleadings or incorporating them in the pleadings. The annexed schedule is particularly convenient if the special damages are lengthy.

26 The words used in this pleading annex the schedule to the pleading. It therefore becomes part of the pleading and evidence can be brought at trial to substantiate the claims, but only the claims listed on the schedule.

If the plaintiff finds difficulty in obtaining evidence of the value of one or several items of special damage, it is not good practice to delay issuing proceedings and so risking falling foul of the Limitation Act. Good practice is to list the item and write 'tba' (to be advised) or similar words under the value column.

27 In some personal injury cases medical evidence will show that the plaintiff's health, though currently improved, will or may deteriorate in the future as a result of the personal injury. Depending on the strength of the medical evidence, the plaintiff is faced with a choice. She can ask for provisional damages under s 51 County Courts Act 1984 or she can ask for damages to reflect the full extent of her injuries at the time of the trial. The power of the county courts to grant provisional damages is under CCR Ord 22 r6A.

28 Provisional damages, under s 51 County Courts Act 1984, mean that the plaintiff asks for damages to be assessed assuming that her condition will not deteriorate, but it also gives her the later

opportunity to apply for further damages at a future date if her condition does deteriorate.

If a claim is made for provisional damages, CCR Ord 6 r1B states that the particulars of claim shall include the claim and the facts that the plaintiff relies on to support the claim. The evidence relied on in this pleading will be in the medical report which is part of the pleadings by annexation under the Particulars of Injury. If the medical evidence is comprehensive, it is only necessary to give general facts when pleading provisional damages.

The order for provisional damages is limited. It has to specify the type of deterioration and the period in which an application for provisional damages may be made. If the plaintiff's health deteriorates, it is possible to make only one application for further damages and this must be because of deterioration of health as specified in the original order for provisional damages. It must also be within the time limits specified in the original order.

The alternative to pleading provisional damages is to put forward as evidence the prognosis of the medical expert that will be relied on at trial by the plaintiff. This may mean that the plaintiff will be awarded a larger sum at the trial, but will not have the opportunity to go back to court to claim more money should her health deteriorate at a later date.

Before making a decision as to whether or not to claim provisional damages, it may be necessary to seek the advice of medical and financial experts as well as discussing the alternatives with the plaintiff.

29 The claim for interest must be specifically pleaded: CCR Ord 6 r1A. Details of the rates of interest in the county courts on special and general damages are on p 192 at note 13.

30 This states the value of the claim. By art 5 High Court and County Courts Jurisdiction Order 1991 where a personal injury claim is for less than £50,000, the action must commence in the county court.

31 This contains a summary of the remedies that the plaintiff is claiming. Included here is the claim for provisional damages. Interest can be claimed in a number of different ways; the way it is pleaded here is just one example.

Defences to a claim for breach of statutory duty and negligence

For the purposes of this chapter, we have assumed that there is no defence under the Limitation Act. We therefore assumed that Mrs Jones issued and served proceedings within three years of the accident taking place.

We also have appreciated that causation cannot be in issue and so must be disregarded, nor can the lack of foreseeability for the accident be mounted as a defence since all the defendants knew of the problems with the hot water system.

That being so, the defences of the four defendants now have to be considered.

The first and second defendants' defences

We assume that the company cannot deny that it is an occupier under the Act, nor can it deny that Mrs Jones is a visitor. Further, in the light of *Wheat v Lacon* (1966) (above) it cannot deny that the second defendant is an occupier as well as an employee.

FIRST DEFENCE: STATUTORY WARNING

A possible defence under the Act is that a warning was given to Mrs Jones. This defence is set out at s 2(4)(a). The first defendant has evidence to show that it gave instructions that a sticky label was to be positioned above every hot water tap in the home warning that the water was very hot.

The second defendant will say that acting on company policy she instructed a member of staff to place the warning notices above every hot tap in the home. She will also give evidence to the fact that she had discussed the problems of the hot water system with Mrs Jones who was well aware of why the staff at the home no longer used the hot water.

The case law on warnings suggests that they must be specific about the immediacy of the danger (*Rae v Mars (UK) Ltd* (1990)). This the defendant will have to prove at trial.

The statutory defence will not be effective unless the defendants can prove that the warning was '... enough to enable the visitor to be reasonably safe ...'.

SECOND DEFENCE: FAULT OF ANOTHER

This can lead many defendants down the 'not my fault guv' route. The possibilities are that the fault was that of either the plumber or Mr Turner, both of whom could be held to be independent contractors. This also is a statutory defence under s 2(4)(b) Occupiers' Liability Act.

The first and second defendants must prove firstly that the damage caused was '... due to the faulty execution of any work of construction, maintenance or repair by an independent contractor employed by the occupier ...'.

Secondly the first and second defendants must prove that they '... had acted reasonably in entrusting the work to an independent contractor ...'.

Lastly they must prove that they had taken such steps as was reasonable '... in order to satisfy himself that the contractor was competent and that the work had been properly done'.

If the report into the accident showed either the third or fourth defendant as wholly or partly responsible, the defence of the first and second defendant could be drafted along the lines indicated below.

The defendants can prove the second limb, above, that is, that they acted reasonably in entrusting the work to Mr Turner, since he had successfully owned and managed and maintained the home for a number of years and was a competent contractor.

Whether they can prove the third limb, that is, that they had taken steps to satisfy themselves that the work was properly done, could be more difficult and would depend on the evidence of what instructions they gave Mr Turner.

THIRD DEFENCE: CONTRIBUTORY NEGLIGENCE

A further defence to all common law negligence claims is contributory negligence. While not acting as a total defence if it succeeds it will reduce the total damages awarded at trial by a stated percentage.

The ground for so reducing damages is the Law Reform (Contributory Negligence) Act 1945. This states in s 1(1) that:

Where any person suffers damage as the result partly of his own fault and partly of the fault of any other person or persons ... the damages recoverable ... shall be reduced to such extent as the court thinks just and equitable having regard to the claimant's share in the responsibility for the damage ...

The Act applies only to actions in tort. It is open to the occupier as a qualified defence even if the right is not given in the Act. A 50% contribution was ordered in *Stone v Taffe* (1974) which was a case concerning liability under the Occupiers' Liability Act.

Fourth defence: *Volenti non fit injuria*

Under s 2(5) Occupiers' Liability Act, if the plaintiff willingly accepts the risks which caused him or her damage the maxim *volenti non fit injuria* will not be excluded by the Act.

In order to establish the defence, the plaintiff must be shown not only to have perceived the existence of danger, but also to have appreciated it fully, *Merrington v Ironbridge Metal Works Ltd* (1952), and voluntarily accepted the risk, *Cutler v United Dairies (London) Ltd* (1933).

The plaintiff may argue that it was her job to check on the facilities at the home, but the defendants will say that in trying the taps she was exceeding her duty and voluntarily taking on the risk.

The last matter to consider is joining the first and second defendants in a joint defence. Since the second defendant is an employee of the first defendant and both are being sued in negligence and for breach of statutory duty, they will have a common defence. It is sensible, and cheaper, to serve a joint defence in this particular case.

Sample defence of the first and second defendants

IN THE EAST LONDON   Case No
COUNTY COURT

BETWEEN

EDITH JONES   <u>Plaintiff</u>

and

(1) GOLDEN HOMES PLC
(2) STELLA LITTLE
(3) ALLAN TURNER
(4) FRED JACKSON
(Trading as Pipeworks)   <u>Defendants</u>

DEFENCE OF THE FIRST AND SECOND DEFENDANTS [1]

1. Paragraph 1 of the Particulars of Claim is admitted, save it is not admitted that the visit of the Plaintiff to the home was to inspect the plumbing of the home. [2]

2. Paragraph 2 of the Particulars of Claim is admitted save it is denied that the Third Defendant was employed by the First and/or Second Defendant. At all material times the Third Defendant was an independent contractor. [3]

3. Paragraph 3 of the Particulars of Claim is not admitted. [4] The Plaintiff was warned on the said day by the Second Defendant in the presence of the Third Defendant of the danger of the system. Further, a warning notice was placed by the Second Defendant on 5th April 1995 above the hot water taps in each and every bathroom and above every basin in the home. Such warnings were in all the circumstances enough to enable the Plaintiff to be reasonably safe. [5]

4. The First Defendant and the Second Defendant deny that they, their servants or agents were negligent or in breach of statutory duty as alleged in paragraph 4 of the Particulars of Claim or at all. [6] It is further denied that the said accident was caused by the alleged or any negligence or breach of statutory duty on the part of the First or the Second Defendant, their servants or agents. [7]

5. The Third Defendant was at all material times an independent contractor hired by the First Defendant to manage, maintain and

repair the exterior and the interior of the home. The Fourth Defendant was an independent contractor engaged by the Third Defendant to repair the system. [8]

6. The First and Second Defendants acted reasonably in entrusting the work and maintenance to the Third and Fourth Defendants [9] and took all reasonable steps to satisfy themselves that the Third Defendant was competent to supervise the maintenance of the home. [10]

7. If, which is not admitted, a duty of care was owed to the Plaintiff by the Third and Fourth Defendants, [11] the said accident was caused by the negligence of the Third and Fourth Defendants. [12]

PARTICULARS OF NEGLIGENCE OF THE THIRD DEFENDANT

The Third Defendant was negligent in that he:

(a) Knowingly allowed the system to fall into disrepair.

(b) Knowing that the system was in disrepair failed to mend it or to make any or any adequate arrangements for the repair of the system.

(c) Failed to instruct the Fourth Defendant or any other expert to repair the system.

(d) Failed to disconnect the system.

(e) Failed to warn the Plaintiff that the system was in disrepair.

(f) In all the circumstances acted negligently.

PARTICULARS OF NEGLIGENCE OF THE FOURTH DEFENDANT

The Fourth Defendant was negligent in that he:

(a) When instructed failed to repair the system adequately or at all.

(b) Failed to give any or any adequate warning to the First or Second Defendant that the system was in disrepair.

(c) Failed to disconnect the system.

(d) In all the circumstances acted negligently.

8. Further or alternatively the said accident was caused by or contributed to the negligence of the Plaintiff. [13]

PARTICULARS OF CONTRIBUTORY NEGLIGENCE

The Plaintiff:

(a) Failed to heed the oral warning about the system given to the Plaintiff by the Second Defendant in the presence of the Third Defendant.

(b) Turned on the hot water tap when she knew or ought to have known that the system was in disrepair.

(c) Failed to take care when she turned on the tap.

(d) Failed to heed warning notices.

(e) Failed to take any or any proper care for her own safety.

9. Further or alternatively the Plaintiff willingly accepted the risks of such damage by reason whereof the First and Second Defendants owe no duty in respect of such risks as alleged in the Particulars of Claim or at all. The Plaintiff is therefore not entitled to maintain her claim against the Defendants. [14]

PARTICULARS

The Plaintiff was warned about the system as stated in paragraph 2 hereof.

[15]

10. The Defendants make no admissions as to any of the matters alleged in paragraphs 7 and 8 of the Particulars of Claim. [16]

[17]

                                                        Signature

Dated etc

Notes

1   Heading is the same as on the plaintiff's particulars of claim. The title to the defence pleading is however the defence of the first and second defendants. The reason why they are joined in defending the action is referred to on p 250.

2   This admits most of para 1 of the particulars of claim. However, the defendants do not know what the purpose of the plaintiff's visit was to the home. They therefore do not admit that particular sentence. This will mean that the plaintiff has to give evidence to support that part of her claim.

3   This admits most of para 2 of the particulars of claim. However they wish to deny that they employed the third defendant, Mr Turner. It will be part of their defence that the fault lay with either the plumber, the fourth defendant, or with Mr Turner, the third defendant. Both of these defendants will be claimed by the first and second defendant to be independent contractors and they will bring proof of this to the trial.

4   This is not admitted. This means that the plaintiff will have to give evidence as to the facts she alleges in this paragraph and she will be subject to cross-examination by the defendant's barrister or solicitor.

5   The defendants cannot deny that the accident took place but they now have the chance to put their side of the story. Their defence to this part of the pleading is that despite a verbal warning, and despite a notice above the hot water taps in the bathroom, the plaintiff insisted on turning on a hot water tap. This is the first defence which is discussed on p 262.

6   The first sentence is a denial of the alleged fact that the first and second defendants were negligent or in breach of a statutory duty under the Occupiers' Liability Act. Note that the name of the Act does not have to be repeated in the pleading.

7   The second sentence is denying causation. The defendants are stating that the cause of the accident was not their negligence. Since servants and agents have been included quite rightly in the particulars of claim, it is good practice to deny that they also were negligent, or caused the accident.

8   This starts to give the defendants' side of the story. The defendants have decided that the fault lies not with them, but with others, namely their independent contractors, the plumber and Mr Turner. This is the second defence which is discussed on p 263.

    This paragraph gives further information as to the status of the third and fourth defendants. The first and second defendants will prove at trial that they were independent contractors and not employees.

9   In order for the second defence to be successful, not only must the defendants prove that the damage caused to a visitor was the work of an independent contractor, but that the defendants had acted reasonably in entrusting the work to such a contractor. The first part of this sentence is pleading to this fact.

10 The second limb of this statutory defence is that the defendants ought to satisfy themselves that the contractor was competent and the work had been reasonably done. The second part of this sentence addresses this.

    It is likely that the first and second defendants will raise in their evidence that, since Mr Turner had successfully run the home for a number of years before it was purchased by the first defendant, it was reasonable to assume that he was competent to continue to do so.

The particulars of negligence of the third defendant must be specifically structured to show how he in particular was negligent. Similarly, the particulars of negligence of the fourth defendant, the plumber, must be crafted to reflect how his actions or omissions were negligent.

11 In the first part of the sentence of this paragraph they do not admit that the duty of care is owed. By doing this, they leave it to the plaintiff to prove the duty of care in negligence.

The duty of care in negligence is more difficult to prove than the duty of care under the Occupiers' Liability Act. Obviously the Occupiers' Liability Act cannot apply to the plumber and Mr Turner, so the first and second defendants will make life harder for the plaintiff by not admitting the duty of care.

12 Having denied causation in para 3 of the defence, in the last part of the sentence, the defendants state who they hope to prove caused the accident.

13 This is the pleading which reflects the third defence on p 263. This defence is often referred to as a partial defence. This is because it is not possible for a court to find that a plaintiff can be totally contributorily negligent: s 1(1) Law Reform (Contributory Negligence) Act 1945.

The claim in contributory negligence must be pleaded by the defence, and the particulars give details of how and why the defence hopes to prove that the plaintiff was at least partially responsible for the damage resulting from the accident.

At trial the judge has the power under s 1(1) Law Reform (Contributory Negligence) Act 1945 to reduce the damages recoverable ' ... to such extent as the court thinks just and equitable having regard to the claimant's share in the responsibility for the damage ... '.

At trial the lawyer must be prepared to argue not only that the plaintiff was partly responsible for the accident, but also to what extent the damages should be reduced because the plaintiff was partly to blame.

14 This is the pleading which reflects the fourth defence on p 264. This is a different defence to contributory negligence. The basis of the defence is that the plaintiff, knowing of the risk, voluntarily incurs the risk. This is because, while acting in such a manner, they may or may not exercise the utmost care for their safety. While the extent of that care defines the extent of the contributory negligence, it does not go to the defence of *volenti*.

Therefore here the defendants must prove that the plaintiff not only knew of the danger, but fully appreciated this danger and in the light of this full appreciation accepted the risk of turning on the hot tap.

This requires a high level of proof. Examples where the defence of *volenti* have not succeeded are shown in case law. For instance, a passenger travelling in a car does not necessarily accept the risk of negligent driving even though he knows that the driver is under the influence of alcohol, *Dann v Hamilton* (1939), or is a learner, *Nettleship v Weston* (1971). Whether this can be proved by these particular defendants will be left for the lawyer to decide.

15 It is not necessary to plead to paras 5 and 6 of the particulars of claim since they refer to the third and fourth defendants.

16 This is a paragraph not admitting the extent or the existence of the claim by the plaintiff for special, general or provisional damages.

This means that the plaintiff will have to bring evidence to prove both the existence of the loss for which she is claiming damages and the amount that she thinks that the claim is worth and, further, whether the court should grant provisional damages.

17 It is not necessary to plead to interest in para 9 of the particulars of claim. Nor is it necessary to plead to the prayer.

Possible defences for the third defendant

The third defendant is only defending the negligence action. He cannot be liable under the Occupiers' Liability Act as he is not an occupier within the meaning of the Act.

It is usually worthwhile before drafting a defence to go through a checklist of possible defences.

The usual defences to a negligence claim are:

* The plaintiff cannot successfully prove all the elements necessary in the cause of action. In negligence this is to establish a duty of care, breach of the duty and damages flowing from the breach. There appears to be no possibility of mounting a defence to break these elements in this case.

* Arguments that limit the amount of damages as lack of foreseeability, lack of causation, failure to mitigate losses, a counter-claim or claims of contributory negligence. The only possibility here is contributory negligence.

- Statutory defences as under the Limitation Act 1980 which are not applicable here.
- Possible claims against a third party or other defendants which in this case is worth considering.
- A possible further defence here is the legal status of the third defendant. If he can prove he is an employee of the first defendant, then the first defendant company will be vicariously liable for his negligent acts or omissions which occurred in the course of his employment.

The third defendant's defence

This will be:

(a) the third defendant was an employee of the first defendant; and
(b) the first, second and fourth defendant were responsible for the accident; and
(c) the plaintiff contributed to the negligence; and
(d) the plaintiff will have to prove the negligence, and the extent of her loss and the damages she is claiming because the third defendant will not admit these.

Sample defence of the third defendants

IN THE EAST LONDON
COUNTY COURT   **Case No**

BETWEEN

EDITH JONES   <u>Plaintiff</u>

and

(1) GOLDEN HOMES PLC
(2) STELLA LITTLE
(3) ALLAN TURNER
(4) FRED JACKSON   <u>Defendants</u>
(Trading as Pipeworks)

DEFENCE OF THE THIRD DEFENDANT [1]

1. Paragraphs 1 and 2 of the Particulars of Claim are admitted. In particular the Defendant admits that he was at all material times employed by the First Defendant. [2]

2. Paragraph 3 of the Particulars of Claim is not admitted. [3]

3. The Third Defendant denies that he was negligent as alleged in paragraph 4 of the Particulars of Claim or at all, and denies that the said accident was caused by the alleged or any negligence on the part of the Third Defendant. [4]

4. If, which is not admitted, a duty of care was owed by the First, Second and Fourth Defendants to the Plaintiff, the said accident was caused by the First, Second and Fourth Defendant. [5]

<u>PARTICULARS OF NEGLIGENCE OF THE FIRST</u>
<u>AND SECOND DEFENDANTS</u>

The First and Second Defendants were negligent in that they:

(a) Failed to approve plans for the repair of the system which were drawn up by the Third Defendant.

(b) Failed to authorise expenditure for the repairs to the system.

(c) Failed to allow the Third Defendant to engage a competent workman to repair the system.

(d) Failed to allow the Third Defendant to turn off the system.

(e) In all the circumstances failed to undertake their duty of care.

PARTICULARS OF NEGLIGENCE OF THE FOURTH DEFENDANT

The Fourth Defendant was negligent in that he:

(a) When instructed failed to repair the system adequately or at all.

(b) Failed to give any or any adequate warning to the First, Second and Third Defendants that the system was dangerous.

(c) Failed to disconnect or turn off the system.

(d) Failed to return to complete the work on the system, thus leaving the system in a dangerous state.

(e) In all the circumstances failed to undertake his duty of care.

5. Paragraph 5 of the Particulars of Claim is denied. [6]

6. Further or alternatively, the said accident was caused by or contributed to the negligence of the Plaintiff. [7]

PARTICULARS OF CONTRIBUTORY NEGLIGENCE

The Plaintiff:

(a) Failed to heed the oral warnings given by the Third Defendant as to the dangerous state of the system.

(b) Turned on the tap knowing the system was in an unsafe condition.

(c) Failed to take due care when she turned on the tap.

(d) Failed in the above circumstances to take any or any proper care for her own safety.

7. No admission is made as to the alleged or any pain, injury, loss or damages suffered by the Plaintiff, or as to the amount thereof. [8]

[9]

Signature

Dated etc

Notes

1 Heading as the draft defence of the first and second defendants. The heading however must state it is the defence of the third defendant.

2 This admits paras 1 and 2 of the particulars of claim. To signal that his defence will be based on note (a) on p 271 he highlights his admission that he was employed by the first defendant company at the time of the accident.

3   By not admitting the actions that the plaintiff states gave rise to the accident, this means that these will have to be proved by the plaintiff at the trial.

4   This is a denial that the third defendant was negligent and the second sentence denies that any alleged negligence caused the accident. He is therefore denying causation.

5   He does not admit that a duty of care was owed to the plaintiff. This leaves the plaintiff having to prove this to the satisfaction of the court. The second sentence states that the defence will be based on note (b) on p 271 that the three other defendants were responsible for the accident.

6   This is the denial by the third defendant of the breaches of the duty of care alleged by the plaintiff. He has denied the breaches because he can bring evidence to show that either the breaches did not arise, or, if they did arise, they arose because they were the fault of someone else.

7   Paragraph 6 continues to give the third defendant's side of the story. This paragraph is his defence (c) on p 271 that the plaintiff was at least in part responsible for the accident. Contributory negligence is discussed on p 263.

8   This is a statement that the third defendant does not admit to the plaintiff's injuries, losses, or amount of general or special damages. It is the final element in his defence (d) on p 271.

9   It is not necessary to plead to paras 4 and 6 of the particulars of claim as they refer to the first, second and fourth defendants.

Similarly it is not necessary to plead to the interest in para 9 of the particulars of claim. Nor is it necessary to plead to the prayer.

The fourth defendant's defence

We will assume that the fourth defendant had not looked at the summons and the particulars of claim when they arrived in the post. He is now in a panic and the solicitor he instructs soon realises he needs an extension of time to draft and serve a defence. The fourth defendant, a plumber, who is now in extreme financial difficulties, may also be eligible for legal aid so more time is needed to make an application for the grant of a legal aid certificate and receive the offer of legal aid.

An extension of time of five working days is granted by the plaintiff's solicitor on the telephone. This is not enough, so the solicitor has only one choice. He drafts a holding defence.

A holding defence

This is a defence which should only be filed and served when there is no time to draft a full defence. It is an option that should be taken only in extreme circumstances, when it will prevent the disastrous consequences of the plaintiff obtaining a judgment in default of the requirement to serve the defence 14 days after service.

Judgment in default is obtained in the county court under CCR Ord 9 r6(2) when the claim is for unliquidated damages. The damages will then be assessed at a later hearing.

Sample holding defence

IN THE EAST LONDON COUNTY COURT   **Case No**

BETWEEN

EDITH JONES   <u>Plaintiff</u>

and

(1) GOLDEN HOMES Plc

(2) STELLA LITTLE

(3) ALLAN TURNER

(4) FRED JACKSON   <u>Defendants</u>

(Trading as Pipeworks)

DEFENCE OF THE FOURTH DEFENDANT

---

1. Paragraph 1 of the Particulars of Claim is not admitted. [1]
2. Paragraph 2 of the Particulars of Claim is denied. [2]
3. Paragraphs 3, 4 and 5 of the Particulars of Claim are not admitted. [3]
4. Paragraph 6 of the Particulars of Claim is denied. [4]
5. Paragraphs 7 and 8 of the Particulars of Claim are not admitted. [5]

Signature

Dated etc

Notes

1 Is not admitted because this defendant has no knowledge of anything alleged in that paragraph of the particulars of claim, and wishes the plaintiff to prove her allegations.
2 Is denied because the last sentence does not agree with the fourth defendant's somewhat limited instructions.
3 Is not admitted because the fourth defendant has no personal knowledge of any of the matters alleged in these paragraphs.
4 Is denied because the fourth defendant says he was not negligent.
5 Is not admitted because the fourth defendant has no knowledge of the plaintiff's injuries, the amount of her claim or the fact that she has suffered loss and damage because of her injuries.

The best that can be said about this defence is that it stops judgment being entered by the plaintiff against the fourth defendant.

It does not state for the benefit of the court, the plaintiff and the other defendants, the basis of the fourth defendant's defence.

One of the purposes of pleadings is to isolate the unresolved elements in a dispute. This pleading, it is obvious, does nothing to show the plaintiff what the fourth defendant is going to allege as his defence.

This is not an elegant way of pleading a defence. It is however sometimes necessary, but the drafter of such a defence must realise it is only a temporary measure, and he or she will need to file a full defence as soon as possible.

Chapter 11

Drafting in a Nuisance Case

Scope of chapter

One type of problem on which legal advice is often sought arises where a lay client is aggrieved by the conduct of a neighbour. While the best advice to such a client may be to settle the matter amicably if possible, some disputes between neighbours do result in litigation.

We looked at one such dispute in Chapter 7. There the conduct complained of was the felling of a tree in a neighbour's garden which resulted in damage to the client's property. In that case, the client was able to bring an action in negligence to recover his losses. However, conduct which interferes with enjoyment of the land a client owns or occupies may also give rise to an action in private nuisance.[1]

The purpose of this chapter is to outline the nature of this action and to show how to approach drafting in the context of such a claim.

Nuisance

The nature of the action

Private nuisance may be defined as an activity, omission or state of affairs which wrongfully interferes with a person's use or enjoyment of land which he or she owns or occupies.[2]

Such interference may take the form of encroachment on another's land as where the branches of a tree overhang a neighbour's land. In other cases the nuisance alleged consists in causing physical damage to a neighbour's land or property on it. This might occur, for example, where water flooding from a blocked drain destroys vegetables growing on a neighbour's land. Frequently, however, the nuisance consists in activities which interfere with a neighbour's comfort, causing annoyance to him. Examples of such activities are making

---

[1] An activity or state of affairs may be a nuisance at common law or made a nuisance by statute. At common law a nuisance may be a public nuisance or a private nuisance. Only the latter type of nuisance is considered in this chapter.

[2] Wrongful interference with an easement, for example, obstruction of a right of way, or other right enjoyed in connection with land constitutes nuisance.

unreasonable noise, causing vibration or causing smoke to spread over another person's land.

In most cases the conduct of a person alleged to be causing a nuisance is in itself lawful. It is the resulting interference with another's use or enjoyment of land which renders the conduct in question actionable in nuisance. In deciding whether or not it is so actionable, the court will consider whether or not the use the defendant is making of his land is unreasonable in the light of its adverse effect on the plaintiff's enjoyment of his land. Other related factors taken into account are the character and extent of such interference. Its duration is also relevant, though temporary interference may be actionable if substantial.

Remedies

Where proceedings are brought arising out of conduct alleged to constitute a nuisance, the remedies which may be sought are damages and/or an injunction.

DAMAGES

Where the conduct complained of causes damage to the plaintiff's property, damages may be awarded on the basis of diminution in the value of the property. Where the damage consists of interference with the plaintiff's enjoyment of the land by causing discomfort and inconvenience to the plaintiff, rather than damages to his or her property, damages may be awarded for loss of amenity, as in a personal injury case.[3]

INJUNCTION

Where the nuisance is alleged to be a continuing one an additional or alternative remedy is an injunction restraining the defendant from continuing the conduct or state of affairs said to constitute nuisance. In many cases the plaintiff will seek a prohibitory injunction restraining the defendant from doing certain proscribed acts. In some cases, however, the appropriate remedy will be a mandatory injunction which orders the defendant to do some act, for example to demolish a fence erected by the defendant which obstructs the plaintiff's right of way. The remedy sought will be a final injunction to prevent any future nuisance of the kind described in the order.

However, immediate relief may be sought in the period between issuing proceedings and trial of the action, by an application for an

---

3 *Bone v Seale* [1975] 1 All ER 787 CA.

interlocutory or interim injunction. In cases of exceptional urgency an injunction may be sought before proceedings have been issued.

Defences in a nuisance action

IGNORANCE OF THE NUISANCE

An occupier of land from which a nuisance emanates cannot be held liable if the nuisance was created by another and the occupier neither knew nor ought to have known of its existence.

CONSENT

Proof that a plaintiff specifically agreed to accept the nuisance will constitute a defence provided that negligence by the defendant is not alleged.

CONTRIBUTORY NEGLIGENCE

The Law Reform (Contributory Negligence) Act 1945 applies to nuisance and provides a defence except where the defendant deliberately creates a nuisance.

STATUTORY AUTHORITY

A defendant is not liable for nuisance which is the inevitable result of its activities if those activities are authorised by a statute.

PRESCRIPTION

It is in theory a defence that the nuisance alleged has continued for over 20 years, though this defence is unlikely to succeed in practice.

Drafting in a nuisance case

Drafting on behalf of the plaintiff

WHO CAN SUE?

The first step is to establish that the client is competent to bring proceedings in nuisance. It has long been the rule that only a person having a freehold or leasehold interest in the land affected can sue in nuisance. However, in *Khorasandjian v Bush* (1993) 3 WLR 496, a majority of the Court of Appeal held that a child living at home with her parents could obtain an injunction to restrain harrassing telephone calls notwithstanding that she had no proprietary interest in the property. The plaintiff may, therefore, be the owner or tenant occupying the land or, it appears, a member of the occupier's family, such as a wife or child, who is living at the property.

WHO CAN BE SUED?

Next, the appropriate defendant or defendants must be identified. Anyone who creates a nuisance may properly be sued. He or she need not be in occupation of the land on which the nuisance originates. However, in such a case the occupier of that land may also be sued if, having actual or presumed knowledge of the existence of the nuisance alleged, he or she takes no steps to prevent or minimise it.

WHICH COURT?

Once the correct parties have been identified, it is necessary to check in which court the action should be brought. As mentioned earlier on p 146 the jurisdiction of the High Court and the county courts is concurrent in matters of tort, but in selecting a venue the rules with regard to allocation for trial must be borne in mind. A straightforward case may well be appropriate for the county courts, but one involving complex issues of law or fact and/or a claim for substantial damages should be brought in the High Court, normally in the Queen's Bench Division.

The statement/particulars of claim

As is the case in pleading any cause of action, the framework of the pleading is provided by the essential elements which must be established if the claim is to succeed. In a case of nuisance these are:

(1) wrongful conduct

(2) by another

(3) causing

(4) interference with use and/or enjoyment of the land

(5) by the owner/occupier of that land (as extended by *Khorasandjian v Bush*)

(6) resulting in loss and/or damage.

Where it is alleged that the nuisance consists in causing damage to a neighbour's land, or property on that land, the existence of damage is an additional element which must be proved at trial. Where, however, the nuisance consists of an encroachment on a neighbour's land, damage is presumed to exist and need not be proved. Nor is it necessary to establish damage where the alleged nuisance consists in interfering with a neighbour's comfort by creating noise, vibration, toxic fumes or similar conduct. In such cases, the discomfort and annoyance caused constitute damage.

In a simple case of nuisance caused by noise, the statement/particulars of claim must therefore plead the following matters:

THE PLAINTIFF'S RELEVANT STATUS: (5) ABOVE

Since the plaintiff must normally establish a legal interest in the land allegedly affected by the nuisance complained of, his or her status as occupier of that land must be pleaded. Normally this is dealt with in the opening paragraph. A typical example is:

> The Plaintiff is and was at all material times the owner (lessee) of premises known as ... at [address].

THE DEFENDANT'S RELEVANT STATUS: (2) ABOVE

Since the nuisance alleged to affect the plaintiff's land must emanate from some other land, the defendant's relevant status will be his or her occupation of, or presence upon, such land at the time of the wrongful activities for which he or she is alleged to be liable. The examples below show how the defendant's relevant status is pleaded in two common situations.

(a) Where the nuisance complained of is caused by the activities of a neighbour on his or her land:

> The Defendant is and was at all material times the owner and occupier of the neighbouring land at [address].

(b) Where the nuisance complained of is caused by the activities of a building contractor working on the land:

> The Defendant is a building contractor and as such was at all material times engaged in works of demolition and construction on a site at [address].

In this way the matters identifying the person causing the nuisance at (2) above are pleaded. This may be done in the paragraph pleading the plaintiff's relevant status, or in a separate paragraph.

THE CONDUCT ALLEGED TO AMOUNT TO NUISANCE: (1) ABOVE

The next matter which must be pleaded is the nuisance itself. That is the conduct which is alleged to interfere with the plaintiff's enjoyment of or use of the land. In a case where it is alleged that work done by a building contractor causes excessive noise and vibration, the facts of nuisance might be pleaded as follows:

> During the course of the said works the Defendant his servants or agents by using pneumatic drills wrongfully caused excessive noise to come from the said site into the plaintiff's said premises.

Where necessary details of the conduct alleged to constitute nuisance may be given under the heading of particulars, as illustrated at p 287.

CAUSATION AND LOSS AND/OR DAMAGE: (5) AND (6) ABOVE

As indicated earlier, in some types of nuisance cases damage need not be proved. Nevertheless, the fact that interference with the plaintiff's use and/or enjoyment of the land has resulted in loss and/or damage must be pleaded. The examples below illustrate how this may be done:

(a) Where the damage consists of the annoyance and discomfort caused to the plaintiff:

> By reason of the matters complained of, the Plaintiff and his family have been and are being caused nuisance and the Plaintiff has thereby suffered damage.

(b) Where it is alleged that the nuisance complained of has caused physical damage to the plaintiff's property and consequent loss to the plaintiff:

> By reason of the matters complained of, the Plaintiff's said premises have been damaged and the Plaintiff has thereby suffered loss and damage.

PARTICULARS OF SPECIAL DAMAGE

> (a) cost of repairs due to the subsidence of
>   Plaintiff's house estimated at   £
>
> (b) cost of repairs to Plaintiff's said fence estimated at   £

This example also illustrates the basic rule that particulars must be pleaded of any special damage alleged.

The remedies sought

INJUNCTION

Where this remedy is sought, the ground for the claim to an injunction must be set out in the body of the statement/particulars of claim by pleading that the nuisance is a continuing one and will so continue unless the defendant is restrained by an injunction. The examples that follow show how these matters are pleaded:

(a) claim for a prohibitory injunction to restrain nuisance by a building contractor:

By a letter dated [date] the Plaintiff requested the Defendant to abate the nuisance complained of but the Defendant refused to do so and threatens unless restrained by injunction to continue to carry out the aforesaid activities causing the said nuisance.

(b) claim for a mandatory injunction to compel the defendant to cut his trees so as to remove the branches which overhang the plaintiff's land:

By a letter dated [date] the Plaintiff requested to Defendant to cut the said trees and/or to take such other steps as would prevent the branches from encroaching over the Plaintiff's said premises and thereby causing nuisance and annoyance to the Plaintiff, but the Defendant has refused to do so and unless restrained by injunction threatens and intends to continue the said nuisance.

The claim for an injunction must also be pleaded in the prayer, as in the example below.

DAMAGES

A claim for damages must also be pleaded in the prayer. It should be remembered that where the claim exceeds £5,000 this must be pleaded.

INTEREST

As in other tortious actions, the claim for interest under s 35A Supreme Court Act 1981 in the High Court or s 69 County Courts Act 1984 in the county court must be pleaded in the body of the statement/particulars of claim and repeated in the prayer.

THE PRAYER

An example of a prayer claiming damages, an injunction and interest in an action in nuisance brought in the county court is set out below:

AND the Plaintiff claims:

(1) Damages;

(2) An injunction to restrain the Defendant from allowing the branches of any tree on his said land so to encroach on the Plaintiff's said land as to cause a nuisance; and

(3) Interest pursuant to section 69 of the County Courts Act 1984.

The application for an interlocutory injunction

Where nuisance is alleged, it may be appropriate for the plaintiff to apply to the court for an interlocutory injunction to restrain the conduct complained of in the period between issuing proceedings and the hearing of the action.

The process of making an application and the drafting skills required have already been described in Chapter 4. It will be remembered that in the county court the application is made by completing the prescribed Form N16A, but that in the High Court there is no prescribed form of application. In both cases the applicant must put before the court a draft of the operative terms of the order.

As emphasised earlier, the order itself must be drafted with great care. The wording necessary to ensure that the defendant cannot evade the effect of the order by acting through others has already been discussed, and is illustrated again below. It should also be borne in mind that the order must make clear precisely what it is that the court says the defendant may not, or, in the case of a mandatory order, must do. Any vagueness or ambiguity is likely to give the defendant a loophole enabling him or her to evade the effect of the order.

To illustrate these points in the context of a nuisance action, let us suppose that the householder is being driven to distraction by the weekend activities of a do-it-yourself enthusiast neighbour. The householder is desperate to prevent the neighbour from hammering and using his electric drill throughout Saturday and Sunday, including the evenings.

If the householder brings a county court action, and seeks an interlocutory injunction, the wording of an appropriate draft order might read as follows:

> That the Defendant [name] be forbidden (whether by himself or by instructing or encouraging any other person) from using at his premises known as [address] a hammer or electrical drill or any other electrical or mechanical tools so as to cause a nuisance by noise to the Plaintiff.

Such an order identifies precisely the nature of the nuisance complained of by the plaintiff. At the same time the words 'or any other electrical or mechanical tools' inform the defendant that he cannot evade the effect of the injunction simply by substituting another tool.

The application for such an order must be accompanied by an affidavit setting out the evidence relied on by the applicant. Here again, as discussed at Chapter 5 special drafting skills are required. These are best illustrated in the context of a particular case.

Drafting in practice – a simple nuisance case

Drafting on behalf of the plaintiff

THE PROBLEM

The client in this case, Mrs Rose Andrews, has sought advice with regard to an all too common problem; noise created by a neighbour. The following information has been obtained in an interview with Mrs Andrews.

The client's account

The following statement was taken from Mrs Andrews by her solicitor.

'I live in Rose Court which is a small block of flats located in private grounds overlooking a park. The situation is a very secluded, peaceful one and most of the residents are, like myself, retired. I have lived there for 24 years. In the past the flats have always been very quiet and relationships between the residents have always been very good. There has always been a very pleasant atmosphere in the past.

The flats are owner-occupied. The flats are leasehold, on a 999 year lease, and there is a management company which acts on behalf of the owners. The residents have formed a committee which has meetings with the management company to ensure that things run smoothly.

The flats do not often change hands. However, several months ago the flat directly adjacent to mine went up for sale. We always become very anxious when that happens and hope someone suitable will move in. Then in June last year, Mr Young purchased the flat and moved in.

It was clear from the outset that he was not going to fit in at Rose Court. He is a rather loud, brash young man. I don't know why he moved into this kind of community. I don't know what he does for a living. He seems to have plenty of money as he has a very expensive car, but he certainly doesn't work regular hours.

Almost from the very first day he moved in Mr Young has frequently played loud music at weekends and quite often he does so into the early hours of the morning, keeping me awake. One of the other residents, Mrs Francis, says Mr Young has a very powerful hi-fi system. The music is often so loud that I can't hear my own radio or television properly.

However everything became much worse about two months ago when a young woman moved into Mr Young's flat. I met them both in the grounds once, and Mr Young introduced her as his girlfriend. Since she moved in matters have deteriorated badly.

At first whenever I complained to Mr Young about the noise he was very civil and co-operative and did reduce the volume of the music. But after his girlfriend moved in the noise has become really quite unbearable and Mr Young has recently behaved quite aggressively when I have had to complain.

Matters reached a head two days ago. On Tuesday 20 January 1996, Mr Young was playing music very loudly most of the evening and was still doing so at 2 am. I am really quite nervous of going out of my flat at night, but I just had to go and complain. I rang his door bell and knocked on his door several times, very loudly, but he simply refused to answer the door. I went on ringing the bell. I knew they were in there because I could hear laughter. Eventually I heard someone approaching the door, but instead of opening it, Mr Young just shouted at me through the door. He was very abusive. I have never been spoken to like that in my life. Then he went away and turned the music up even louder.

The following day I learned that several other residents had been disturbed by the noise. It seems that one or two people have complained on earlier occasions. Mrs Wicker who lives at Flat 7 told me that. The whole incident made me feel quite ill, and I visited my solicitors for advice as soon as I felt well enough to do so, on Monday 22 January 1996.'

The legal advice

In all the circumstance of this case it seemed to Mrs Andrews' solicitor that to solve this problem it might be necessary to seek a permanent injunction to restrain Mr Young from playing music so loudly as to cause a nuisance to Mrs Andrews. The expenses associated with bringing an action are not a problem for Mrs Andrews, and it was explained to her that the court would also be asked to award her, if she succeeds at trial, damages for the nuisance caused and the costs she incurs in bringing the action.

It was agreed that, before initiating proceedings, Mrs Andrews' solicitor would send a letter before action to Mr Young asking him to cease from playing the music so loudly, and warning him that legal action would be taken if he failed to do so. If this did not produce the required result, a summons would be issued in the county court and an interlocutory injunction would be sought to restrain Mr Young from causing nuisance by playing music loudly in the period up until trial.

The letter was sent at the end of January, but no reply was received. Accordingly proceedings must be issued. The particulars of claim and an application for an interlocutory injection, together with an affidavit in support are set out below.

Sample particulars of claim

IN THE   **COUNTY COURT** [1]   **Case No** [2]

BETWEEN [3]

ROSE ANDREWS   <u>Plaintiff</u>

and

JAMES YOUNG   <u>Defendant</u>

PARTICULARS OF CLAIM [4]

1. The Plaintiff is and was at all material times [5] the owner and occupier [6] of the ground floor flat ('Flat 1') [7] of the premises known as Rose Court, Park View, Portsea. [8] The Defendant is and was at all material times the owner and occupier [9] of the ground floor flat ('Flat 3') adjacent to Flat 1 at the said premises. [10]

2. The Defendant moved into Flat 3 in or about June 1995 and since that date [11] has wrongfully [12] caused or permitted excessive noise to come from Flat 3 into Flat 1.

<u>PARTICULARS</u> [13]

On or about three evenings a week and during every weekend since the said date the Defendant has caused or permitted music from a record player and/or tape recorder and/or radio to be played very loudly from about 9 pm until 1 or 2 am the following morning.

3. By reason of the matters complained of the Plaintiff has been caused annoyance and discomfort and has thereby suffered damage.[14]

4. The Plaintiff has on numerous occasions orally and by a letter dated 22 January 1996 requested the Defendant not to cause or permit music to be played so loudly and for so long or so late, but the Defendant has refused to do so and threatens unless forbidden by injunction to continue the said nuisance and/or to permit the said nuisance to be continued. [15]

5. Further the Plaintiff claims interest pursuant to section 69 of the County Courts Act 1984 on the amount found to be due to the Plaintiff at such rate and for such period as the court thinks fit. [16]

AND the Plaintiff claims: [17]

(1) Damages; and

(2) An injunction forbidding the Defendant whether by himself of by instructing or encouraging any other person to continue the said nuisance; and

(3) Interest pursuant to section 69 of the County Courts Act 1984.

                                              Signature [18]

Dated [19]

Notes

1   Court in which proceedings are brought.

2   Case number allocated by court office.

3   Title of case. The full names of the parties must be pleaded if known.

4   Description of pleading.

5   The phrase 'at all material times' is a brief and convenient way of pleading that the allegation to which it relates applies throughout the period during which the matters alleged in the pleading occurred.

6   Occupation or possession by the plaintiff of the land affected by the nuisance is normally an essential element of the claim (see p 280) and so the plaintiff's ownership of the land must be pleaded. Similarly the fact that a plaintiff is a leaseholder of affected land is pleaded where appropriate.

7   For conciseness a shortened form of the address is introduced here so that it may be substituted for the full address when the premises are subsequently mentioned.

8   The land affected by the nuisance must be identified. This is usually done by pleading the full address.

9   Neither ownership nor occupation by the defendant of the land from which nuisance he or she creates emanates needs to be proved. However, the plaintiff must plead the facts which explain the defendant's presence on the land and this may be done, where appropriate, by pleading the defendant's ownership and/or occupation of that land. Where a defendant is sued as occupier of

land on which another creates a nuisance, his or her occupation must be pleaded. These facts are pleaded immediately after the plaintiff's occupation of the land either in the same or in a separate paragraph.

10 The land from which a nuisance emanates must be identified. This is usually done by pleading the full address.

11 The period during which the nuisance occurred must be defined.

12 This may be included to emphasis the tortious nature of otherwise lawful conduct.

13 Sufficient details of the conduct alleged to be nuisance must be given to make clear the plaintiff's case. These may be pleaded under the heading 'Particulars' if this assists clarity.

14 Loss and damage resulting from the alleged nuisance must be pleaded. Annoyance and discomfort are pleaded here because they constitute the damage where the nuisance alleged is excessive noise.

15 This paragraph lays the basis for the claim for an injunction by pleading facts which show that the nuisance is a continuing one and is likely to continue unless restrained by an order of the court. Where appropriate, as here, the plaintiff can demonstrate the need for an injunction to restrain the defendant by proving details of requests the plaintiff has made for the noise to be reduced which have been ignored by the defendant.

16 A claim for interest must be pleaded to show the basis on which, rate at which and period for which the claim is made. This wording is standard in a tortious action where no special damages are claimed.

17 The prayer must plead every type of relief sought and the claim for interest must be restated.

18 Signature of barrister, solicitor or litigant in person who drafts the pleading.

19 The date of service and address of the plaintiff's solicitor, if any, must be pleaded here.

Application for an injunction on Form N16A

In preparing Mrs Andrews' application to the county court for an injunction to restrain Mr Young, her lawyer must as indicated above complete prescribed Form N16A. To do so they must draft the operative terms of the order and a copy of these must be put before the court.

In the example below Form N16A is completed to show a draft injunction which might be appropriately sought in the present case.

N. 16A
General form of application for injunction
Order 13, rule 6(3), Order 47, rule 8(2)
[*Introduced* 1991]
[*Title – Form* N. 16]

Seal

Notes on completion *Tick whichever box applies*	☑ By application in pending proceedings ☐ In the matter of the Domestic Violence and Matrimonial Proceedings Act 1976
(1) Enter the full name of the person making the application	The Plaintiff ~~(Applicant/Petitioner)~~(1) *ROSE ANDREWS* applies to the court for an injunction order in the following terms:
(2) Enter the full name of the person the injunction is to be directed to	That the Defendant ~~(Respondent)~~(2) *JAMES YOUNG* be forbidden (whether by himself or by instructing or encouraging any other person)(3)
(3) Set out here the proposed restraining orders (If the defendant is a limited company delete the wording in brackets and insert "Whether by its servants, agents, officers or otherwise"	*from playing or permitting to be played a record player or a tape recorder or a radio at the Defendant's premises at Flat 3, Rose Court, Park View, Portsea, so as to cause a nuisance by noise to the Plaintiff.*
(4) Set out here any proposed mandatory orders requiring acts to be done	~~And that the Defendant (Respondent)~~(4)
(5) Set out here any further terms asked for including provision for costs	And that(5) *the Respondent shall pay the costs of this application*
(6) Enter the names of all persons who have sworn affidavits in support of this application.	The grounds of this application are set out as in the sworn statement~~(s)~~ of (6) *Rose Andrews* This ~~(these)~~ sworn statement~~(s)~~ is ~~(are)~~ served with this application.
(7) Enter the names and addresses of all persons upon whom it is intended to serve this application	This application is to be served upon(7) *JAMES YOUNG* *Flat 3, Rose Court, Park View, Portsea*
(8) Enter the full name and address for service and delete as required	This application is filed by(8) *[insert solicitor's name]* (the Solicitors for) the Plaintiff (~~Applicant/Petitioner~~) whose address for service is *[insert solicitor's business address]*
	Signed Dated

This section to be completed by the court

* Name and address of the person application is directed to

To *
of
This application will be heard by the (District)Judge
at
on   the   day   of   199   at   o'clock
If you do not attend at the time shown the court may make an injunction order in your absence
If you do not fully understand this application you should go to a Solicitor, Legal Advice Centre or a Citizens' Advice Bureau

The Court Office at *[insert court office address]*
is open from 10 am to 4 pm. When corresponding with the court, address all forms and letters to the Chief Clerk and quote the case number.

The plaintiff's affidavit

This affidavit must put before the court the evidence on which Mrs Andrews relies in support of her application for an interlocutory injunction. It is therefore based upon the statement that she has given to her solicitors.

The broad approach to drafting an affidavit has been discussed earlier. In essence, an effective affidavit is comprehensive in that it puts before the court all the relevant admissible evidence that the deponent can give, accurate in that it reproduces that evidence without invention or exaggeration and concise in that it contains only relevant matters and does not waste words. It is also reader friendly in that the evidence is presented within a clear structure and in a logical and, so far as practicable, chronological order making it easy for the reader to assimilate.

It will be recalled that the content of an affidavit can broadly be categorised as follows:

(1) Formal parts

(2) Required information

(3) Relevant background

(4) The facts of the matter complained of

(5) Why the applicant is entitled to the relief sought

(6) Why the application is made *ex parte* (if appropriate).

The outline below indicates in relation to each applicable category the relevant information which can be drawn from Mrs Andrews' statement:

REQUIRED INFORMATION

- identity of plaintiff: Rose Andrews
- purpose of affidavit: in support of her application for an interlocutory injunction
- whether it contains hearsay: here it does so in that it will refer to what other residents have told her.

RELEVANT BACKGROUND

- details of where plaintiff lives and how long resident there
- character of community of Rose Court
- sale of Flat 3 and purchase by Mr Young in June 1995.

FACTS OF THE MATTER COMPLAINED OF

- details, in chronological order, of the problem with noise due to Mr Young playing music loudly.

WHY APPLICANT IS ENTITLED TO RELIEF SOUGHT
- details, in chronological order, of complaints to Mr Young and his reaction
- verbal complaints
- letter of 22 January 1996 from Mrs Andrews' solicitors.

The example that follows, illustrates how an affidavit might be constructed from this information, bearing in mind the qualities of an effective affidavit set out above.

Sample affidavit

> Filed on behalf of the Plaintiff
> Deponent: R Andrews
> 1st Affidavit of deponent   } 1
> Date of swearing:
> Date of filing:

IN THE   COUNTY COURT   Case No
BETWEEN

> ROSE ANDREWS   Plaintiff ⎫
> and   ⎬ 2
> JAMES YOUNG   Defendant ⎭

AFFIDAVIT OF ROSE ANDREWS [3]

I, Rose Andrews, of Flat 1, Rose Court, Park View, Portsea, the above-named Plaintiff, MAKE OATH and say as follows: [4]

1. I make this affidavit in support of my application for an interlocutory injunction against the Defendant. The matters deposed to herein are true to the best of my knowledge and belief, and are within my personal knowledge unless expressly stated to the contrary. [5]
2. I am the owner and occupier of the premises known as Flat 1, Rose Court, Park View, Portsea. The Defendant owns and occupies the flat adjacent to mine and known as Flat 3, Rose Court, Park View, Portsea. [6]

3. Rose Court is a small block of flats located in a secluded and quiet location and many of the residents are, like myself, retired. Relationships between the residents have always been harmonious. [7]

4. The Defendant purchased and moved into Flat 3 in about June 1995. Almost immediately he began to play music very loudly at weekends. The music is often played so loudly that I am unable to hear properly my own radio or television. In addition the Defendant frequently plays the music into the early hours of the morning without reducing the volume, and so keeps me awake. I am told by another resident and believe that the Defendant has a very powerful hi-fi system which is capable of playing music at a very high volume. [8]

5. At first when I complained to the Defendant about the noise, he responded by turning the music down. However, the situation deteriorated in about November 1995 when a young woman moved into Flat 5 with Mr Young. Since that date the noise has increased and Mr Young's response to complaints has become aggressive. [9]

6. Matters came to a head on Tuesday 20 January 1996. Mr Young had been playing music very loudly during the evening and was still doing so at 2 am. I was unable to sleep because of the noise, and though I do not like to go outside my flat after dark, I went upstairs to complain. Although I rang the doorbell and knocked on the door of Flat 3 several times, Mr Young did not answer the door. Eventually he did come to the door but did not open it. Instead he shouted abuse at me through the door. I heard him walk away from the door and then the music became even louder. [10]

7. The following day I spoke to other residents who told me, and I believe it to be true, that the noise had disturbed them too. I was told by Mrs Wicker who lives at Flat 7 and believe that there have been complaints about the noise by other residents. I did not take any further action that day with regard to the problem as the incident of the previous evening had made me feel ill. [11]

8. On Thursday 22 January 1996 I visited my solicitor and, on their advice, instructed them to write to the Defendant seeking a written undertaking that he would cease to play music in his flat so loudly as to cause a nuisance. I am told by my solicitors and believe that they have not received any reply to that letter.[12]

9. I believe that unless restrained by this court from so doing, the Defendant will continue to play music so as to cause a nuisance. I therefore ask this Honourable Court to grant me the requested relief. [13]

Sworn etc [14]

Notes

1   Markings. See above, p 111.

2   Heading as in particulars of claim (see p 288, notes 1–3).

3   Description. This is not essential. If included it may be in various forms of wording. See above p 111.

4   The commencement contains the deponent's name, address, occupation, or description, and the declaration of oath. Here the applicant has no employment and is described by referring to her status in the proceedings.

5   The first substantive paragraph conventionally contains a description of the applicant's status in the proceedings, (unless already given, as here) and states the purpose for which the affidavit is made. It also states the deponent's belief as to the truth of its contents and whether or not the affidavit contains hearsay.

6, 7 Background to the matters complained of. Paragraph 2 states the fact that the plaintiff occupies Flat 1, which gives rise to her right to bring an action in nuisance.

8, 9, 10, 11 The facts of the conduct alleged to cause the nuisance and details of complaints made by the plaintiff to the defendant. Paragraph 4 includes hearsay as does para 7.

12 The facts which show that the plaintiff's attempts to solve the problem without a court order have failed and that the order is necessary to restrain the defendant's conduct.

13 The inference that a court order is necessary is drawn from the facts set out at para 9. There is also the conventional request for the injunctive order as set out in the application.

14 The *jurat*.

Drafting on behalf of the defendant

When Mr Young is served with the summons and particulars of claim, and/or the application for an interlocutory injunction together with Mrs Andrews' affidavit, his reaction is anything but conciliatory. He immediately visits his solicitor and instructs him to fight all Mrs Andrew's claims. A statement taken by Mr Young's solicitor reads as follows.

The Defendant's account

'I have read the Particulars of Claim served on me by Mrs Andrews' solicitor and it is a lot of nonsense. I do not play my music system any more loudly than is acceptable. In fact the noise that comes out of some of the other flats is a lot worse than any I make because some of the residents do not hear very well and don't realise how loud their televisions and stereos are. The only reason Mrs Andrews doesn't make a fuss is that they are her cronies and they play bridge together. Also they play classical music but I play popular music which Mrs Andrews doesn't like.

I bought my flat in Rose Court in June 1995 and moved in on 21 June. It wasn't precisely what I wanted, but it was a very good deal. The owner was a middle-aged businessman. He said he had to sell in a hurry because he had financial difficulties. He certainly accepted my offer, which I pitched a bit low, very quickly.

I realised soon after I moved in that it wasn't really my sort of place. There are a few youngish couples, but most of them are fairly staid. In any case, the building is really controlled by the older residents. Several of them run the management committee.

Actually, I have always got on reasonably well with most of the residents. In fact it was one of them who told me that the real reason my flat was sold in such a hurry was that the owner had been driven out by Mrs Andrews. Apparently, she made his life a misery complaining about him banging doors, and stamping around the flat, and playing his radio too loud. Now she's trying the same trick with me.

It is true that initially we were able to co-exist. I tried to play my music so that it wouldn't be too loud in her flat, and turned it down on the couple of occasions she complained. Even so, it really wasn't that loud. Also, the flats are very well constructed so that not too much noise can be heard in neighbouring flats.

In early November last year, my girlfriend, Sarah, moved into the flat with me. Since then Mrs Andrews has become quite obsessive about noise from our flat. One of the other elderly ladies told me that Mrs Andrews doesn't approve of people living together when they are not married. Perhaps that is what it is all about. No one else has ever complained to me about any noise from my flat.'

The defence

On the basis of the information provided by Mr Young, his solicitor drafts the following defence.

Sample defence

IN THE   **COUNTY COURT**   **Case No**

BETWEEN

ROSE ANDREWS   <u>Plaintiff</u>

and

JAMES YOUNG   <u>Defendant</u>

1

DEFENCE

1. Save that it is denied that the Defendant has caused or permitted excessive noise to come from Flat 3 into Flat 1 as alleged or at all, paragraphs 1 and 2 of the Particulars of Claim are admitted. The Defendant moved into Flat 3 on 21 June 1995. [2]

2. No admissions are made as to the nature, cause and extent of the alleged or any annoyance, inconvenience and damage sustained by the Plaintiff as alleged in paragraph 3 of the Particulars of Claim. [3]

3. It is admitted that the Plaintiff has asked the Defendant on no more than two occasions not to play music loudly, but it is denied that the said music was being played so loudly as to cause nuisance by noise to the Plaintiff. On each occasion, the Defendant complied with the Plaintiff's request. It is further admitted that the Defendant received a letter dated 22 January 1996 sent by the Plaintiff. Save as aforesaid paragraph 4 of the Particulars of Claim is denied.[4]

4. In the premises it is denied that the Plaintiff is entitled to the relief claimed in the Particulars of Claim and/or any relief.

Signature

Dated etc

Notes

1   The heading is simply reproduced from the particulars of claim. The description of the pleading changes to 'Defence'.

2   The facts stated in para 1 of the particulars of claim and the allegation in para 2 that the defendant moved into Flat 3 in about June 1995 are not controversial and must be admitted. Even if Mr Young does not know whether or not Mrs Andrews actually owns

Flat 1 this fact can safely be admitted. Nothing turns on whether she is the owner, since her right to sue arises from her status as occupier of the flat.

The allegation in para 2 as to noise must however be denied since it is Mr Young's case that he neither played music loudly himself, nor allowed anyone else to play music loudly to the extent that this would have caused a nuisance to Mrs Andrews.

To ensure that any possible allegation as to noise that Mrs Andrews may seek to prove is traversed, the defence denies that Mr Young caused or permitted noise not merely as alleged in the particulars of claim but in any way at all.

For clarity and conciseness, the defence deals with paras 1 and 2 of the particulars of claim together. Thus the allegations as to noise are denied and the uncontroversial facts, indicated above, are admitted. In addition, and for clarity, the defence pleads the precise date on which the defendant moved into Flat 3.

3   The defendant admits in this paragraph that complaints were made. However the defence limits the damage of para 4 of the particulars of claim by stating when the complaints arose and how the defendant responded to the complaints.

4   The defence concludes by traversing the plaintiff's allegations as to annoyance, discomfort and damage and the allegation that any annoyance, discomfort or damage suffered was due to the defendant's conduct. Since it is not within the defendant's knowledge whether the plaintiff has suffered any annoyance, discomfort or distress, these claims are not admitted.

It is the defendant's case, however, that his conduct did not cause nuisance to the plaintiff by playing music loudly or in any other way. Consequently causation is denied.

Chapter 12

Drafting an Action in Trespass to Land

Scope of chapter

Ownership and occupation of land has been central to the historical development of civil law. Land often represents the largest capital investment for its owners; it also represents emotional bonds as it can be, and often is, a home and a refuge. When ownership or occupation is challenged it often produces stressful disputes between neighbours. In many cases the best advice you can give a client is to settle the dispute without going to law.

In Chapter 7 we looked at a neighbour dispute where a tree belonging to one property owner crashed into the greenhouse of another property owner. The claim in that case was pleaded in negligence and we showed how the plaintiff was able to plead the case to recover the loss he suffered because of the negligence of the neighbour.

In Chapter 11 we looked at another neighbour dispute. The action there arose in nuisance. In that case the plaintiff was unable to peacefully enjoy her land because of the excessive noise caused by her neighbour. That chapter showed how to plead an affidavit, an injunction and a particulars or statement of claim to support a case at law.

This chapter looks at claims where there is no nuisance and no negligence, but when another person enters and remains on the owner's or occupier's land.

The purpose of this chapter is to outline the nature of these claims, the possible defences and to show how to approach drafting in the context of an action in trespass.

Trespass

The nature of the action

Trespass to land can be defined as any unjustifiable intrusion by one person upon land in the possession of another.

The slightest crossing of the boundary is sufficient to establish a claim. It is therefore trespass to drive a nail into the wall of a neighbour, to grow creeper up another person's wall or to dump rubbish on someone else's land.

In order to claim and win a case in trespass, it is not necessary to prove that the plaintiff has suffered any damage or loss. This is one of the major differences between an action in trespass and actions in negligence and nuisance where loss and damage have to be proved. For this reason it is often said that trespass is actionable *per se*.

Trespass can be unlawful or criminal. It is unlawful to throw stones at a person's greenhouse. It is also potentially a criminal offence. But if the police did not have enough evidence to take a criminal action, the plaintiff could sue the thrower of the stones in trespass and claim damages.

Because there is a lower standard of proof in civil law than in criminal law, this is a realistic possibility.

However, in most cases of trespass to land the conduct that causes the trespass is in fact a civil offence. The poster that claims 'Trespassers will be prosecuted' is not strictly true. Prosecutions are criminal actions. Trespassers are usually sued in the civil courts and this book is solely concerned with civil actions in tort.

When deciding if a trespass has been committed, the duration of the trespass is not material. This is because a new cause of action arises each day as long as the trespass continues. It is therefore not possible for a defendant to claim that by taking no action the plaintiff agreed with the trespass. The duration of the trespass may however be relevant when the amount of damages to be awarded is assessed.

Remedies

Where an action in trespass to land is brought, the remedies available are damages and/or an injunction and/or a declaration.

DAMAGES

Even where no actual loss has been sustained, the court can award damages. The extent of the damages awarded are usually assessed under one of the following heads:

(a) Where there has been no damage to the landowner, but the trespasser has profited, the damages are the value of profit gained by the trespasser while on the land. An example of this is the lost letting value of a squatted building.

(b) Where there has been physical damage to the land, the damages are not the replacement value, but the amount by which the value of the land has diminished. This is called the diminution value and the overriding principle is to put the plaintiff in the state he or she was in before the trespass.

It is also possible for exemplary or aggravated damages to be awarded. However, exemplary damages are usually only awarded where the trespass was an oppressive, arbitrary or an unconstitutional action by servants of the government. Aggravated damages can and will be awarded, if, for instance, the trespasser was noisy, insulting or threatening.

INJUNCTION

This is often the most useful remedy if the trespass is a continuing one. Injunctions may be granted on an interim basis, or at the end of the case. The court will grant an interim injunction before the case goes to trial, if, on the balance of convenience, it is just to do so, and if the granting of the interim injunction does not prejudice the defendant.

The two kinds of final injunction available are mandatory and prohibitory. The courts are more likely to order a prohibitory injunction. This could be, for example, an order to restrain the trespasser from crossing the plaintiff's land. A mandatory injunction could, for example, order the removal of a wall built on the plaintiff's land.

It is the judge who decides whether an injunction should be granted and even if the plaintiff wins the case against a trespasser, it is entirely a matter for the discretion of the judge as to whether an injunction is granted. Chapter 4 contains a detailed discussion on injunctions.

DECLARATION

Since trespass is a tort that claims or alleges a wrongful entry onto the land of the owner or occupier of that land, it follows that a trespasser will often claim that he or she has a right to enter, pass through or stay on the land. It is therefore sometimes advisable to ask the court to state in the final order the rights to the use of the land of the various parties. This order is termed a declaration and will be a final order that can be used to prove title in conveyancing when the property is sold.

Defences

The following are the defences available in an action for trespass.

JUSTIFICATION

If the entry onto another person's land was granted by a licence or easement or custom, this is a complete defence. It is also in some circumstances justification if the trespass was to abate a nuisance, for example, entry to stop the spread of fire. If however a licensee remains on the land after his licence is revoked or expires, he or she becomes a trespasser.

NECESSITY

This defence is not much favoured by the courts. The defence will only be accepted if the defendant can show that it was necessary to enter onto another person's land to preserve life or property. It will not be accepted if the entry was because of the defendant's negligence.

STATUTORY AUTHORITY

A number of Acts of parliament give a right of entry onto property of another person. The most important of these are given to the police under the Police and Criminal Evidence Act 1984. They cover, for instance, rights to enter and search premises. Under the Access to Neighbouring Land Act 1992, a neighbour has the right to enter another person's land in order to carry out reasonably necessary preservation work on his own property which otherwise could not be reached.

PUBLIC WAY

A person who uses the highway for passing or repassing is not a trespasser. But the misuse of the public highway can amount to trespass. Consequently the public have no right to hold public meetings or picket on a public highway. Statute, however, provides a defence by giving a limited right to peacefully picket under s 220 Trade Union and Labour Relations (Consolidation) Act 1992.

MISTAKE

It is not a defence that the trespass was due to a mistake of either fact or law.

LIMITATION

The general rule under s 2 Limitation Act 1980 is that the action for trespass must be brought within six years after the trespass occurred.

ADVERSE POSSESSION

Ownership of the land might be lost and a trespasser can acquire the title to the land if he or she remains in possession of the land for 12 years. However, the trespasser cannot acquire possession if he or she were given a licence by the owner to occupy that land.

Drafting in a trespass to land case

Drafting on behalf of the plaintiff

WHO CAN SUE?

The first step is to establish that the client has the right to bring an action. Since trespass to land concerns the occupation and ownership of land, the right to sue lies with those who possess these legal rights. Therefore only the person who has a legal or equitable title or has physical possession of the land can sue. However a lodger in a private house cannot bring an action in trespass because though he or she might have the use of the rented rooms they are not in possession of the land.

WHO CAN BE SUED?

Provided that the trespasser can be identified, there are no limitations as to who can be sued.

WHICH COURT?

Both the High Court and the county court can hear cases where the matters in issue are tortious acts. The choice between the two will depend on a number of factors including the value of the claim, the urgent necessity for an injunction, the complexity of law and the desirability of the case to be heard by a local judge.

The statement/particulars of claim

The elements that have to be established to prove a case in trespass to land are listed below. These essential elements will establish the framework of the pleading.

(1) wrongful entry

(2) by another

(3) on the land

(4) of the owner or occupier of that land.

Earlier in this chapter we pointed out that it is not necessary to establish that damages resulted from the trespass in order to found a successful claim in trespass. However, it is desirable, if a claim is being made in damages, to specify the damages claimed. This is to enable the defendant to mount a defence.

In a simple case of trespass to land, the statement/particulars of claim must therefore plead the following matters:

THE PLAINTIFF'S RELEVANT STATUS: (4) ABOVE

Since the plaintiff must prove that he or she has a right of ownership or occupation to the land that has been trespassed upon, his or her status must be pleaded. This is usually pleaded in the first paragraph.

A typical example is:

> The Plaintiff is and was at all material times the [owner or tenant] in possession of land and premises known as [address].

THE RELEVANCE OF THE DEFENDANT: (2) ABOVE

The status of the defendant is not in issue in trespass, but it is necessary in the pleading to explain how or why the defendant was on the plaintiff's property. If the defendant had remained on the property after a licence had been revoked, the date of the licence and the date of revocation should be pleaded.

This is usually pleaded in the second paragraph of the statement/particulars of claim.

THE CONDUCT ALLEGED TO AMOUNT TO TRESPASS: (1) AND (3) ABOVE

This is the act of trespass itself and details the times and the dates of the trespass. If the trespass concerns the alleged unauthorised use of a footpath then the pleading should refer to a plan on which should be drawn the footpath, for example:

> Since about [date] the Defendant has on [dates] wrongfully entered and crossed the Plaintiff's said land by way of the path shown on the plan annexed hereto and coloured pink.

The use of 'said' in this paragraph saves the drafter repeating the details of the plaintiff's land; the land in issue having been set out in the first paragraph.

LOSS AND/OR DAMAGE

As noted above, it is not necessary to establish loss and damage to be successful in a claim in trespass. But if the plaintiff is claiming damages for loss, it is necessary to plead them. Some examples are shown below:

(a) Where it is alleged that the trespasser has caused physical damage and therefore loss to the plaintiff:

> By reason of the matters aforesaid, the Plaintiff's property has been damaged and the Plaintiff has thereby suffered loss and damage.

PARTICULARS OF LOSS AND DAMAGE

Cost of repairing 20 yards of fencing   £

1 new gate   £

Value of 10 growing oak trees   £

It is perfectly acceptable that these particulars could be headed 'Particulars of Special Damage'.

(b) Where it is alleged that the trespasser has caused financial loss by continuing to remain on the land after the licence has been revoked:

By reason of the matters aforesaid the Plaintiff has been deprived of the use of the said garage and has thereby suffered damage. A reasonable charge for the use of the said garage would be £   a week.

It is important to remember that claims for aggravated and exemplary damages must be claimed and supported in the pleading and the claim must be repeated in the prayer.

The remedies sought

INJUNCTION

As with pleadings in nuisance discussed at p 277 of this book, when an injunction is sought, the reason why the court is asked to grant this injunction must be given in the particulars or statement of claim. The most usual reason is that the trespass is a continuing one, and the plaintiff believes that it will continue unless the defendant's action is restrained by an injunction. The following examples show how to plead this information:

(a) claim for a prohibitory injunction to stop the plaintiff's land being crossed:

The Plaintiff on numerous occasions has requested the Defendant not to enter and cross his land, but the Defendant has ignored these requests and threatens and intends unless restrained by injunction to repeat the acts complained of.

(b) claim for a mandatory injunction to compel the defendant to remove a wall built on the plaintiff's land:

By letter from the Plaintiff's solicitors dated [date] the Plaintiff by his solicitors requested the Defendant to remove the said wall but the Defendant has failed to do so.

The claim for an injunction must also be pleaded in the prayer as in the example set out below.

DAMAGES

As discussed above, the claim for damages must give details of what the plaintiff claims has been lost. These can be listed as 'Particulars of Special Damage' or, as above, 'Particulars of Loss and Damage'. In a case of trespass these figures should be readily available and stated in the particulars or statement of claim. The evidence to support these figures will be relied on at trial.

The claim for damages must be repeated in the prayer.

DECLARATION

An action in trespass concerns the rights to the use of the land in dispute. Therefore an injunction coupled with a declaration is often one of the most effective remedies. In order for the declaration to be granted, it is not necessary to plead it in the body of the statement/particulars of claim. It is however necessary to plead it in the prayer.

The terms of the declaration sought must be specific. An example is given below under the discussion of the prayer.

INTEREST

As in other tortious actions, the claim for interest under s 35A Supreme Court Act 1981 in the High Court, or s 69 County Courts Act 1984 in the county court, must be pleaded in both the body of the statement/particulars of claim and repeated in the prayer.

THE PRAYER

An example of a prayer claiming damages, an injunction, a declaration and interest in an action in trespass brought in the county court is set out below:

AND the Plaintiff claims:

(1) Damages;

(2) An injunction forbidding the Defendant whether by himself or by instructing or encouraging any other person from entering or crossing the Plaintiff's said land;

(3) A declaration that the Defendant is not entitled to enter or cross the Plaintiff's said land; and

(4) Interest pursuant to section 69 of the County Courts Act 1984.

The application for an interlocutory or interim injunction

The act of trespass may be one that is causing the land owner/occupier acute distress, or it may be a matter that the land owner feels can wait to be decided at trial.

If the client instructs the solicitor to obtain immediate relief, and the solicitor or legal adviser feels that the client has a good case, it may be advisable to apply for an interim or interlocutory injunction that will restrain the trespass between the issue of proceedings and the hearing at trial.

In order to obtain a hearing for this interim or interlocutory injunction, it is necessary to draft the following documents:

- An affidavit. This has been discussed in Chapter 5 and on p 291 in Chapter 11 where advice is given on drafting an affidavit in support of an injunction to restrain a nuisance. The same principles of drafting apply, should the case concern trespass to land.
- An application. This will be on form N16A in the county court, or in the form of a general application in the High Court. The skills necessary to draft an application are discussed in Chapter 4. You will find you can use these skills to draft an application in a case concerning trespass to land.
- A draft order setting out the terms of the interlocutory order stopping the trespass. This is discussed in depth in Chapter 4 where rules and advice on drafting an injunction are set out. Both the advice and the rules apply in actions for trespass to land.

Drafting in practice – a simple trespass case

Drafting on behalf of the plaintiff

THE PROBLEM

The client in this case, Mr John Steven, has sought advice with regard to a dispute with his neighbour over the boundary to his garden.

THE CLIENT'S ACCOUNT

The following statement was taken from Mr Steven by his solicitor.

'Last year I inherited Lime Cottage, Green Lanes, Oldbury from my aunt who had lived there most of her life. I am her only living relative and live and work about 30 miles away in Newtown in Westchester.

When I first inherited the cottage, I thought I would keep it and either use it for weekends or let it. But I soon found out that the house and the garden were in a terrible state, because, for a number of years, my aunt had been very crippled with arthritis.

I therefore decided to sell the cottage because I couldn't afford to repair it.

A number of people have been interested in buying the cottage, but the problems over part of the garden which was my aunt's vegetable plot have deterred them.

The garden at Lime Cottage is quite large and part of it had been used by my aunt, even during my lifetime, as a vegetable plot. However, as she had become more crippled she had given up gardening, and had allowed her neighbour, James Grover, to grow vegetables on the old vegetable plot. I think that he gave her some of the vegetables he grew in return for the use of her land. He certainly did odd jobs for her as she grew older.

My aunt did not discuss her financial affairs with me. When I asked her about the plot she said "Jim and I have an agreement, but it will all come to you when I die".

I have spoken to James Grover on a number of occasions about this plot, and asked him to stop using it. On solicitor's advice I have written to him revoking his licence. However he still continues to cultivate this land, and has threatened to sue me if I damage any of his vegetables, fruit or flowers, or touch the greenhouse he has put on my aunt's land.

James has won a number of medals for his flowers and vegetables, and he specialises in growing dahlias. He is, I think, a national judge. Unfortunately, his own garden is too small for this greenhouse.

The people in the village all side with James and are barely civil to me.

To try to break the deadlock, I have offered to sell the plot of land to James at my estate agent's valuation. This was based on the difference in the value of Lime Cottage with and without the plot and this came to £5,000.00.

James told me that it is agricultural land which down here is about £1,500 an acre and therefore the value is £750. In any case, he says, he has no intention of buying it; he hasn't any money and he thinks he has every right to go on using the plot because "your aunt gave me permission as long as I lived".

I cannot continue like this. James will not negotiate with me or with my solicitors. He doesn't answer letters and refuses to speak to me. The estate agents say that I can sell the cottage without the land, but I will have to reduce the price considerably.

My solicitors tell me that if I sold the cottage without the plot of land I would have to pay to put in a fence to separate Lime Cottage garden from the plot of land. I can't believe I am hearing this. Why should I pay for that thief, James Grover, to keep my land?

I want to get James off my land as soon as possible.'

The legal advice

The file was passed from the probate department to the litigation department after Mr Steven had obtained probate of his aunt's estate and the assets were distributed.

It was obvious from the deeds that Lime Cottage and all the land, including the vegetable plot, had been owned by Mr Steven's aunt, Mrs Lily Grimes. It was now owned by Mr Steven following his aunt's death, and he had been the executor of the will that had given him Lime Cottage. Therefore, in law, Lime Cottage and the land surrounding it was now the property of Mr Steven. Further, there was nothing in the papers passed to the solicitors to indicate any written agreement about the plot of land.

It was agreed, before starting the legal case, that Mr Steven's solicitor would send a final letter before action to Mr Grover asking him to leave the land, dismantle his greenhouse and remove his plants by a specified date. Further, a separate 'Without Prejudice' letter would be sent to Mr Grover repeating the offer of sale of the plot for £5,000. The offer would be expressed to last for a specified number of days, and would then automatically lapse if not accepted.

If these did not produce the required result, a summons would be issued in the county court.

Mr Steven and his solicitor also discussed whether to apply for an interlocutory injunction to take effect before the trial. It was agreed that they would not do this as it would not help Mr Steven. He needed a final decision in order to settle the future of the cottage and the land.

The letter was sent at the end of March, but no reply was received. Accordingly proceedings were issued. The particulars of claim are set out below.

Sample particulars of claim in a simple trespass case

IN THE   **COUNTY COURT** [1]   Case No [2]

BETWEEN

JOHN STEVEN   <u>Plaintiff</u>

and

JAMES GROVER   <u>Defendant</u> [3]

PARTICULARS OF CLAIM [4]

1. The Plaintiff is and was at all material times the owner of land known as Lime Cottage, Green Lanes, Oldbury, ('the land'). The land is shown on the plan annexed hereto and coloured pink. [5]

2. On a date unknown in 1987 the Defendant with the consent of the previous owner and occupier of the land entered and remained on part of the land ('the disputed land'), shown on the said plan and coloured green. Further, the Defendant on a date unknown, erected a greenhouse on the land. [6]

3. The land passed to the Plaintiff by grant of probate dated 23 November 1994. [7]

4. On 25 February 1995 in writing through his solicitors and orally the Plaintiff revoked the consent of the previous owner as from lst March 1995 and requested the Defendant to remove the said greenhouse and leave the disputed land. [8]

5. Thereafter the Defendant wrongfully continued to use the disputed land and wrongfully continues to use the same. Further the Defendant has failed to remove the said greenhouse. [9]

6. By reason of the matters aforesaid the Plaintiff has been deprived of the use of the disputed land and has thereby suffered damage. A reasonable charge for the use of the disputed land would be £5 a week. [10]

7. Further the Plaintiff claims interest pursuant to section 69 of the County Courts Act 1984 on the amount found to be due to the Plaintiff at such rate and for such period as the court thinks fit. [11]

AND the Plaintiff claims: [12]

(1) An injunction forbidding the Defendant whether by himself or by instructing or encouraging any other person from occupying the disputed land;

(2) A declaration that the Defendant is not allowed to occupy the disputed land;

(3) An order that the Defendant do forthwith pull down and remove the said greenhouse;

(4) Damages;

(5) Interest pursuant to section 69 of the County Courts Act 1984.

Signature [13]

Dated etc

Notes

1   Court in which the action is brought. This will be the local county court.

2   Case number which is inserted by the court office.

3   Heading is the names of the parties.

4   Description of the pleadings.

5   Material facts that are necessary for the plaintiff to establish an action for trespass to land. The facts in this paragraph are:

(a) the plaintiff's ownership of the land;

(b) the identity of the land;

(c) a reference to a plan annexed to the summons identifying the land by colour code.

6   General explanatory paragraph. This has been drafted so that the defendant can agree with this paragraph. It explains how the defendant came to occupy the land and refers to a colour code on an annexed plan to delineate the land which is the subject of the action.

The plaintiff uses the phrase 'at a date unknown' to indicate he has no knowledge of the dates of the erecting the greenhouse and the original occupation by the defendant of the disputed land. In this case, these dates are not material facts so the defendant is therefore unlikely to take issue with this paragraph.

7   Plaintiff's right to the land. This establishes the material fact as to how the plaintiff became the legal owner of the land. It is unlikely that the defendant will dispute this. This fact could have been incorporated into para 1, but it would have made para 1 unnecessarily clumsy.

8   Material fact establishing that the occupation by the defendant was wrongful from a specified date.

9   Material fact establishing that the wrongful occupation is continuing.

10 Loss and damage are not material facts to establish the tort of trespass to land. However, if the plaintiff wishes to claim for the

loss he has suffered, he must give the basis for how he calculates his loss.

11 The claim for interest is pleaded as required in the body of the pleading.

12 The prayer pleading the remedies sought and re-pleading the claim for interest. Note that the prayer pleads both for an injunction to stop the present tort and a declaration to stop any future claim that the defendant may make on the disputed land.

13 The signature of the barrister or the solicitor or litigant in person who drafted the pleading.

Drafting on behalf of the defendant

We have discussed earlier at pp 40–46 the general principles and approaches to drafting a defence in tortious actions. The same principles apply to drafting a defence to trespass to land and you should now be able to attempt to draft a defence yourself.

We therefore now set out below the statement given by the defendant to his solicitor and would ask you to try to draft a defence on the basis of these instructions. Our draft defence and brief explanatory notes will be found at p 314 in this book; after you have drafted your defence you can compare it with ours.

The defendant's account

'I have read these Particulars of Claim and I want to put my side of the case.

I have lived next door to Mrs Grimes for many years and I was very sad when she died. She was a wonderful gardener and she and I were great friends. The last few years before she died were particularly difficult for her, because she couldn't bear to see her garden getting more and more overrun.

However, long before that she let me take over her vegetable garden. The first arrangement was that I would grow vegetables there and give her any that she wanted.

Then, sometime in about 1989 or 1990 she suggested that I put up a greenhouse on this land, so I could grow tomatoes and keep my dahlias over the winter. At first I didn't want to spend the money on a greenhouse, but she told me that I could use her vegetable plot for as long as I lived. She was very keen on the idea, and in fact after it was built often used to go and sit in the greenhouse in the winter.

As she got more frail, I was worried because our agreement was not in writing. When I raised it with her, Mrs Grimes said that all the village knew she wanted me to use to land as long as I lived. However, eventually she gave me a piece of paper on which she had written in her own handwriting and signed and dated:

> 'I, Lily Grimes, have agreed with James Grover that he can use my vegetable plot as long as he lives.'

I must admit I don't like her nephew, Mr Steven. He very rarely came to see his aunt, and he didn't help her at all when she got arthritic and frail. It was her friends in the village who looked out for her all the time. Not that we expect anything for that, because she was our friend.

However, I was very annoyed when he tried to make me pay £5,000 for the vegetable plot. I pointed out that the land wasn't worth anything like that and I haven't got that kind of money and, anyway, his aunt said I could use the plot as long as I live.'

Question for self-testing

Having read that statement, perhaps you can then look at each paragraph of the particulars of claim and work out to how to traverse the material facts and put the defendant's side of the story.

PARAGRAPH 1

This paragraph sets out the material facts by identifying the plaintiff's land and establishing the plaintiff's right to this land. Is there anything in this paragraph that you would wish to take issue with? Anything that you want the plaintiff to establish?

PARAGRAPH 2

This explanatory paragraph contains no material facts. Do you want to give the correct dates of occupation of the vegetable plot and the date the defendant put up the greenhouse?

PARAGRAPH 3

This paragraph states a material fact. You therefore have to decide whether you wish the plaintiff to prove this fact, or whether you wish to admit it, so that the plaintiff does not have to bring the proof to the court.

PARAGRAPH 4

This material fact, the alleged unlawful occupation, has to be proved by the plaintiff if he wishes to establish his case. How do you wish to deal with this material fact? You could also consider if this is a suitable place to give the defendant's story.

PARAGRAPH 5

This paragraph points to a continuation of the tort. How do you intend to deal with this?

PARAGRAPH 6

The paragraph deals with the plaintiff's alleged loss and the damages he is claiming. How should this be treated?

PARAGRAPH 7

The defendant is not required to plead to the claim for interest.

PARAGRAPH 8

The defendant is not required to plead to the prayer.

Sample defence to the action in trespass to land on p 310

IN THE   **COUNTY COURT**   **Case No**

BETWEEN

JOHN STEVEN   <u>Plaintiff</u>

and

JAMES GROVER   <u>Defendant</u>

DEFENCE

1. Paragraphs 1, 2 and 3 of the Particulars of Claim are admitted. [1]

2. The Defendant denies that the Plaintiff revoked the Defendant's right to occupy the disputed land as alleged in paragraph 4 of the Particulars of Claim. By an oral agreement on or about 1987 which was later evidenced in writing, the previous owner of the land granted the Defendant the right to occupy the disputed land and to build and retain his greenhouse on the disputed land for the lifetime of the Defendant. [2]

3. The Defendant admits the acts complained of in paragraph 5 of the Particulars of Claim but denies that any of the same were wrongful. The Defendant did the said acts by virtue of the said agreement and not otherwise. Save as aforesaid, paragraph 5 of the Particulars of Claim is denied. [3]

4. No admission is made as to the alleged or any loss in paragraph 6 of the Particulars of Claim or as to the amount and causation thereof. [4]

5

Signature

Dated the   day of   199

by J S Willis & Co of [address]

Solicitors for the Defendant

Notes

1   Paragraph 1 is admitted if the defendant does not disagree with the plan, the extent of the area coloured pink, and the plaintiff's ownership of the land.

   Paragraph 2 is admitted, and not amended to include the correct dates because the defendant's solicitor takes the view that the dates are not in issue. The defendant, it is assumed, agrees with the extent of the area covered green.

   Paragraph 3 is admitted because the defendant does not consider it critical to take issue as to title in the land passing under the will of the plaintiff's aunt. Should this be in doubt, the defendant should not admit this paragraph.

   Note: Admitting facts not in issue is encouraged by the judges. The drafter of pleadings should be aware that judges can award costs against those parties who lengthen a trial by not admitting facts which are not in issue which later have to be proved at trial. It is for this reason that paras 1, 2 and 3 in this model have been admitted.

2   Paragraph 4 is denied and the defendant gives the reason for his defence. This is justification, which is referred to on p 301 of this chapter. The defendant states that he has been granted a license to use the land for as long as he lives and, acting on that license, and with the agreement of the deceased, he spent his money and erected a greenhouse. In legal terms he is claiming license by estoppel.

3   Paragraph 5 is admitted to the extent that the defendant agrees that he occupied the plaintiff's land, but denied as to the effect of this occupation.

4   Paragraph 6 is not admitted. The amount claimed and the causation is also specifically not admitted. It is, alternatively, perfectly acceptable to deny this paragraph of the particulars of claim.

5   Paragraph 7 of the particulars of claim and the prayer are not pleaded to.

Chapter 13

Drafting in an Action in Trespass to the Person

Chapter 12 dealt with drafting a claim for damages for unlawful interference with the possession of land, that is trespass to land, and a defence to such a claim. In this chapter we shall look at drafting in cases involving unlawful interference with the person, that is trespass to the person.

Conduct which falls within the tort of trespass to the person takes three basic forms, namely, assault, battery, and false imprisonment. This chapter will therefore discuss typical claims relating to each of these forms of trespass to the person. Where assault and/or battery is alleged, one remedy frequently sought is that of an injunction, and the drafting of a claim for an injunction and the application for an interlocutory injunction and supporting affidavit in such a case will also be considered.

In order to enable you to practise what you have learned in this and the preceding chapter we shall close with a case study in trespass to the person and trespass to land. This will provide you with sufficient basic information about the case to make it possible for you to draft the particulars of claim and an application for an interlocutory injunction together with the affidavit in support. Sample documents are included and are annotated to give guidance on what should be included in these documents.

Actions in trespass to the person

Assault

THE NATURE OF THE ACTION

An assault is an act which causes another person reasonably to apprehend that force will immediately be inflicted upon his or her person.[1] The person who feels threatened need not experience fear, but he or she must believe that the threat is one capable of being executed. Thus a violent gesture by a person who is unable to get near to the person at whom the gesture is directed is not an assault.[2]

---

1 *Read v Coker* [1853] 13 CB 850; *Collins v Wilcock* [1984] All ER 374, 377.
2 See, for example, *Thomas v National Union of Mineworkers (South Wales Area)* [1985] 2 All ER 120.

THE ELEMENTS OF ASSAULT

The elements of assault may therefore be listed as follows:

- act
- causes
- another person
- reasonably to apprehend immediate[3] violence.

Damage is not an element that must be proved in order to succeed in an action for assault. Even in the absence of damage an action may be brought and nominal damages awarded. However, where the intending plaintiff has suffered no damage it may be sensible to advise him or her against pursing a claim in damages unless on the facts of the case a claim for aggravated or exemplary damages is appropriate. In some such cases, of course, proceedings are issued with the object of obtaining an injunction, there being no intention to proceed with the action for damages.

Battery

THE NATURE OF THE ACTION

While the essence of assault is the threat of force, battery is an act which actually inflicts unlawful force on another person.[4] The degree of force involved may be slight; merely to touch another person in anger is sufficient.[5] Physical contact between the wrongdoer and his or her victim is not, however, essential. Even throwing water on another person may constitute battery.[6] Nor is it necessary to establish a hostile intention on the part of the wrongdoer, though he or she must have intended to commit the act in question.

Thus a prank which gets out of hand may constitute battery. Similarly a surgeon who operates without a patient's consent may be sued for battery even though he or she intervenes to help rather than harm the patient. It should be noted, however, that the kind of physical contact which, even though it may be unwelcome to a particular individual, is accepted as a normal part of daily life, for example being jostled in the street, will not normally constitute battery.[7]

---

3   The apprehension of immediate violence is taken to embrace the belief that the threat will be executed.
4   *Collins v Wilcock*, above.
5   *Cole v Turner* [1704] 6 Mod 149.
6   *Pursell v Horn* [1838] 8 A & E 602.
7   *Cole v Turner*, above.

THE ELEMENTS OF BATTERY

The elements of battery may be listed as follows:

- act
- inflicting
- unlawful force
- against another person.

As with assault, damage is not an essential element of the action, and the comments with regard to bringing an action in assault where no damage has been suffered apply equally to an action for battery.

THE RELATIONSHIP BETWEEN ASSAULT AND BATTERY

Many incidents constitute assault without battery occurring, and, though less common, battery may be committed without involving any assault. An example of the latter is where a person is hit from behind.

False imprisonment

THE NATURE OF THE ACTION

False imprisonment occurs when a person is completely deprived of liberty for a period of time, however short, without lawful cause. The person imprisoned need not be aware of his or her imprisonment. Thus a person may be falsely imprisoned while asleep.[8] Nor need the restraint have been imposed by physical force. It is sufficient if the person imprisoned is restrained by fear of the application of force or submits to legal authority.[9]

There is, however, no false imprisonment where a person is lawfully detained, as, for example, where an arrest is made in accordance with the provisions of the Police and Criminal Evidence Act 1984. Moreover, it appears that where a person has been lawfully imprisoned under s 12(1) Prison Act 1952, it is not open to that person to challenge the conditions under which he or she is detained by means of an action for false imprisonment.[10]

---

[8] In such a case only nominal damages would be awarded if no harm was suffered by the plaintiff.

[9] *Warner v Riddiford* [1858] 4 CB (NS) 180.

[10] *Hague v Deputy Governor of Parkhurst Prison; Weldon v Home Office; R v Deputy Governor of Parkhurst Prison ex p Hague* [1992] 1 AC 58 HL. An action for false imprisonment may, however, be brought against a fellow prisoner or a prison officer acting outside the scope of his authority.

THE ELEMENTS OF FALSE IMPRISONMENT

The elements of false imprisonment may be listed as follows:

- complete restraint of a person's liberty
- by another
- by the use or threat of force or by confinement.

As with the other forms of trespass to the person, damage is not an essential element of false imprisonment. However, whereas in cases of assault or battery the absence of damage may make it undesirable to bring proceedings, where false imprisonment is established substantial damages may be awarded even where the plaintiff has suffered no physical injury.[11]

Remedies[12]

The remedies which may be claimed in an action for trespass to the person are damages and, in an appropriate case, an injunction to restrain further trespass.

Interest

A claim may be made under s 35A Supreme Court Act 1981 in the High Court and s 69 County Courts Act 1984 in the county courts for interest on any damages awarded.

Defences to an action in trespass to the person

The main defences to an action in trespass to the person are consent, self-defence and lawful arrest. These are outlined below.

Consent

Conduct which would otherwise constitute trespass to the person may not be actionable if the victim consented to such conduct. However a defence based on consent will fail if it is established that the victim's express or implied consent to physical contact or the use of force against him or her did not extend to contact or force of the type, or to the extent, which occurred. Thus, for example, forceful physical

---

11   See, for example, *Hayward v Metropolitan Police Commissioner* (1989) *The Times*, 29 March (£1,750 for four and a half hours detention) and other examples cited in *Clerk and Lindsell*, *op cit*, 17-58, note 88.

12   Trespass to the person is not only actionable in the civil courts but is also a criminal offence. Criminal proceedings are, however, outside the scope of this work.

contact between players is to be expected during a rugby match, but a player's implied consent to such behaviour does not extend to the use of such force as could not reasonably be expected.[13]

Self-defence

Where a defendant can show that an alleged trespass to the plaintiff's person was necessary in order to protect the defendant's own person or property this will constitute a complete defence provided that the amount of force used was no greater than was appropriate in the circumstances.

Lawful arrest

At common law any citizen may take reasonable steps, which may include forcibly detaining a person, to stop conduct which constitutes a breach of the peace or to prevent what he or she reasonably believes to be an imminent breach of the peace. A breach of the peace occurs when an individual is assaulted or public alarm and excitement is caused. A private citizen may also arrest a person without a warrant under s 24 Police and Criminal Evidence Act 1984 if an 'arrestable offence' has been committed. An arrest by a police constable will be lawfully made under a warrant or in accordance with the provisions of the Police and Criminal Evidence Act 1984 or subsequent legislation such as the Public Order Act 1986.[14]

Limitation

Since expiry of the relevant limitation period is a complete defence to an action in tort, both plaintiff and defendant must be aware of the date on which an action will become statute barred. In an action for intentional trespass to the person the limitation period is six years from the date on which the cause of action accrued whether or not a claim is made for damage for personal injury.[15]

---

[13] For a detailed analysis of the defence of consent in actions for battery, and particularly in medical cases, see *Clerk and Lindsell, op cit*, 17–05ff.

[14] An account of the complexities of this defence are outside the scope of this work. Reference should be made to works such as *Clerk and Lindsell, op cit.*

[15] *Stubbings v Webb* [1993] 1 All ER 322 HL.

Drafting in a case of trespass to the person

Drafting on behalf of the plaintiff

WHO SHOULD BE SUED?

In many cases the person sued will be the person who committed the act of trespass. However an employer may be vicariously liable for the tort of an employee, and in medical cases the appropriate defendant will be the relevant Area Health Authority or National Health Service Trust. In false imprisonment cases brought against the police, the appropriate defendant is the Chief Officer of Police of the relevant police area who is liable for any tort committed by constables[16] who are under his direction and control and acting in the purported performance of their duties.

WHICH COURT?

The general considerations which apply when deciding in which court an action in tort should be commenced and tried should be borne in mind. To recap briefly, the High Court and county court have concurrent jurisdiction in matters of tort regardless of the amount of any claim for damages, but if the action includes a claim for damages for personal injury, proceedings must be commenced in the county court unless the value of the action exceeds £50,000. The value of the action also determines the court to which it is allocated for trial unless the High Court, or where appropriate the county court concerned, decides otherwise.[17]

THE STATEMENT/PARTICULARS OF CLAIM

The basic division of the statement/particulars of claim into paragraphs pleading the cause or causes of action and the prayer setting out the relief or remedies claimed will now be very familiar to you. As you will also recall it is the elements of the cause or causes of action, pleaded in logical order, which provide the basic structure of the first section of the pleading but that any other material facts which must be pleaded in order to lay the basis for the claims made in the prayer must be incorporated into this section of the pleading.[18]

With these basic points on structure in mind, we shall examine how to plead claims for assault, assault and battery, and false imprisonment.

---

[16] The term includes all ranks of a police force and special constables.
[17] See above, p 146.
[18] See above, p 82.

Pleading a claim for assault or assault and battery

As explained above, in a claim for assault the basic elements of the cause of action which must be pleaded are as follows:

- act
- causes
- another person
- reasonably to apprehend immediate violence.

The elements of an action in battery are:

- act
- inflicting
- unlawful force
- against another person.

In pleading the elements of assault and/or battery sufficient details must, of course, be given to enable the defendant fully to understand the case made against him or her.[19]

In some cases the facts of an assault and/or battery are sufficiently plain and uncomplicated for it to be possible to plead all the elements of the cause of action in a single paragraph, as in the example below alleging assault:

1. On or about the 10 September 1995 the Plaintiff was walking along Morton Street, Bickerton, Cumbria when the Defendant waylaid her and raised his fist so that the Plaintiff apprehended the immediate use of violence.

Contained in this sample paragraph are the material facts which establish the elements of an action in assault, as the table below shows:

the defendant raised his fist	: act
so that	: causes
the plaintiff	: another person
apprehended immediate violence	: to apprehend immediate violence

Additional material facts (the date and place of the wrongful conduct) are pleaded so that the defendant will be able to identify when and where the incident is alleged to have occurred. These are, therefore, details supplied to enable the defendant fully to understand the plaintiff's case.

In other cases the material facts which establish the background to the alleged assault and/or battery must be set out before the conduct

---

[19] See above, p 34.

complained of is pleaded. This is illustrated in the example below which pleads an alleged battery which by its nature also involves assault:

1. The First Defendant is in the business of organising jazz festivals. At all material times the Second and Third Defendants acted as servants or agents of the First Defendant.

2. On 2 July 1995 the Plaintiff attended a jazz festival ('the Festival') organised by the First Defendant at Cowley Fields, Bridgeton, Wiltshire.

3. The Second and Third Defendants acted as stewards at the Festival.

4. During the course of the Festival a scuffle broke out amongst members of the audience close to where the Plaintiff was standing whereupon the Second and Third Defendants wrongfully seized the Plaintiff and forcibly ejected him from the Festival and onto the street.

In this example the first three paragraphs plead details identifying the defendants and the time and place of the alleged wrongful conduct. Note that para 1 states the relationship between the first defendant and the second and third defendants. This, if proved, establishes the liability of the first defendant for torts committed by the second and third defendants in their capacity as his servants or agents. The phrase 'at all material times' establishes that the second and third defendants were acting in that capacity, and that consequently the first defendant was so liable, at the time of the alleged wrongful conduct.

The fourth paragraph contains the facts which establish the elements of battery as set out in the table below:

the second and third defendants seized and forcibly ejected from the festival and onto the street	act inflicting
wrongfully (seized etc)	: unlawful force
the plaintiff	: on another

The additional facts pleaded in para 4 further explain the context in which the allegedly tortious conduct occurred, clarifying the plaintiff's case that he was wrongfully ejected from the festival when stewards reacted to an incident in which the plaintiff was not involved. These facts, together with those relating to time and place alleged in para 2 are, of course, details supplied to enable the defendant fully to understand the plaintiff's case.

Pleading a claim for false imprisonment

As you will recall, the elements of false imprisonment are as follows:
- complete restraint of a person's liberty
- by another
- by use or threat of force or by confinement.

In the example that follows, the elements of false imprisonment are contained in the second and third paragraphs.

1. The Defendant was at all material times the tenant of a room on the second floor of premises known as 'Seaview', Winsley Street, Brighton, the property of the Plaintiff.

2. At about 6 pm on 19 November 1995, when the Plaintiff knocked at the door of the Defendant's room, the Defendant forcibly dragged the Plaintiff into the room and then left the room, locking the door which was the only means of egress therefrom and thereby imprisoning the Plaintiff until 11 pm on that day.

3. By reason of the matters aforesaid the Plaintiff was deprived of her liberty and thereby suffered loss and damage.

[PARTICULARS OF SPECIAL DAMAGE]

4. Further the Plaintiff claims interest pursuant to section 69 of the County Courts Act 1984 on the amount found to be due to her at such rate and for such period as the court thinks fit.

AND the Plaintiff claims:

(1) Damages;

(2) Interest pursuant to section 69 of the County Courts Act 1984.

The facts which are pleaded in paras 3 and 4 in order to establish the elements of the tort are set out in the table below:

the defendant	:	another
locked the door of the room and thereby imprisoned the plaintiff	}	confined the plaintiff
and the plaintiff was thereby deprived of her liberty (para 3) [completely] since the door was the only means of egress (para 2)	}	completely restraining the plaintiff's liberty

The reference in para 2 to the door being the only means of egress is included because if any means of escape is available to the victim, the false imprisonment is not complete and no action lies.

The allegation in para 2 that the defendant 'forcibly dragged the plaintiff into the room' lays the basis for an additional claim for damages for assault and battery. The facts of false imprisonment cases will often support such an additional claim, or a claim for assault if only the threat of force is used to restrain the plaintiff.

Additional facts are pleaded either to clarify the case for the court, as in para 1 which pleads the relevant status of the plaintiff and the defendant, or to enable the defendant fully to understand the plaintiff's case, as when the date and time of the alleged torts are pleaded in para 2.

This example also illustrates the way in which the remainder of the statement/particulars of claim setting out a claim for damages for trespass to the person should be pleaded. The sub-heading 'PARTICULARS OF SPECIAL DAMAGE' included in brackets in para 3 should of course only be inserted in cases where the plaintiff has suffered special damage. It should be noted that in a false imprisonment case substantial damages maybe awarded even in the absence of any claim for special damage or any additional claim for assault or battery.

Pleading a claim for damages for personal injury arising from trespass to the person

Where the plaintiff has suffered injury as a result of the alleged conduct constituting trespass to the person, particulars of the injuries suffered must be pleaded as in any other case involving a claim for damages for personal injury. After the facts establishing the elements of assault or battery or false imprisonment, as the case may be, have been pleaded, the allegation of injury may be pleaded, together with the allegation that the plaintiff has suffered loss and damage, and the particulars of injury and special damage are set out below:[20]

4. By reason of the matters aforesaid, the Plaintiff has suffered personal injury, loss and damage.

PARTICULARS OF INJURIES

(give details of the injuries suffered and refer to the medical report served with the statement/particulars of claim)

---

[20] For further details on pleading injury consult Chapter 8.

PARTICULARS OF SPECIAL DAMAGE

Please see attached schedule of damages (or Please see attached statement of damages).

Pleading a claim for an injunction

Where the plaintiff in an action based on trespass to the person intends to seek the remedy of an injunction at trial, the facts on which the claim for injunctive relief is based must be pleaded in the statement/particulars of claim and the claim itself pleaded in the prayer.[21]

The basic facts on which the claim for an injunction is based are, of course, those which establish the tort alleged. In theory the particulars/statement of claim ought also to include an allegation that the defendant threatens to continue the tortious conduct unless restrained by the court. This may be expressed as follows:

4. The Defendant threatens and intends unless restrained by the Court to repeat the acts complained of herein.

In practice, at least in the county court, this paragraph seems to be unnecessary.

Drafting in relation to an application for an interlocutory injunction

The principles which apply to drafting the application for an interlocutory injunction or preparing a draft order in High Court or county court proceedings are discussed fully in Chapter 4. Examples illustrating the ways in which the operative terms of an order in an action based on trespass to the person are set out below:

(a) From using violence against the plaintiff;

(b) From threatening, harassing or pestering the plaintiff;

(c) From molesting the plaintiff, whether by actual or threatened violence, or by harassing or pestering her;[22]

---

[21] See further above at p 81.

[22] This example which appears in Fricker, *Emergency Remedies and Procedures* (2nd edn, 1993), at p 516 is alternative to, or may be preferred as being more precise than, example (b).

Drafting an affidavit in support of an application for an interlocutory injunction

The approach to drafting an affidavit in support of an application for an interlocutory injunction is discussed fully in Chapter 5.

Drafting on behalf of the defendant

Drafting a defence

The rules and practice in relation to drafting defences have been discussed generally in Chapter 3 and illustrated in relation to particular torts in subsequent chapters. Consequently no detailed discussion of drafting a defence is included here. To assist the reader, however, an example illustrating how to present a defence to a claim for damages for assault and battery is set out below.

THE DEFENCE OF SELF-DEFENCE

This can be illustrated in the context of a straightforward claim for damages for assault and battery. The relevant paragraphs of the particulars of claim are as follows:

1. On 2 March 1995 at about 3 pm the Plaintiff was present at a football match held at the Padlow Rangers Football Ground at Pool Street, Padlow, when the Defendant wrongfully assaulted the Plaintiff and beat the Plaintiff by wrongfully punching and striking the Plaintiff.

2. By reason of the matters aforesaid, the Plaintiff has suffered injury, loss and damage.

A defence to this claim might consist of a general denial that the defendant assaulted the plaintiff as alleged together with an allegation that if the defendant did so assault the plaintiff he acted in self-defence. This defence might be pleaded as follows:

1. Save that it is admitted that on 2 March 1995 at about 3 pm the Plaintiff and the Defendant were present at the said football match, paragraph 1 of the Particulars of Claim is denied. In particular if which is not admitted the Plaintiff was assaulted as alleged, it is denied that it was the Defendant who so acted.

2. At about the time alleged the Plaintiff wrongfully assaulted the Defendant by punching him in the head and thereafter threatened to strike the Defendant again.

3. Further or alternatively to the extent that the Plaintiff may establish that the Defendant did lay hands on the Plaintiff, the Defendant will aver that he did so in necessary self-defence to protect himself from further assault by the Plaintiff and in any event used no more force that was reasonably necessary in the circumstances.

Note the phrase 'if which is not admitted' which enables the defendant to plead, inconsistently, that the plaintiff was not assaulted but that, if he was assaulted, it was by someone other than the defendant. The defence of self-defence pleaded in para 3 is further to the matters pleaded in para 2 but alternative to the denial in para 1 that the plaintiff was assaulted.

If it is admitted that the defendant assaulted the plaintiff, but alleged that he did so in self-defence the defendant might plead as follows:

1. On the date and at the time and place alleged in paragraph 1 of the Particulars of Claim the Plaintiff wrongfully assaulted the Defendant by punching him on the head and thereafter threatened to strike him again. Thereupon the Defendant in necessary self-defence to protect himself from further assault by the Plaintiff pushed the Plaintiff away using no more force than was reasonably necessary in the circumstances.

Once the defence to the plaintiff's allegation of assault and battery has been set out, the defendant might complete his defence by traversing the plaintiff's allegation that he has suffered injury, loss and damage as a result of the alleged assault as follows:

4. No admissions are made as to the extent, nature and/or cause of the alleged or any injury, loss or damage sustained by the Plaintiff.

In addition a paragraph could be included denying the plaintiff's entitlement to the remedy claimed. This might read:

5. In the premises it is denied that the Plaintiff is entitled to the relief claimed.

Where the defendant has himself suffered injury and/or loss and damage as a result of the alleged assault by the plaintiff a counterclaim may be pleaded. In the defence set out above this might be presented as follows:

6. Paragraphs 1 and 2 of the Defence are repeated.

7. By reason of the matters set out in paragraphs 1 and 2 hereof, the Defendant has suffered injury, loss and damage.

[PARTICULARS OF INJURY]

[PARTICULARS OF SPECIAL DAMAGE]

Case study: *Powers v Rawlings*

Question for self-testing

Set out below are the particulars of claim and an application for an interlocutory injunction in Form 16A together with an affidavit in support in the case of *Powers v Rawlings*. These documents illustrate some of the points made in this chapter. In addition, the particulars of claim illustrates matters raised in Chapter 3 which dealt with the drafting of pleadings and in Chapters 4 and 5 which dealt, respectively, with drafting interlocutory injunctions and affidavits.

Ms Powers' version of the facts of the situation which has resulted in her bringing an action in trespass and assault are given below. Following this there is a brief account of the legal advice given to Ms Powers when she consulted her solicitor with regard to her problem with Mr Rawlings, and some notes on claims in trespass and assault.

You may find it helpful, using Ms Powers' account, to practise drafting the particulars of claim, an application for an interim injunction and an affidavit in support of this case. Our version of these documents (pp 333–38) has been annotated to help you check that you have recognised what needs to be included in them.

Ms Powers' account of events

Ms Powers visited her solicitor, Hilary Smith, who is employed by the firm of Fawcett, Williams & Saunders, on 2 November 1995. She was very distressed and said that this was due to an incident the previous day involving a former boyfriend, Jonathan Rawlings. According to Ms Powers, Mr Rawlings had accosted her in the street as she was walking home at about 11.30 pm and threatened to hurt her badly if she ever went out with another man. Ms Powers said there had been a similar incident a few days earlier on 26 October, when she had been walking home from work. The words used by Mr Rawlings on that occasion had been almost identical to those used by him on 1 November.

Both incidents had occurred in Hodge Street, which is the street in which Ms Powers lives. On being questioned by her solicitor, Ms Powers said that she rents a flat in Frimley Buildings, where she has lived since 1987. The address of her flat is No 2, Frimley Buildings, Hodge Street, Halifax HX5 3BA.

Ms Powers told her solicitor that she had known Mr Rawlings since 1992. They met at a Christmas party and got on very well. The relationship developed very quickly and in January 1993 Mr Rawlings moved into the flat at No 2, Frimley Buildings where he lived with Ms Powers until May 1994.

According to Ms Powers, soon after Mr Rawlings moved into her flat he started to become aggressive towards her. He had a violent temper, as she now saw for the first time, and on several occasions slapped and punched her when she disagreed with him on trivial matters.

However, in early 1994, Mr Rawlings began to spend less time with Ms Powers and was often absent from the flat at night. Then in May 1994 he moved out of the flat. He told Ms Powers that he was moving in with a woman who lived in a house further down Hodge Street. Ms Powers has seen him coming out of the house with the woman on a number of occasions as she walks to work at about 8 am.

Ms Powers was initially upset when Mr Rawlings left her, but in early 1995 she met another man who has become a close friend.

Ms Powers was very surprised when one evening in August 1995 Mr Rawlings telephoned her, told her that he had ended his relationship with the other woman, and asked if she would let him return to the flat to live with her. Ms Powers said that she would not do so, and Mr Rawlings then became very angry and said that he would make her change her mind.

Nothing more was heard from Mr Rawlings until 10 October when he turned up at her flat and asked if he could talk to her. Ms Powers told him that she would not allow him to enter the flat and asked him to go away and leave her alone. Mr Rawlings, however, became very angry because she closed the front door. He kicked the door, swearing repeatedly, and calling her very unpleasant names. Ms Powers told Mr Rawlings she was going to call the police and he left.

Five days later there was another incident. Ms Powers went out for the evening with some friends from work, and when she arrived home she found Mr Rawlings had forced open the front door of the flat and was sitting inside the flat waiting for her. When Ms Powers asked Mr Rawlings to leave he grew very angry and raised his hand as if to hit her. Ms Powers moved away quickly, but Mr Rawlings caught her. He then put his hands round Ms Powers' throat for a second or two and then pushed her away from him and left.

It was after this incident that Mr Rawlings stopped Ms Powers twice in Hodge Street and threatened her. She told Mrs Smith that she is now very frightened as to what he might do next, and is certain he will try to break into her flat again and that he will attack her. She asked Mrs Smith what could be done to protect her against Mr Rawlings.

Ms Powers told Mrs Smith that she believes that Mr Rawlings is now living with a male friend at 40 Weigh Lane, Halifax.

The solicitor's advice

Mrs Smith advised Ms Powers that she could obtain protection by bringing proceedings against Mr Rawlings in the county court. She explained that the court could be asked to make an order to restrain Mr Rawlings from entering Ms Powers' flat without her consent, or attempting to do so, and to protect Ms Powers from actual or threatened violence by Mr Rawlings. Mrs Smith discussed such a cause of action fully with Ms Powers and explained to her that once proceedings have been issued, she could apply for an interim injunction to restrain Mr Rawlings' wrongful conduct in the period up to trial.

Notes on the nature of the action

This action is based on two torts: trespass to the person and trespass to land. Brief notes on each of these torts are given below.

Notes on trespass to the person

Trespass to the person takes three forms: assault, battery and false imprisonment. An *assault* is an act which indicates an immediate intention to inflict violence on another person who believes that the threat of violence could be executed. There is no assault if the threat is made in circumstances in which it could not be carried out and abusive language which does not create a reasonable apprehension of immediate violence does not constitute assault. *Battery* is an act of unlawful violence against another person. *False imprisonment* occurs where a person is deprived of their liberty unlawfully, even if only for a very short period of time.

The remedies available in an action for trespass to the person are damages and/or an injunction.

Notes on trespass to land

Trespass to land consists of interference with a person's possession of land. Most actions involve deliberate interference with land, but trespass can be committed by mistake, for example where a person trespassing genuinely, but wrongly, believes that his or her entry on that land in question is authorised. Trespass should be distinguished from nuisance, but where the distinction is a fine one the claim may be formed alternatively in trespass and nuisance.

The remedies available in a claim based on trespass are damages and/or an injunction and/or a declaration. An example of a claim for the latter remedy might be where a declaration is sought that the defendant is not entitled to remain on a defined area of land belonging to the plaintiff.

Before drafting a claim in trespass to land you should consult Chapter 12.

Pleading a claim in trespass to the person and trespass to land

(1) Sample particulars of claim

IN THE HALIFAX COUNTY COURT   Case No

BETWEEN

SARAH LOUISE POWERS   <u>Plaintiff</u>   1

and

JONATHAN RAWLINGS   <u>Defendant</u>

PARTICULARS OF CLAIM ²

1. The Plaintiff is and was at all material times the tenant of the property known as Flat 2, Frimley Buildings, Hodge Street, Halifax ('the Flat'). [4]

2. On 10 October 1995 the Defendant came to the Flat. When the Plaintiff refused to allow the Defendant to enter the Flat the Defendant kicked the door several times and shouted abuse at the Plaintiff.

3. On 15 October 1995 the Defendant came to the Flat while the Plaintiff was out and forced open the front door and entered the Flat without the Plaintiff's consent. When the Plaintiff returned to

the Flat the Defendant threatened to hit the Plaintiff and put his hands round her throat.

4. On 26 October and 1st November 1995 the Defendant waylaid the Plaintiff in Hodge Street and threatened her with violence.

AND the Plaintiff claims: [6]

(1) An injunction forbidding the Defendant whether by himself or by instructing or encouraging any other person:

    (a) to assault, molest or otherwise interfere with the Plaintiff; [7]

    (b) to enter or attempt to enter the Plaintiff's said property;

(2) Costs. [8]

Signature [9]

Dated etc [10]

Notes

1 *Heading.* It is easy to make mistakes in the heading, so check that you have completed it correctly. A county court action in which an injunction is sought is a fixed date action and must be commenced in the county court for the district in which the defendant resides or carries on business or in which the cause of action wholly or in part arose: CCR Ord 4 r2(1)(a) and (b). The application must be made in the court where the action is proceeding.

2 *The description of the pleading.* Here, too, it is easy to make a mistake and put statement of claim when the action is brought in the county court and particulars of claim when it is brought in the High Court.

3 The paragraphs of the pleading are numbered consecutively.

4 This paragraph pleads the relevant status of the plaintiff. A plaintiff who brings an action in trespass must plead his or her right to occupy the land or premises concerned. Note the use of an abbreviated description of the plaintiff's property.

5 Paragraphs 2–4 set out the acts of the defendant alleged to give rise to an action in trespass and an action for assault. Check that you pleaded all the incidents relied upon by the plaintiff and that you have included the relevant dates. Note that you could have pleaded trespass and assault generally. The specific incidents alleged would then have been pleaded under the heading 'PARTICULARS' as in the example below:

    2. On various occasions since [date] the Defendant has wrongfully entered the said property and has assaulted the Plaintiff.

PARTICULARS

(1) On [date] the Defendant .... } details of alleged trespass

(2) .... } and assault

Alternatively, trespass and assault could be pleaded generally in separate paragraphs and particularised separately or together.

6 *The prayer*. Claims for damages for trespass and assault could be included.

7 Each injunction claimed could be set out in a separate paragraph if preferred.

8 Costs need not be pleaded. If you decide to include the claim for costs it should be pleaded last, as here.

9 *Signature* of litigant acting in person or solicitor or barrister who drafts the pleading.

10 *Date* of pleading.

(2) Sample notice of application for interlocutory injunction

N. 16A
General form of application for injunction
Order 13, rule 6(3), Order 47, rule 8(2)
[*Introduced* 1991]
[*Title – Form* N. 16]

Seal

Notes on completion
Tick whichever box applies

(1) Enter the full name of the person making the application

(2) Enter the full name of the person the injunction is to be directed to

(3) Set out here the proposed restraining orders (If the defendant is a limited company delete the wording in brackets and insert "Whether by its servants, agents, officers or otherwise"

(4) Set out here any proposed mandatory orders requiring acts to be done

(5) Set out here any further terms asked for including provision for costs

(6) Enter the names of all persons who have sworn affidavits in support of this application.

(7) Enter the names and addresses of all persons upon whom it is intended to serve this application

(8) Enter the full name and address for service and delete as required

☑ By application in pending proceedings

☐ In the matter of the Domestic Violence and Matrimonial Proceedings Act 1976

The Plaintiff (Applicant/Petitioner)(1) *SARAH LOUISE POWERS* applies to the court for an injunction order in the following terms:

That the Defendant (Respondent)(2) *JONATHAN RAWLINGS* be forbidden (whether by himself or by instructing or encouraging any other person)(3)

(1) *to molest the Plaintiff whether by actual or threatened violence or by other conduct likely to injure her physical or mental health;*

(2) *to trespass on the Plaintiff's home or property at Flat 2, Frimley Buildings, Hodge Street, Halifax*

And that the Defendant (Respondent)(4)

And that(5)

The grounds of this application are set out as in the sworn statement(s) of (6) *SARAH LOUISE POWERS*

This (these) sworn statement(s) is (are) served with this application.

This application is to be served upon(7)
JONATHAN RAWLINGS
40 Weigh Lane, Halifax

This application is filed by(8) *Fawcett, Williams & Saunders* (the Solicitors for) the Plaintiff (Applicant/Petitioner) whose address for service is   *56a Powder Street*
                           Halifax HX3 2YY

Signed   Dated

This section to be completed by the court

* Name and address of the person application is directed to

To *
of
This application will be heard by the (District) Judge
at
on   the   day   of   199   at   o'clock
If you do not attend at the time shown the court may make an injunction order in your absence
If you do not fully understand this application you should go to a Solicitor, Legal Advice Centre or a Citizens' Advice Bureau

---

The Court Office at *Prescott Street, Halifax, West Yorkshire HX1 2JJ* is open from 10 am to 4 pm. When corresponding with the court, address all forms and letters to the Chief Clerk and quote the case number.

(3) Sample affidavit in support of application for interlocutory injunction

Filed on behalf of: Plaintiff
Deponent   : SL Powers
No of Affidavit : 1st
Date sworn   :
Date filed   :
} 1

IN THE HALIFAX COUNTY COURT   **Case No**

BETWEEN

SARAH LOUISE POWERS   <u>Plaintiff</u>
and
JONATHAN RAWLINGS   <u>Defendant</u>
} 2

3

I, SARAH LOUISE POWERS, of Flat 2, Frimley Buildings, Hodge Street, Halifax, MAKE OATH and say as follows:[4]

1. I am the Plaintiff in the above action and make this affidavit in support of my application for interlocutory injunctive relief against the Defendant as set out in the Notice of Application herein. The facts stated in this affidavit are true and are within my personal knowledge. [5]

2. I am and have been for 8 years the tenant of Flat 2, Frimley Buildings, Hodge Street, Halifax.

3. In December 1992 I met the Defendant at a Christmas party and in January 1993, he came to live with me at my flat. While the Defendant was living with me, it became clear that he had a violent temper. He began to behave very aggressively towards me and on several occasions he slapped and punched me when I disagreed with him on minor matters.

4. In May 1994 the Defendant left me and since that date he has been living with another woman at a house in Hodge Street. However, in August 1995 the Defendant telephoned me, told me that he had left the other woman and asked if he could return to live with me at my flat. When I said that he could not do so, the Defendant became angry and said that he would make me change my mind.

5. On 10 October 1995 the Defendant came to my flat and asked if he could talk to me. I told him that I would not let him in as there was nothing more to be said and asked him to go away and leave me alone. I closed the front door of the flat. The Defendant then became very angry. He kicked the front door of the flat several

times and shouted at me through the door using foul and abusive language. When I threatened to call the police, the Defendant left.

6. On 15 October 1995 I went out for the evening with some friends. When I returned home, the front door of my flat had been forced open and the Defendant was sitting inside my flat. When I asked the Defendant to leave he became very angry again, and raised his hand to hit me. I moved away quickly but the Defendant caught me. He put his hands round my throat for a few seconds and then pushed me away from him and left.

7. For about 10 days I did not see the Defendant, but on 26 October 1995 he stopped me in Hodge Street as I was returning from work. I told the Defendant to leave me alone and he raised his hand as if to hit me, but I ran past him towards my flat. The Defendant shouted after me that he would hurt me badly if I ever went out with another man.

8. A few days later, on 1 November 1995 the Defendant again stopped me in Hodge Street as I was returning home at about 11.30 pm and repeated the threat made on 26 October 1995. [6]

9. I fear that the Defendant will continue to threaten and harass me and will attempt to enter my flat again and I therefore ask the court to grant me an injunction to restrain him from doing so. [7]

SWORN at: 56b Prince Street, [8]
Halifax, HX3 2YY the 9th day   (*signature*)
of November 1995, before me

(*Signature*)
Solicitor

Notes

1 Markings.
2 Heading, see p 334, note 1.
3 A description of the document could be inserted here. See above, p 111.
4 The commencement. See above, p 112.
5 The first substantive paragraph. See above, p 112.
6 Paragraphs 3–8 set out the background to the matters complained of and the facts of the conduct on which the claim for an injunction is based.
7 Paragraph 9 draws the inference that a court order is necessary and includes the conventional request for the injunction orders sought.
8 The *jurat*, see p 111.

References

Access to Justice. Interim Report to the Lord Chancellor on the Civil Justice System in England and Wales (June 1995).

Bean, D, *Injunctions* (London: Longman, 1994, 6th edn).

Butterworths County Court Precedents and Pleadings (London: Butterworths, 1995).

Charlesworth and Percy on Negligence (London: Sweet & Maxwell, 1990, 8th edn).

Clerk and Lindsell on Torts (London: Sweet & Maxwell, 1995, 17th edn).

County Court Practice, The (London: Butterworths, 1995 edn).

Curran, P, *Personal Injury Pleadings* (London: Sweet & Maxwell, 1995).

Encyclopaedia of Forms and Precedents, The (London: Butterworths, 1989, 5th edn).

Fricker *et al*, *Family Courts: Emergency Remedies and Procedures* (Bristol: Jordan, 1993, 2nd edn).

Hendy *et al*, *Personal Injury Practice* (London: Legal Action Group, 1994, 2nd edn).

Holborn, G, *Butterworths Legal Research Guide* (London: Butterworths, 1993).

Jacob and Goldrein, *Pleadings: Principles and Practice* (London: Sweet & Maxwell, 1990).

Kemp and Kemp, *Quantum of Damages* (London: Sweet & Maxwell, 1995).

Kessler, J, *Drafting Trusts and Will Trusts* (London: Sweet & Maxwell, 1992).

Odgers *et al*, *High Court Pleading and Practice* (London: Stevens, 1991, 23rd edn).

Radevsky, A, *Drafting Pleadings* (Croydon: Tolley, 1995, 2nd edn).

Stott, D, *Legal Research* (London: Cavendish, 1993).

Supreme Court Practice, The (London: Sweet & Maxwell, 1995 edn).

Index